HALLOWEEN NATION

Also by Lesley Pratt Bannatyne

Halloween: An American Holiday, An American History
A Halloween How-To: Costumes, Parties, Decorations, and Destinations
A Halloween Reader: Poems, Stories, and Plays from Halloweens Past
Witches' Night Before Halloween (illustrated by Adrian Tans)

HALLOWEEN NATION

Behind the Scenes of America's Fright Night

LESLEY PRATT BANNATYNE

PELICAN PUBLISHING COMPANY

GRETNA 2011

Library of Congress Cataloging-in-Publication Data

Bannatyne, Lesley Pratt.
Halloween nation : behind the scenes of America's fright night / Lesley Pratt Bannatyne.
p. cm.
Includes bibliographical references and index.
ISBN 978-1-58980-680-1 (pbk. : alk. paper) 1. Halloween—United States.
2. United States—Social life and customs. I. Title.
GT4965.B295 2011
394.2646—dc22
2010029008

All uncredited photographs are courtesy Lesley Pratt Bannatyne

Printed in China
Published by Pelican Publishing Company, Inc.
1000 Burmaster Street, Gretna, Louisiana 70053

For haunters, everywhere

Contents

Acknowledgments

You can't write about any community without its permission, so it is to Halloween lovers that I owe my biggest gratitude. For everyone who opened their home, haunt, heart, and hearse; for those who talked for hours about the things they collect, build, chase, and practice, I'm proud to know you.

Thanks must also go to my husband, Gary, photographer, reader, editor, and slayer of clichés, for being such a fun traveling companion these past two zombie-and-pumpkin-filled years. I owe a debt of gratitude to Rebecca Venable, without whom I'd never have discovered many wonderful Halloween artists, and Pam Tole, Ed Gannon, Debbie Thompson, Rosemary Ruley Atkins, Tom Lee, Jeanne Youngson, Elizabeth Dobrska, Leonard Pickel, and Jeanne Escher-Pickel for helping me connect with many of the people and events whose stories fill chapters of this book. Thank you Tina Reuwsaat for being so kind and generous with resources, and thank you Janet Meyers for talking me through chapters as we walked the length of Highland Avenue in Somerville every Sunday morning at ten. To Pelican, for all they do, I am deeply grateful. Lastly, I thank Meg Ruley and Kate Kelly, without whom, twenty years ago, this train might never have left the station.

Introduction

 I'm at the very edge of a New Hampshire cornfield squinting up at a fifteen-foot-tall tree that's staring right back at me. Someone's carved a face into its trunk, and the tree's branches look like skeletal arms stretching out to block my way. The late afternoon sun rakes hard across the landscape, and, for a second, the tree glows an angry, otherworldly red.

"Sometimes when we're out here working at night you can hear coyotes howling," calls Eric Lowther as he traipses ahead of me through the cornfield that's a big part of his Halloween attraction, Haunted Overload. Lowther is explaining what he has left to do here in the four weeks before it opens to the public. We pass by several pairs of giant clown feet wrapped in plastic and squeeze around a ten-foot-tall jack-o'-lantern half-hidden under a tarp. A furry monster claw sits on a tree stump near a heap of oversized skulls waiting for bodies. From way off in the distance, I can hear workers pounding finish nails into coffins.

What strikes me, and what's struck me hundreds of times over the past twenty years I've been researching Halloween, is this: there are probably five hundred hours of work left here between now and opening night, and the people at Overload will do anything to make sure it gets done. Lowther himself won't sleep much. And when the time comes, his crew won't be paid a lot for standing in the cold and damp of late October wearing sweaty wolf masks as they wave cars through the parking lot. They do this because they love to do this. They love the dark; they love to scare people; they love to be a part of a big, public event; and, more than anything, they love Halloween.

11

So much that's been written about Halloween has been about the holiday's history or about how to decorate, cook, and costume for it (guilty, all counts), but there's not been much written about what it is today, who makes Halloween, and why. It's not like the guy sitting next to you on the train is going to let on that he spends most of every summer growing a giant pumpkin that he really hopes David Letterman will explode on late night TV. Or spends weekends painting latex onto molded clay trolls' feet to decorate his yard come October. Or three months on a *Ghostbusters'* costume for World Zombie Day. But Halloween today is so much about this kind of individual passion and creativity that I got curious.

What actually does go on behind the scenes at prop shops and national Halloween conventions, quiet commemorations of pagan Samhain, or the wickedly raucous Salem Witches' Ball? What motivates someone to collect so many Halloween vintage curios that when he sells his collection he's made enough money to finance a house? Or to dedicate a life to creating a spectacle that happens one night a year? Or even to tattoo a jack-o'-lantern on a hip? How is it that this overly commercialized, religiously contentious, and politically fractious holiday unites us in a community based on fantasy and fear; and what draws us together on this one night when we open our doors to strangers?

With these questions in hand, I spent two years talking with the people for whom Halloween is much more than just another holiday: pumpkin growers, dark artists, haunted house designers, fear scientists, monster builders, pumpkin ale brewers, pranksters, ghost hunters, cyber haunters, spooky font developers, horror burlesque dancers, parade organizers, horror movie actors, and zombie fiction authors. I'll admit that staring at severed, moldy ears in August in southern Indiana was a little unsettling. And squatting in an airless, pitch-black laundry room in New Hampshire waiting for an angry ghost was a little tense. Then again, being swept up by two thousand zombies shuffling through Pittsburgh's Monroeville Mall was a real highlight. So was walking up the middle of Sixth Avenue in New York City in the midst of two million celebrants in the Village Halloween parade and hearing burlesque artist Devilicia explain the tassel-twirling act she does with eyeballs.

You'd have to have been living off the grid to miss the Halloweening of America that's been happening over the past few decades. This we owe not just to commerce (all holidays are market driven to a point; it's part of what gets us on the same page), but to cultural events in the not-too-distant past. Without the costumed

street parties in the gay community of San Francisco in the 1960s, we might not have the spectacular Halloween parades we have now. Without second-wave feminism, we may never have heard of how modern pagans mark the holiday. Without a renaissance of the occult, there'd be no fascination with the world of spirits. Without a clinical, hands-off relationship with our dead, there'd be no curiosity about death. Without our post-Vietnam, post-9/11 worldview, there'd be no need to fight back against a pervasive fear that seems to come from everywhere and nowhere at once. Without the Internet, there'd be no network, no way to form a national tribe.

Halloween is not only simpatico with the counterculture mind-set familiar to boomers, but also with more recent alt-cultures such as Goth and metal, that share with Halloween a darker aesthetic fine honed on romance and rebellion. At the same time, Halloween is no small part a kind of nostalgic time travel. If the light and the leaves and the weather are right, we're transported back to where we can almost see our friends running around in Zorro capes, or the flick of a monster's tail in the shadows.

Adults today are clear about the fact that they're not giving Halloween up. Not the chocolate, not the creatures, and certainly not the costumes. Halloween isn't important because it has a history. It's important because it's still relevant.

This book attempts to look at contemporary Halloween through a modern lens. What does Halloween mean right now and what purpose does it serve? Who creates it? Do ghosts and witches still connect our world to the next? And what imp of the perverse makes us run toward the dark, rather than away from it, on this one, extraordinary night?

When I go back to Haunted Overload during Halloween, it is completely transformed. I make my way through the cornstalks, now brittle and bleached white like bones in the light of a half moon. Ahead, I can hear the screams of people who went in before me, I can see the horns of giant monsters piercing the blanket of fog. From somewhere, far away, I hear growls and whispers. Inside, Halloween waits. You coming?

Part I. Celebrate!

Zombie dancers, Village Parade, New York City, 2008. (Photograph by Brian Lin)

Chapter One
What Does Halloween Celebrate?

Four days before Halloween the iParty store looks like Best Buy on Black Friday. People paw through wigs and racks of witch-wear while staff rush around directing them to pirate hooks and lightsabers. A massive guy in a football jersey squeezes past me with his purchase. I sneak a quick look, and nope, I wouldn't have guessed. He's picked out a bright yellow marshmallow Peep suit.

"Look at all these," complains a young dad as he frowns at the ravaged racks of prepackaged costumes. "There's no creativity. No one knows what Halloween means anymore."

Respectfully, sir, I disagree.

Yes, it's true that Halloween's a monster of an industry. We grow 1.5 billion pounds of pumpkin each year and spend somewhere around $7.4 million on costumes for our pets. There are Halloween-y skulls on our mouse pads, fangs on our kids' stuffed animals, and claws on energy drink labels. We have so much Halloween we've exported it to places as unlikely as Catalonia, Sweden, and Slovenia, where it's either lambasted as cultural imperialism or, even in a slightly more generous light, seen as an American commercial holiday cut off from its roots and without meaning.[1]

But who gets to say what Halloween means? And is there something we can all hold in our fists and say, now this, *this,* is Halloween?

Most accounts of the holiday start in a misty Celtic or vaguely Catholic past, and truth to tell, much of the current contention about Halloween comes from our trying to source it back to a prehistoric (e.g., pagan) time.[2] But it's just as possible to look at Halloween as a living and breathing festivity, something we create each year. Old World Halloween doesn't—for most of us—give meaning to our actions on October 31. Rather, we bring meaning to Halloween when we come together to celebrate.

So . . . what *are* we celebrating when we celebrate Halloween?

Possibility

Joseph Boo, Halloween tattoo artist

"There's something really magical about Halloween in the truest sense of magic. All bets are off. When you're a kid, everything changes at Halloween. The leaves turn colors, it's colder, school starts, it gets darker earlier. The whole world changes, and maybe kids don't make the connection that it's a season, they just know that Halloween is coming. That's what people tap back into as adults. Into that innocence, that purity, that wonderful lack of restraint. Dudes well into their 40s and 50s will get all excited about Halloween tattoos. It goes back to when you were young and things were a lot more open, when anything, no matter how profound, was possible."

"I love Halloween. It is the only community holiday left. At what other time do neighbors visit each other and interact as they do on Halloween? I do not host zombie walks except during the Halloween season. I'm not certain I could get into that."

—Dan Burrello, Asheville, North Carolina, zombie walk organizer

Tolerance

Griffin von Hallenborg, custom fang maker

"I'd live it every day if I could. On Halloween, people accept you for how you're presented. Nobody judges you. You can wear a suit of armor or girls' underwear and everyone says, 'Isn't that great, how creative.' But if it's after Halloween, they're like, 'That guy's a freak.' If you look at magazine ads, everybody has to be hot and sexy, and, I dunno, the standards that people are expected to live up to are tough and cruel. Halloween is more how the world should be on an everyday basis. People are more accepting and generous and everyone's happy. They should have at least four or five Halloweens a year."

"I was really hoping you'd outgrow this stuff some day."

–von Hallenborg's mom

Driving Away Evil Spirits

Garrison Keillor, humorist and native of Anoka, Minnesota, "Halloween Capital of the World"

The Village Parade attracts around two million spectators and forty to sixty thousand costumed marchers, making it the largest Halloween-night event in the country.

Halloween night on the subway. (Photograph by Brian Lin)

"We were told that George Green started the big Anoka Halloween with the parade and the Pumpkin Bowl and that vandalism was the reason for it, which we found very interesting since we were good kids and never vandalized anything, which meant that our fathers and uncles had been vandals and never told us. I come from a Sanctified Brethren family, and I knew that fundamentalist boys have a lot of wild oats to sow, and I had picked up veiled references to outhouses being tipped and Model Ts being disassembled and reassembled atop a shed. I begged for more details and never got any.

"For us there were mighty few shenanigans on Halloween—a roll of toilet paper now and then, maybe a potato in a tailpipe, maybe a mailbox banged up. Nothing like an outhouse being tipped over while the owner was inside. That was dramatic. Think about it. You are in the act of opening your bowels and suddenly you are plunged forward onto your hands and knees in the dark. And if you have a lantern with you—good God.

"Halloween gives us a chance to impersonate evil and that is a rare opportunity. Of course you can dress up as a princess or a clown or cowboy, but that isn't nearly as much fun as being a monster, witch, zombie, vampire or demonic person, or some combination of any of those. You can put on a black cape and smear burnt cork under your eyes and cackle or groan or screech and purport to eat human flesh and it's very satisfying, much more so than impersonating righteousness is.

"We are driving away evil spirits, and we are celebrating life

itself by hauling out morbid icons and playing with them. . . . We can talk about old age and decrepitude and what our funerals will be like, and it's all very much fun, so long as we're fairly young and in good shape, which we are. And talking about death is a way of warding it away."

Merriment

Diane C. Arkins, Halloween author

"Halloween is about the actual *act* of celebrating *in and of itself;* a spirited occasion for taking down one's hair (or patented plastic Collegeville face mask as the case might be!), setting caution to the wind, and making as much 'merry' as possible on an especially bewitching autumn eve."

"It's like going to drama school but no one's making fun of you."
—Angela Cannistraro, body-piercing artist

Horror

Debbie Rochon, horror movie actress

"Most of us live our lives in fear, myself included; our government and schools teach us to fear, unintentionally I think (and intentionally sometimes). Halloween is about good fear rather than bad fear, being scared in a good way. And independence, for kids anyway. When they go to horror movies at Halloween, it's exciting for them; they have to be a certain age to get in. And all the things that teens go through are represented in horror movies, as well as a certain amount of sexuality. It's like a celebration of adulthood for teens."

"I guess I look at things that are monstrous as just things that have been able to grow outside of rules. So finding monstrosities betoken a sort of freedom, I guess.
—Al Ridenour, Los Angeles Cacophony Society

Uncorking the Bottle

Michael Einziger, guitarist/composer, Incubus

"I think the world at large is kind of putting on a show most of the time. And Halloween is the opposite. Everyone's acting how they really want to act. On Halloween, it's almost like we're uncorking the bottle. We're unwrapping a present. I think Halloween's a really good example of how creative and open people can be. People tend to be very buttoned-up and, you know, it's good for people to kind of go nuts. We all have to sometimes."

"Halloween serves an important function in that there are scary things in the world and what we do on Halloween to a certain extent is we make fun of it."

—David Zald, psychology professor

Dark, Spooky Magic

Chad Savage, dark artist and visual designer

"Many of my generation were lucky enough to be kids at the right time in America when Halloween was the way it's still depicted in the movies and in fiction, before it became so horror-oriented and paranoid. Back when it was about trick-or-treats, ghosts, goblins and witches, *It's the Great Pumpkin, Charlie Brown,* and so forth. For us, Halloween was (is) magic. Dark, spooky magic. The decorations, the dark, the sense of adventure a kid gets trick-or-treating, the sense of community created when everybody in a neighborhood gets into it, decorates, and comes out to give candy to the trick-or-treaters; these things weave magic. It's palpable; you can feel it in the crisp autumn air, and you can feel it in your chest. I think it's the spooky part that really sets it all apart from other holidays—the thrill, the low-level fun, edgy feeling that maybe, just maybe, there really is something with fangs and claws out there, hungry and waiting.

"As a result, we Halloween kids have grown up loving the holiday, and now we're making it our own. We're reclaiming it from the corporations and companies that somehow turned it into a blood-and-guts holiday in the '80s and '90s, and bringing it back around to the fun side in an attempt to give our kids the experiences we had, and instill in them the same sense of spooky magic and dark wonder that we enjoyed. We're celebrating our collective youth when we celebrate Halloween. We're celebrating our children, and giving them something to remember fondly when they're older. In some ways we're celebrating one of the last vestiges of magic and mystery in the world, however you choose to define those words."

"It's not having adult figures yelling at you for doing something strange. Halloween is licensed strange."

—Richard Blewett, married on Halloween 1986 to Dyan and who celebrates every wedding anniversary in costume, sipping champagne, and handing out candy

Opposite: *Scarecrow at Haunted Overload, 2009.* (Photograph by Dan and Suzanne Plumpton of Artifact Images)

Imagination
Jonathan Maberry, award-winning horror writer

"Halloween allows me to be a kid, to openly and innocently immerse myself in the joy of magic and the unexpected. Halloween has always been my favorite holiday, and goblins and ghouls will always be my friends because it was into their world I escaped [as a child] to be free from the real world. Now I get to write about goblins and ghouls to make my living. And so, yeah, every Halloween I give thanks to everything that lives out there in the dark. . . . I celebrate Halloween as a kind of festival of the imagination."

A Chic That Never Grows Old
Ryan Landry, actor, playwright, and Halloweenophile

"I've loved Salem and Halloween since *Bewitched*—I wanted Elizabeth Montgomery to *be* my mother. I grew up in a time when gays weren't as accepted as they are today so Christmas didn't mean a lot to us because it was all about families and a lot of my friends were gay and our families didn't even speak to us. So Halloween ended up being our Christmas. I love it even more as an adult because I can make my own choices about who I want to hang around with and what I determine is candy. I can throw my own parties. And I try to make my house look as haunted as possible all year round—I think it's a chic that never grows old."

Coming Out of Your Own Skin
Devilicia, horror burlesque performer

"What I just loved about Halloween when I was a kid was becoming something else. All the little daydreams I had in my head and my sense of adventure, come Halloween, I could be that thing. I could be a cat burglar; I could be from *Planet of the Apes*. It was like your daydreams were made flesh.

"For the folks who aren't as comfortable with breaking out all the time, Halloween is when you can embrace all that stuff that's inside of you. It's about coming out of your own skin. I'm personally super annoyed by "sexy" Halloween costumes, but at the same time, a lot of the girls that dress like that for Halloween would never dress like that the rest of the year. If that's the monster in them, well then they're letting it loose, and I think that's a healthy thing."

Dragon created by Joe Dorety as part of the Giant Pumpkin Carve, an annual charity event staged at the Fairgrounds in Pilesgrove Township, New Jersey. (Photograph by Sharron Sparks Boyle, courtesy Meals on Wheels)

Things That Return

Mark B. Ledenbach, author and longtime collector of vintage Halloween

"Speaking only for myself, Halloween celebrates those things that return in and around the autumn season: kids to school, new television programs, short days and long nights, logs crackling in the fireplace, long-sleeve shirts, irregular car washings, and the slowing-to-nothing growth of lawns and shrubs."

Freedom

Susan Bartolucci, Halloween folk artist

"To me it is a magical time that engenders joy, playfulness, almost any behavior, and an utter sense of freedom to artistically create whatever strikes my fancy. I like the characters that can be conjured up for the holiday, and the imagery. I like the idea that it is a holiday where old traditions can mingle with new in any order. And I suppose most of all I love the mystery and element of surprise that Halloween brings."

Connection to the Ancestral Dead

Rosemary Ellen Guiley, paranormal researcher and investigator

"Halloween marks a transition in time. The harvests were put away and winter was coming. Out of all the seasonal changes, this is always the most significant for us because winter means a focus on survival. Our instincts go very deep. We're actually girding ourselves for surviving the toughest time of year."

Creativity

Ricky Dick, Halloween costume and haunt designer

"I would say over all, we celebrate creativity. There are those that show it by making one-of-a-kind works of costume art, and there are those that buy something off the rack, but to them, it's about *being* the character that brings out the creativity in them. A small child knows that he needs to be Batman to ring a doorbell and ask for candy. He needs to make the leap of faith that his efforts will be rewarded."

Vandalism

Tom Landry, retired Halloween prankster

"Halloween was all about vandalism, plain and simple. In the

Miss January, from the 2009 Zombie Pin-Up calendar created by myzombiepinup. com. Photography team Robyn Malter and Shalaco Sching create traditional pin- ups with a zombie twist. (Courtesy myzombiepinup.com)

Opposite: *Guerrilla Masquerade Party participant, Seattle, Washington.* (Photo- graph by Dave Matthews)

city, there was a lady—she had her kitchen upstairs—and we'd knock on the door, trick-or-treating, and she'd throw pennies and nickels down. We'd run and grab them. But she was up there putting them on the stove. She was a nasty, nasty lady. We got an empty milk bottle and passed it around and all the boys donated a bit [of pee] and we left it at her door. Next morning the bottle was gone. We like to imagine that some time that day she opened the door and the bottle tipped in."

Fear

Eric S. Brown, horror writer and expert on the undead

"I think we're celebrating fear. It's a time of the year when it's socially acceptable to scare people silly. There are a whole lot of ways to do that. I stay home and rent a ton of horror films and have a massive blood fest. Why? Our world is a really, really dark place. Ninety percent of what you hear on the news is bad news, and some of it has an apocalyptic feeling. On some level, we can all sense deep in ourselves that we may be facing the brink of that apocalypse. For me, if the world ended with a zombie pandemic, it would definitely be the most fun."

Individual Expression

David Skal, cultural historian

"Halloween is a quintessentially selfish holiday—a celebration of personal identity and all its stifled capacity for transformation and transgression. In its modern incarnation, Halloween has emerged as a specifically American celebration of our assumed birthright to 'be anything you want,' at least for one all-too-brief evening."

Death

Kristen Lawrence, composer of Halloween carols

"I like to call Halloween a dichotomy holiday. It's a swirl of serious and silly that formed from reactions to what all people have in common: death. We accept death but also want to deny its finality. And so, I believe, when we celebrate Halloween, we celebrate that colorful heritage of tradition having to do with mortality, death, and the otherworld. We celebrate lives past and present. We celebrate ourselves."

Opposite: *Shance Youmans and Melissa ZeRuth from Tampa, Florida, celebrating Halloween at the Vampire's Ball in Salem, Massachusetts, 2009.*

Part II. Icons of Halloween

Two devils in Grand Central Station, Halloween night.

Chapter Two
Ghosts

". . . look up from your fire
at night and there
will be half a dozen
white faces pressed
against the windowpane"
　　　　　—Danielle Willis, "The Pillow Bone," *Dogs in Lingerie*

The Medium Is In

Tucked way upstate in New York under Lake Erie, almost Ohio, sits a tiny town where the curious come to speak with spirits. Lily Dale is home to two Spiritualist churches as well as forty or so registered mediums, and each year thousands make the trip in hopes they'll receive messages from the beyond.

At the town's gate, a church volunteer hands me a map and smiles. "It's small. You'll find what you're looking for."

What am I looking for? I want to know, in this town where the biggest industry is talking with the dead, if Halloween is marked in any special way. I want to ask if the relationship between Halloween and spirits is reciprocal: we seek the company of ghosts on October 31, but are ghosts really close by? I want to know if it's more possible, as people have told themselves for centuries, to make contact with the dead on Halloween.

The village still has the veneer of its original incarnation as a Victorian summer camp: shingled cottages painted pink and lilac line its tidy, narrow lanes. At the Lily Dale Museum, you'll find a pair of "aura goggles" from 1920, a gavel from the first meeting of the Medium's League, and charred remnants from the Hydesville,

New York, cottage of the Fox sisters, creators of the American Spiritualist movement. (Spiritualists are committed to proving the continuity of life by communicating with those who have passed on; for Spiritualists, death is a different, rather than final, state of being.) A list of the town's most famous visitors hangs prominently on one wall of the museum: Gandhi, Eleanor and Franklin Roosevelt, Susan B. Anthony, Mae West.

And yet the town has tried to keep up with the times. On the day I visit—a sunny afternoon in July—one of the town's residents buzzes past in a gold-colored golf cart while at the same time (miraculously) scribbling on a Sudoku puzzle.

Right away I discover the answer to my question about Halloween being special here: no. A few families in Lily Dale take their children trick-or-treating, but that's it. Fair enough. For many people, Halloween is, after all, a holiday for kids.

The second question, about Halloween and spirit communication, is more complicated. Rev. Janice Dreshman, one of Lily Dale's registered mediums, explains it like this: "Loved ones in spirit (both people and animals) always want to communicate with us if we are open and willing." Physical location does not matter either. "We are talking about a different plane of energy," says Dreshman. "You are working with the energetic vibration of the person on this plane and the loved ones in spirit." If I understand correctly, this means that a) although there may not be a general mass movement of the dead on Halloween, there may be an openness to the spirit world on that night depending on each of us and our own state of mind, and b) a supermarket could technically be as spirit-filled as a graveyard.

Ghosts. We fear them, hunt them, and try to pry secrets from their musty fists. Desperate to make contact, we've used every method we can think of from séances and Ouija boards to daring each other to spend a few hours after dark in an abandoned house. Even science is curious. Take early-twentieth-century physician Duncan MacDougall, for example, who was so determined to prove or disprove the existence of the spirit world that he constructed a scale to weigh consumptives at the time of their death. The difference between a living and a dead body, he theorized, would equal the weight of a soul. MacDougall's scale did in fact give him a figure—¾ ounce—meaning our otherworldly selves have all the heft of a heaping tablespoon of butter.

However, no one has yet proven, empirically, what, if anything, lies beyond death. It's a mystery, an unknown.[1] That is, it is within the domain of Halloween.

Victorian-era cottages on a quiet Lily Dale Street. The community is home to dozens of mediums.

Thirty-two percent of us, according to a 2005 Gallup poll, believe in ghosts. That's three of the ten people standing in front of you at Target, or thirty-two of the one hundred kids in your lecture hall, or, more likely, half of them, since belief is highest among eighteen to twenty-nine year olds. Interestingly, American belief in paranormal events, healing, and communication with the dead surged between 1990 and 2001, a time period that corresponds roughly with the television run of *The X-Files*.[2]

But here's the twist: once you divide body and soul, you actually get two not-so-comforting entities—a corpse and a ghost. (The corpse we'll deal with later.) The ghost, when tied to spirituality and family, belongs to the sweet comfort of Lily Dale. Unmoored, it belongs to the gaping maw of Halloween.

At Lily Dale, I watched an older woman apply her lipstick during a service in the assembly hall. She listened raptly as the medium prepared himself to receive spirit messages. After about ten minutes, she got what she was waiting for. "Rachel, Tom's here with me. He says hello, he sends his love." She smiled, comforted. Surely, words from those who have passed on—no matter if they're real or just imagined—can be heard with the heart. Is that talking with the dead? A few hours later, I see Rachel at the Inspiration Stump message service. She's sitting on the front row of benches in this majestic, outdoor setting, eagerly waiting for another communication from her beloved Tom. You can get a season pass to Lily Dale, and I begin to understand why someone would buy one.

Ghost Tracks

"You think you know everything. But you don't."

—Ronald Kolek, paranormal investigator,
New England Ghost Project

He wears a big Franciscan cross with a skull and crossbones on it that's been blessed by a priest. He carries a relic. "It's saint's blood. I got this from one of the exorcists," he says, leaning over to show me this tiny amulet, no bigger than a bead. "The blood is like a grain of sand and they put it in a vial of holy water."

Ron Kolek is not a frail man—he plays ice hockey at age sixty—but he uses this arsenal of protection because if he were attacked by an angry spirit, well, it wouldn't be the first time. He'll tell you he's been pitched across a room, slimed with black ooze, and he's wrestled with entities that have broken his watch and dislocated his finger. Kolek works with trance medium Maureen Wood, who channels spirits so that Kolek can find out who they are and what they want.

"Did you ever see a trance medium?" Kolek asks me when we meet in the Village Inn in Dracut, Massachusetts. "It's absolutely freaky. Maureen's eyes will disappear. She slowly raises her head and I know there's no one there. Her voice will change." (Trance mediums allow spirits to inhabit their bodies as opposed to mediums, who relay messages from the spirit world.)

Up until 1997, Kolek was a businessman who never thought about ghosts. Then he cut off three fingers in an accident, and while he was in the hospital, doctors discovered a pulmonary embolism working its way through his body. "I had a strange event, it was—you know, I wouldn't say I saw angels or anything—but there was odd stuff. I shrugged it off as medication. When I got out of the hospital, I had all this time on my hands, so I took a course in TV production. We had to do a show, so I chose to do one on ghosts. I was really skeptical. Psychics? I thought they were all fakes. But I found there was a lot of validity to all this stuff."

Kolek and his team have now done three hundred investigations at sites varying from lighthouses to private homes to old New England inns.

"You know, every old restaurant that's called an 'inn' used to be a brothel," says our waitress, stopping by to refill Kolek's coffee. "In cowboy days 'inn' meant food downstairs and women upstairs. This one's haunted."

Kolek smiles ear to ear. He knows. There's a little boy's ghost in the tunnel between the main house and the barn out back. Probably a residual.

A residual haunting, explains Kolek, is an imprint in time; it plays over and over again. You could stand in front of the ghost and it would walk right through you without so much as a glance. In an intelligent haunting, on the other hand, the will is present and the spirit is aware of its surroundings; it knows what it wants. There are spirits that seem to be grounded, stuck to a specific piece of property. Street ghosts are wanderers. But the number one most common spirit manifestation? The messenger ghost. They show up after a death or a tragic event, looking to see if you're okay, or trying to let you know that they are.

According to Kolek, most of us have had some sort of experience with ghosts, no matter what we say. "But no one will talk about them unless you initiate the conversation. I was at the airport and I put all my stuff in one of those plastic trays—my laser thermometer, EMF meter [electromagnetic field meter]—and

Maureen Wood works with a pendulum while Ron Kolek checks the readings on his EMF meter. (Photograph by Laura Wooster)

boom! 'Can you come aside, sir? What do you do with this?' 'I'm a paranormal investigator.' She kept me in there for a half-hour telling me about this ghost she has and how it makes her bed. I went for a colonoscopy. 'What do you do for a living?' The next half-hour he's telling me about the ghosts he has running around his neighborhood. At the dentist, same thing."

Kolek thinks kids may be more sensitive to ghosts than adults, and that it might be an instinct we lose when we grow up. Maybe there really are monsters under the bed and in the closet, he posits; it's just that after being told time and time again that they're not real, the instinct shuts down.

Kolek has lots of theories, and he'll say they are just that—theories—that there are no facts when it comes to ghosts. He theorizes that because there's more energy (e.g., electrical, nuclear) in the world now than there ever has been before, we may be enabling more paranormal activity. That cold spots are essentially energy harvests, where a ghost has reaped a pocket of heat energy to do its work—to materialize or move objects for example—and that's why the temperature drops on his laser thermometer. That's also why batteries drain around spirit activity or plants die. "A woman in Lawrence, Massachusetts, had a ghost on her stairway. She put poinsettias on the steps one night, and when she woke up in the morning, she could actually see the path of the ghost—all the poinsettias were dead. It had taken energy from the plants."

Ghosts, he explains, vibrate at a different frequency than we do. Like the Scalosians.

Scalosians? I'm drawing a blank.

"Did you ever watch *Star Trek?*" Kolek asks. "When they came back from the Scalosians' planet, the crew of the Enterprise thinks they have insects with them. They hear buzzing, but it turns out to be people that vibrate much faster. That's very much the way it could be with ghosts."

But there are many things that still baffle him.

"Why are there no Cro-Magnon ghosts? Even in England, the earliest they get are Romans. And people say a lot of ghosts don't know they're dead—I always find that difficult to understand. How would you not know you're dead? If there was ever a place where people didn't know they were dead it would be Nagasaki or Hiroshima. Those people were living their ordinary lives and then they were gone. But there are no mass hauntings in those places that we know of."

What about evil spirits? I ask. If there are ghosts in the world—and lots of them it seems—are there also demons?

In a word, Kolek admits, yes. As a lifelong, practicing Catholic, he acknowledges the presence of darkness. He tells me that the Vatican has recently increased the number of church-sanctioned exorcists in the U.S. from one to seven. In 1999, he adds, they also rewrote the rite of exorcism.[3]

Why?

Kolek shrugs and tosses off this idea: Maybe it has something to do with Armageddon? With the ultimate battle between good and evil?

Yikes.

He's felt them, the evil ones. "I've looked into their eyes, nose to nose, and not flinched."

For the first time in our conversation that afternoon, we sit for several seconds in silence. Then he starts in again: "It's very, very negative, very dark. Maureen feels it more than I do. It's really hard to describe. It's energy with a noncorporal body. It never had a body."

Again, silence.

"Let's move on."

Kolek starts describing an interesting case in Derry, New Hampshire, which involved a couple with a new baby. "The toys would move by themselves, their bed would shake, and there was a chemical smell coming out of the closet." Kolek brought a Franciscan monk with him to examine the house. There had been a suicide there, but Kolek sensed that wasn't the cause of the trouble. He was convinced it was the baby, that it needed to be baptized. The Franciscan did the baptism, and the disturbances stopped. Kolek doesn't pretend to know why. "Why does holy water work as protection? What if the ghost isn't Catholic? I think it's all about intent."

Monks, holy water, crosses, late-night baptisms. Doesn't the church look askance at communication with the dead? No, Kolek insists: "In the Bible it says the Lord gave the ability for certain people to do this as long as you're true of heart."[4]

Ninety percent of Kolek's cases are about verification; people want to know that they're not going nuts. And although he thinks it's possible to help a spirit move on, he doesn't see that as his job. "I have more concern for the living than the dead, so if there's a spirit that's bothering a human I'll try to protect the humans. It's their world. Sometimes I get criticized for that because I don't treat spirits properly. I believe they're just like humans. If you were an S.O.B in this world you'll be an S.O.B. in the next world. You don't earn my respect because you die. No offense."

And what about Halloween? Is there a bump in ghost activity?

He chuckles. "I got slimed in a Newburyport [Massachusetts] cemetery once on Halloween. It was thick, black, and oozy. I have no clue where it came from. But for the most part, the cemetery was dead, no pun intended. They say on Halloween the veil is the thinnest, but whatever. Calls from the media increase at Halloween, but ghosts are all year.

"When I first started I wanted to prove that ghosts existed. But then I realized there are people out there who, no matter what you do, won't believe. So I said the heck with it. I'll go out and share my experiences with everybody and you can take it for what it's worth."

As Kolek describes the ghost world, I imagine a dimension parallel to ours: a moral universe with good and bad, full of people with big personalities and habits that are hard to break. It seems infuriating that we can't, after all this time and with all that we know, crack through and hear them with our own ears. Kolek sees hope for this in technology.

"Spirits can manipulate their voices onto a digital recorder. Maybe we've finally got the technology that will allow them to communicate."

This I'd like to see.

Spirit Stakeout

It's 10:00 P.M. and I'm standing in the darkened bar of the Windham Restaurant in Windham, New Hampshire, holding an EMF meter gingerly in front of me, when the thing beeps. Across the room, someone else's meter goes off. Then another, and another, until there are five of us standing dumbly in the dark, waving our EMF meters around like TV remotes, trying to pinpoint the source.

This is the first "disturbance" of a New England Ghost Project paranormal investigation at what Kolek calls the most haunted restaurant he's ever seen. We're working late at night because we're looking for lights, orbs, or streaks that could indicate a presence, and you really can't do that when the sun's out.

Maureen dangles her pendulum and starts asking questions. You can use a ring on a string or a needle on a thread or L-rods (rods in the shape of the letter "L"), but they all do the same thing—help you get answers to Yes and No questions. My L-rods are a little impertinent, as they keep swinging around like helicopter blades and poking me in the chest.

"Is this Jacob?" Maureen asks.

Yes, her pendulum's motion affirms.

"May we please ask questions?"

Yes.

The Windham Restaurant was first a colonial farm (1729), then a home (1812), and the restaurant has had three owners since it started serving food, all of whom have reported oddities: faucets seem to turn themselves on, keys go missing, furniture moves, and doors open by themselves. But for some reason—and maybe it's that I'm not alone here—there's nothing spooky-feeling about it. Even when Maureen starts swaying and the spirit "Jacob" slips into her body, it's not the least bit alarming.

Over the course of the night—with Maureen's help—we learn that this spirit, Jacob, is looking to locate a deed or title buried in the basement, but the floor has been covered with cement and he can't get to it. I'm stunned that my first conversation with a ghost looks like it's going to be about inheritance litigation. I'm also embarrassed that I can't stop my L-rods from winging around and poking other people.

There are three categories of hauntings. Lights flickering or strange animal behavior rank as "general" signs of a haunting. Voices, cold spots, or mild psychokinetic phenomena would be stronger signs, and writing on the walls or levitating objects would be in the category of "extreme" signs of a haunting.

I do want to find a ghost, I do. But since this is my first time, I'd be satisfied with anything in the "general" category.

We move to a narrow hallway, and again the meters light up. Ron notices that there are two silent meters, and he asks the spirit to turn those on. He says please. The meters blink on.

Do you have a message for one of the group?

All six of our meters flash.

Is it for Chris?

They flash. Yes, again. Chris, a teenager, is here with his grandmother.

"I'm getting the name 'David,'" Maureen murmurs, pressing her fingers into her temples. She's also getting a killer headache.

The meters pulse wildly, then they go dark, every last one, at the same moment.

"So who's David?" Ron asks.

Chris's grandma is weeping. "Chris's grandfather, dead four years, is David," she says. "And it's Chris's seventeenth birthday today." We all get goosebumps.

Over the next couple of hours, the pendulum swings wildly, the L-rods helicopter, and the EMF meters blink incessantly. If the devices are correct, there's definitely a presence here, and he or she wants to talk. You'd think we'd blurt out the questions we've had since day one, like, is there a God? Have you met him/her? Can you go anywhere you want? Are you alone, or is your world so populated it's like being on the streets of Tokyo? Do you get older? Where are your friends? Can you see my grandmother? Instead, we play an odd game of Twenty Questions. Is any other spirit here with you? More than ten? Less than three?

Maureen finds the spirit of a boy, William, and we learn he has a sister he misses very much. It could be our empathetic circle of humans—cynics probably don't come out at midnight to cram into a tiny, hot laundry room to chat with an eight-year-old spirit—but the sadness was palpable. William's? Ours? I can't say for sure that William exists, but I can tell you that the feeling was real.

Later we're all sitting around a small radio that's been rewired so it scans stations without stopping. Spirits, Ron tells us, can use random white noise to form words and answer questions. The syncopated waves of static sound a bit demonic to begin with, so when Ron asks if a spirit is present and a voice says "Yes," we all hold our breath. "Do you have messages for us?" he asks. Now we're all straining, leaning closer to the radio, hanging on every blip or vowel sound we can make out. Spirits are fascinating and all, but if they've come to talk with one of us specifically, well, that's a lot more fascinating. "Two." Two messages? Messages for two of us? The message is two? "Big guy." A message for the big guy? For two big guys? Ron reminds us that ghosts can lie, too, to entertain themselves. Or play pranks. "Who is president of the United States?" throws out one of the investigative team. "Nixon," says the demon-sounding voice, clear as day.

Later, on the phone, I tell Ron I wished I'd asked better questions of the spirits we made contact with. People do ask about God and death, he says, but you get different answers all the time. Or sometimes it's really just you making manifest what you want and has nothing to do with spirits or truth. You never really know anything for sure, he says. There are always more questions.

We long for communication with the dead but confronting them in ghost form terrifies most of us. Why do we have such a different reaction to, say, "soul" and "ghost"? Aren't they both the essence of us that lives on?

If I asked you to imagine a ghost, I'll bet you could. They're—for the most part—tomb-moldy, aggressive, brooding, eerie. What if I asked you to imagine your soul? None of those words really describes a soul. But what does?

Beginning in 1999, Robert Blackson, a curator at the Reg Vardy

Gallery at the University of Sunderland, England, began a world-wide project called drawyoursoul.org that collected 750 pencil drawings from people, ranging in age from four years old into their eighties, in fifty-two countries. His instructions were simple: "Draw a picture of what you believe your soul looks like." Three-hundred-and-fifty of the drawings were eventually published in the book *Soul,* and although there are some with similarities to ghosts—no feet, for instance—the range of imaginings is, frankly, unghostly. There are illustrations of a soul as a bowl of fruit, a cow, fish bones, and a bar code. There is a drawing of a microwave oven with wings, an untied shoe, a massive spider about to eat a teddy bear, and a bald man floating atop what looks like the Himalayan Mountains. The most poignant for me was a drawing of a man waiting at a bus stop, done by an eighty-year-old in the U.K.

In most renderings, the soul is evolving, burning, floating, or blossoming. Ghosts, on the other hand, are usually depicted as vengeful, lonely, or stuck, in chains even. A soul is hopeful; a ghost, rattling. Is it because "soul" is protected by religion and "ghost" is not? Or that "soul" is us and "ghost" is everyone else? Are we so afraid of strangers, of other people's dead, of retribution, revenge? Or is it, as horror writer P. D. Cacek explains, that the existence of ghosts means something's gone very wrong in the natural order of things. The walking dead take away the comfort of finding peace, the finality of things.

Conjuring Ghosts

"When we become the dark, the shadows seem less frightening."
—P. D. Cacek

"I think the reason most people are afraid of ghosts, or refuse to believe in them," P. D. Cacek tells me, "is because the existence of ghosts—honest to goodness, they're-right-there entities—flies in the face of a good many religious beliefs. In most standard religions the thinking is that when we die, we go to our just rewards (heaven or whatever), and that only damned souls continue to wander. So, basically, a ghost is a damned soul and should be avoided at all costs. That in itself is pretty scary. Another reason may be that if there are ghosts, that means there aren't any just rewards and we all continue on without rest. Another scary thought for some."

Cacek writes a lot about ghosts, half the time from experience.

"Meet me at the portrait," she says, calling my cell phone. We're both at the Logan Inn, in New Hope, Pennsylvania, a colonial-era,

Author P. D. Cacek. (Photograph by James B. Reese)

Washington-slept-here town on the Delaware River. I hang up, follow the dark corridors around to the lobby, and look up to see a huge painting of a couple. Cacek is standing in front of it.

"What do you smell?"

There's a restaurant in the next room, and it smells all kinds of good: roasted meat, mostly.

"I always smell flowers around this portrait," says Cacek. And she briskly whirls about and begins her tour of the town, reputed to be one of the most haunted in America.

Cacek's story "Metalica" won a Bram Stoker Award in 1996 and her "Dust Motes" a 1998 World Fantasy Award. She's always written horror, starting in the first grade when she turned in a story about a Christmas tree that was overjoyed to be cut and decorated, until it understood the implication: a suffocatingly slow, agonizing death. She has always believed in ghosts, talked with ghosts, and written about ghosts. She's lived, says Cacek, in a haunted house with a transvestite ghost who rifled through her closet and with a Mafia-bodyguard ghost who watched over the property. Aaron Burr once walked her home late at night. And there's something sinister about one particular house tucked away on the shore of the Delaware River.

"There—that's it," says Cacek, shoving her hands in her pockets and giving a blue Federal-style colonial a quick nod of her head.

I admit it; I got a shiver just looking at the house.

We moved on, wordlessly.

Cacek reads a lot, too, and again, mostly about ghosts. "The best ghost story in the world is [Shirley Jackson's] *The Haunting of Hill House*—that book can scare you to death. Also *Ghost Story* by Peter Straub. I read this while I was in labor. I was ten centimeters, then back to three, so I had a spinal and kept reading. When I was finally dilated and they came to wheel me to the delivery room, I grabbed onto the door and yelled, 'Wait! I'm almost finished!'"

Whether you believe in ghosts or not, you don't doubt that Cacek does. Strange things have been happening to her since she was a child, like when people would appear to her after they'd died to give her messages for the living. She says she doesn't see them, she feels them. "It's like the feeling you get at the top of a Ferris wheel—that catch in your solar plexus."

(Trance medium Maureen Wood describes the arrival of spirits as a "sizzle" in the air. Either way, if they're nearby, and if you understand how to recognize them, you know.)

Cacek sees ghosts everywhere: in yards, pools of water, crosswalks, and, of course, houses.

But why, I want to know? Assuming they are who she thinks

they are, why do so many spirits stay here? Isn't there another world beyond that's more inviting?

Well, she fires back, what would you do?

I guess, I say, it would depend on what's going on when I die.

"They're the same," she smiles. "Some people move on, others stay. If you believe you're going to heaven, you go to heaven. I'm planning on staying. I'm going to haunt people, and I have a list."

Is it really that clear? What happens to all those things we've yet to repent, acknowledge, learn, when we blunder into death? To all that human momentum that gets interrupted?

"Perhaps that's the hell everyone fears," offers Cacek. "If a person can't let go of the idea that they need to do something or atone, the soul is in torment just like the person was when they were alive. The only difference is the lack of a body to shell the spirit. . . . [S]o it's free to wander, moaning, ranting, railing and/or throwing things off walls. This could explain a number of the more active haunts."

Like Kolek, Cacek sees ghosts as a year-round phenomenon. Also like Kolek, she's found that talking about ghosts outside the Halloween season or the circle of a campfire generally gets an awkward reception.

So why is that? Why do we scare ourselves silly at Halloween, and then pretend ghosts don't exist at other times of the year?

"Halloween is like saying 'nya-nya' to death and the devil. It's aversion therapy for death. We're facing our worst fears by becoming them: death, monsters, the unknown—in a very safe and accepted environment. When we become the dark, the shadows seem less frightening."

Ghosts fill our imaginations on Halloween like no other day. We impersonate them and visit their resting places on cozy, candlelit tours. We even build graveyards and crypts in our front yards. Imagine their surprise to see the old neighborhoods so transformed.

Just because the world is modernized doesn't mean our instincts are. When our forebears watched the earth gasp out its frozen breaths, they told each other stories of the otherworld, of the dead, as a kind of mythological shorthand. The dark season is dangerous, the cold can kill. Come home, batten down the hatches. The shiver we get around Halloween is a warning, and its ghosts are cautionary.

None of this is new. It's been a thousand years since the church taught people to pay attention to ghosts on All Souls' Day.[5] Set at the beginning of winter in northern Europe, the day painted a vivid picture of death's restlessness. Eyelids flipped open under mounds and in mausoleums, and the souls listened hard to make sure the living—with prayers and alms—did all they could to speed the journey from purgatory to heaven.[6] On All Souls', our thoughts were with them. This has stayed with us: *Memento mei.* Remember me.[7] But here's a thought: after all this time on earth, all of these generations, the dead outnumber the living by billions. Maybe it's we who have been forgotten.

Wigs, Requiem for a Music Theorist, and Pirates!

As kids, there was one house where we never dared trick-or-treat. It was set back down a shadowy driveway behind a wrought iron fence, and it had gables like we'd seen in scary movies. My friend Laurie and I had found a great rope swing in the woods behind the house, so we'd trespass all the time. Once, we saw a nun drive away from one of the outbuildings. But we would never glimpse the inhabitants, and we would never, ever, ring the bell on Halloween—until we were eleven.

The house was dark, of course, no porch light. Walking down the driveway, I felt terrified. Should we turn around? We could see a dim glow coming from somewhere on the first floor. We kept going. There was a cow skull on the steps leading up to the wide stone porch. Laurie rang the bell. The door opened—could it have been any more massive?—and a man dressed in black answered, unsmilingly. "We've just come from a funeral," he said in a whisper. "We have no candy." He gently shut the door.

For all the skeletons and peeled grape eyeballs, we'd never once imagined a real dead body on Halloween. Or the grief that accompanies death. I don't remember how we got home. For us, that year, Halloween came to a full stop on those cold stone steps.

When real death and mock-death collide, Halloween pales. The year I turned eleven was one of those years. The year the musician David Lewin died, more than forty years later, was the other.

It's noon, Saturday. I sniff the air of the Halloween Outlet in Worcester, Massachusetts. Ah, yes, a whiff of fog from the fake graveyard mixed with rubber fingers over a base of polyester. Moms with sulky teens are mauling racks of costumes in aisles jammed with skull candelabra, fake weapons and whips, and slimy alien tentacles. And I'm here, as a Halloween author, for a book signing.

Janis, the owner, is surprised to see me.

"I'd completely forgotten! Let me find your books—I know

they're here somewhere. And we're out of tables, but I can put you behind the wig counter. At least it's a flat surface."

I don't mind, really. My wig-counter mate—pregnant, distracted, twenty-something—I'm pretty sure does mind.

Shoppers spot the two of us and belly up to the glass cases. Do I have a neon red devil's wig? (Actually, yes—I sell about six during the afternoon.) What color was Snow White's hair? (Black, chin length.) People rest their bags on my stack of books while we chat. From behind the counter, I can see kids strapping themselves into the store's most extravagant Halloween prop: a life-sized electric chair. The whole thing shakes, sputters, buzzes, and smokes. After each ride, a voice drones, "Justice has been served."

I sell one book, to the owner, Janis. Bless her.

It's 3:30 P.M. I need to be back in Cambridge for the memorial service of a man I admired, David Lewin, a brilliant music theorist who died too soon at age seventy. I swap my witch costume for a serious dress in the ladies' room at the Natick rest stop on the Massachusetts Turnpike.

Outside the doors of a concert hall at Harvard University, I huddle with other latecomers and listen, eyes closed, to a piece of Lewin's piano music. It is charged, galloping, beautiful. Inside, I take a seat amidst nearly a quarter-acre of dark blue and pearls and listen as his colleagues speak about his genius, generosity, and wit.

At the end of the memorial, a dozen singers perform a Requiem. Listening, head bowed, I can imagine—no, see—the music theorist's soul being lifted on a swell of harmonies. The moment is transcendent: we all feel it. Then it's gone. He's gone. And we're left behind in a world that feels somehow diminished.

It's 6:30 P.M. One more costume change. I'm already late for a gathering in Salem of Halloween cohorts, who have decided to dress like pirates. I change back into my witch suit in my office, grab a cardboard pirate hat from a party store on the way, and head for Pickering Wharf. I spot them on a street corner, yelling "Aargh!" at passing cars. My colleagues are pirated to the nines with leather hip boots, eye patches, and fabulous plumed hats. Up close, I see they're dead pirates: their eyes are inked above and below, their lips blackened, faces pasty. We head to a Salem brewery to hobnob. Jim, the lead pirate (he has the hook), hoists our skull-and-crossbones banner on the wall and leads the crew in all the verses of "A Pirate's Life for Me." I take a lot of heat for my cheap hat.

At the next table is Polly. What are the chances, I think, that twenty-four pirates would be seated next to a thirtieth birthday party for a woman named Polly? There is much "Polly want a . . ." and

"Pretty Polly." Finally, Captain Jim cuts her cake with his sword and, as a special bonus, takes off his eye patch and reveals his missing pirate eye (a special contact lens—very effective).

At midnight, the pirates disperse with farewell "Aarghs." I leave my pirate hat at the restaurant—on purpose.

Enough hat changing, literally, for one day. Enough different ways to be dead, to face down death. I need a breath of air, a reprieve from the morbidity that can rise up at Halloween. After all, there are two sides to the holiday. One that reminds us to beware of the darkness ahead, and one that celebrates the season's bounty. Then, it comes. My teenaged daughter, who's long stopped asking me for help with anything, swoops through the living room to say that she wants to be a bunny for Halloween. A bunny! I need to find the perfect ears for her.

To find the Halloween ghosts we recognize, we have to go back in time, but not as far as you'd think. Halloween ghosts (and I do mean ghosts, not big guys on horseback cradling pumpkins) first appeared in American print around the Civil War, when death was a national obsession. Historian Drew Faust makes the point that the casualties of that war approximated the fatalities of the Revolutionary War, the War of 1812, the Mexican War, the Spanish-American War, World Wars I and II, and the Korean War combined. Hundreds of thousands of men were listed as "Unknown," and 40 percent of Yankees and a higher percentage of Confederates died without being named, their bodies destroyed or buried in unmarked graves.[8] It was beyond comprehension: sons, brothers, fathers, husbands, or fiancés who never came back from battle could be dead, ill, or on their way home. The need to know was critical, but information was mostly missing and often false. The grieving tried to find closure any way possible. Is it any wonder that people began to flock to mediums around this time? Where is my son? Is he here with me now? Yes, he is at peace, he is not suffering.

The first Halloween ghosts in American literature were lost shades, trying desperately to find their way home.[1] But is that really possible? And if it were, how would you prove it?

Back from the Dead: The Houdini Code

Every Halloween, a carefully selected group of magicians and historians take a seat around a séance table, join hands, and ask Harry Houdini to come back from the dead. Ring the bell, blow out the candles, unlock the handcuffs. Please, oh please, give us a sign.

If the afterlife were a state of bondage, however gentle, or if it were a permeable place where escape were possible, or even a dimension someone could vibrate into or out of, Houdini would probably be the one to do it. He could break any hold known to man while he was alive. Why not entertain the idea that he might, as he hoped, return? Who's to say where the edge of possible might be?

All magic roads lead to Houdini. Tod Browning, director of the 1932 film *Freaks*, began his career working carnival sideshows performing the buried-alive trick Houdini had made popular. (Houdini, magicians tell me, was buried in the coffin he created for the illusion. Don't try this at home, but here's how it works: part of the top of the box slides open and folds in, allowing dirt to begin to fill the coffin; as the earth shifts, it creates a cavity of loose dirt where you can begin to dig your way out. How fun is that?) The seven-days-underwater or sixty-three-hours-in-a-block-of-ice feats of David Blaine owe Houdini too. What magician would say no to an invitation to attempt to contact the greatest of all, Houdini, via séance ? On Halloween? Not Paul Rosen.

Rosen was Houdini-obsessed from the first time he watched Tony Curtis play the magician in the 1953 movie *Houdini.* He used to talk his dad into driving him from New York City down to the Library of Congress in Washington, D.C., where the teenager would slip on sterile white gloves and sift through the hundreds of books and personal papers that Houdini had donated. As an adult, Rosen scoured antique stores and private collections to amass four hundred pieces of Houdini artifacts and memorabilia, such as an original pair of Houdini's English Darby handcuffs. And Rosen's son is named Ehrich, after Houdini's birth name, Ehrich Weiss. This nearly four-decades-long dedication to Houdini bought Rosen something few of us will ever have: a seat at the table for an official Houdini séance.

The séance back story is legend: Houdini gave a code to his wife, Bess, so if he were able to escape death and return via a séance, she'd know it was really him. Says Rosen, "Houdini actually said to Bess, 'You're going to have a million mediums coming at you saying they contacted me, so here's this code, and until you hear this code you'll know they're all faking it.'" He told her to try for ten years, then stop.[10]

The séances were staged at the exact moment of Houdini's death: Halloween, 1:26 P.M. The last official séance took place in 1936 on the rooftop of the Knickerbocker Hotel in Hollywood. Dr. Edward Saint beseeched the skies above: "We want the evidence, the proof. . . . [I]n the name of humanity and love . . . if there is communication from the great beyond . . . come through with the evidence!"

The Official Houdini Séance, 2008, at Drew University, Madison, New Jersey. American psychic Jane Doherty and Dorothy Young, the last person living to have performed with Houdini, were both present. (Courtesy Bill Radner)

It didn't come that night, and Bess did her best to put the whole idea to rest. The radio broadcast of the séance concludes with her eloquent, terse, and poignant statement: "I do not believe that Houdini can come back to me, or to anyone. I do not believe that ghosts and spirits exist. I now, reverently, turn out the light. It is finished. Good night Harry."[11]

But magicians persevered. Séances continued, worldwide. For the last few decades, Houdini expert Sid Radner has hosted the Official Houdini Séance, which is held in a different Houdini-significant location each year. (Radner owns about 75 percent of all Houdini artifacts, making him the number one collector, says Rosen. David Copperfield is number two.)

The room is dark, usually candlelit. The table is draped in black, and on it are Houdini's personal effects—his spirit horn, handcuffs,

thumb cuffs, photographs of his mother. The inner circle is comprised of a high-profile medium and a handful of individuals who either knew Houdini or those Rosen describes as having one degree of separation. People like magician Bill Bixby, authors, historians, relatives, and even the granddaughter of Margery Crandon, the Boston medium Houdini battled for so many years.

Margery (Mina Crandon), in Houdini's estimation, had fooled the best. Trying to win the cash prize offered by *Scientific American* to anyone who could produce a verifiable (e.g., visual) spirit manifestation, she channeled the spirit of her dead brother, Walter. At least two of the committee—Malcolm Bird, from the magazine, and Society of Psychical Research's Hereward Carrington—thought she might be the real deal. Houdini thought her an outright fraud, and her proof was less and less convincing the more her hands and feet were confined. Harvard psychologist William McDougall was on Houdini's side and eventually claimed that the ectoplasm (spiritual energy made manifest) she produced was really part of a sheep's lung Margery had smuggled into the séance in a body cavity. (The sheep's tissue wasn't, surprisingly, all that unique. Other mediums had used rubber bladders, cotton rubbed with goose grease, or strips of tripe for their spirit emanations.[12]) Margery never received the money.

Houdini, a master at making something look impossible, was in a unique position to ferret out tricks. It made him crazy to see magic used to fabricate spirit communication, and it made him even crazier to see the grief-stricken pay to be fleeced—especially after the death of his own mother.

"He was very, very close to his mother, Cecilia Weiss," Rosen says. "They had a bond that . . . I couldn't describe it. . . . When she died, he was devastated. He spent every waking moment of his life trying to contact his mother."

He couldn't.

And to this day, according to Rosen, no séance has produced a viable message from Houdini. That's not to say that things are always quiet. At one séance, Rosen remembers, a book supposedly fell off a shelf and opened to a page with Houdini's picture on it. And at another, people said it rained for five minutes right on top of the house where the séance was held and nowhere else in the city.

"These are interesting, and as much as I want to believe, I don't think Houdini can control the weather. And if he could, why didn't he walk in and say, 'Here I am.' Between you and me, if he found a way, he'd do anything in his power to make a show of it."

Magic and mediumship have always been based on similar principles. "Whether I'm making a card appear from a pumpkin or bringing back your dead grandfather, there's something being

Opposite: *Houdini's "Margie Box." Restrictive devices such as this one were designed to limit the movement of mediums and test their real abilities at séances.* (Courtesy American Memory Project, the American Variety Stage Collection: Vaudeville and Popular Entertainment 1870-1920, Prints and Photographs Division, Library of Congress)

done and you don't know how I'm doing it," explains Rosen.[13] Yes, the mind plays tricks, and if you believe hard enough, you'll see exactly what you're looking for.

The fact that Houdini died on Halloween—the one day each year set aside to think of all that is weird—is a fabulous coincidence.

"It was a fateful day to die," concedes Rosen. "In a lot of the writings on his death, it's often, 'Houdini died on Halloween,' and not the date, October 31, 1926. My guess is that even back then the sense was that Halloween was a strange day for Houdini, of all people, to die on. Actually, the odds were very against him to die then. He got to the hospital two weeks before, and the docs didn't think he'd last twenty-four hours, but he held on."

(And, adds Rosen, the theory about Houdini dying from experimental drugs is what he calls a new urban legend. Houdini died of what's usually been reported, peritonitis caused by appendicitis.)

The séance is now more of a tradition than a spiritual event, Rosen explains. The commemoration of Houdini happens also at 1:26 P.M. on Halloween, when up to forty members of the Society of American Magicians hold what is known as a "broken wand ceremony" at Houdini's family plot in Machpelah Cemetery in Queens, New York. Basically, according to Rosen, you say a prayer and break a little wooden wand in half to show that the deceased's spell is broken. It's a religious ceremony for magicians, by magicians.

They continue the séance because it keeps Houdini's name alive, and it can attract the likes of CNN, the *New York Times,* and *People* magazine.

"We get a lot of good press out of the séance and that's what it's about."

But isn't it still possible? Suppose time passes differently in the afterlife? Maybe on Houdini's one hundredth anniversary a medium will come up with the tiniest, most esoteric fact that only historians would know—wouldn't that be the proof the inner circle is looking for?

"If we ever had contact, it would be the greatest thing."

So here then is an attempt to view ghosts through a prism. Tilt it one way and a ghost hunter balances on the narrow basement steps of a colonial-era farmhouse, waiting for his electromagnetic field meter to signal some sort of disturbance. Turn the prism just a fraction and a horror writer in New Hope, Pennsylvania, walks home late at night, convinced she's accompanied by a colonial-era ghost. Again, and mourners imagine the soul of a colleague ascending to another realm on the notes of a Requiem. Tilt once more, and a circle of magicians waits every Halloween for

Houdini to send the string of words that proves death is not final.

It's we on Earth who think more of ghosts at Halloween, not the other way around. Ghost hunters say there's no spike in spectral activity on October 31, and mediums basically agree. In America, there's only one group of people who believe that the spirit world emerges at Halloween. Witches.

Insider Info: Is Your House Haunted?
Ron Kolek, paranormal investigator, New England Ghost Project

There are many telltale signs that you may live in a haunted house. Each sign in itself does not constitute proof that your house has spirits; it's always best to look for the natural cause. But if you can't find a cause, or if you experience several of these, it may indicate you have spirit activity going on. To inspect, call a paranormal investigator near you; many perform investigations as a public service.

- Cold spots (may be caused by drafts or vents)
- Unexplained noises (may be caused naturally by a heating system, the house settling, or sounds outside that carry into the house)
- Doors or windows that seem to open or close by themselves (poor latches or soft or uneven floors)
- Tapping in the walls (small animals such as mice and squirrels)
- The feeling of being watched (a boosted electromagnetic field caused by high tension wires or faulty wiring can have this effect on the human body)
- Strange behavior in pets (illness, a change in diet, or animals in the walls)
- Voices (voices may come from either outside the house or from radio, television, etc., and could be heard due to poor insulation or sound being carried through vents or heating ducts)
- Lights or water faucets turning on or off by themselves (could be faulty switches or taps)
- Odd odors (dead animals in the walls, drafty windows, or a problem with the sewage system)
- Shadows (sometimes the result of an optical illusion or the headlights of a car going by)
- Disappearing objects (forgetfulness)
- The feeling you are being touched (low humidity in the house can cause this sensation)

A witch prop at Barrett's Haunted Mansion, Abington, Massachusetts.

Chapter Three
Witches

"As a witch, I'm appalled by the way society views us. On the one hand, we are portrayed as silly, green-skinned hags flying on broomsticks across children's Saturday cartoons. On the other, we are used as scapegoats for all the bizarre cult crimes and violent rituals staged by misguided individuals who think they are practicing witchcraft."
—Laurie Cabot, "Official Witch of Salem,"
New York Times, October 31,1989

Why is it that, each Halloween season, half a million people flock to Salem, Massachusetts, to bask in the incense of pagan shops and rub elbows with witchcraft? Do witches, even in today's science and technology-obsessed America, possess an occult mojo that creeps us out and fascinates us at the same time? What is magic's place in this world where Internet thieves can grab our credit cards from two continents away and we can find a lost pet using a GPS chip? And what do witches *do* on Halloween anyway?

Old World Witchery

"How long has she been in town, like five minutes? You really need some street cred to be a rock star witch around here."
—Overheard in a witch shop in Salem, Massachusetts

The Witches' Ball, Salem: Rob Zombie's "Living Dead Girl" beats in the background as wait staff cruise through Hawthorne Hotel's elegant ballroom with silver trays of hors d'oevres. Ten-foot-tall skeletons constructed of balloons drift lazily overhead on

Witches in a pedi-cab during the Salem Haunted Happenings Parade, 2008.

Opposite: Christian Day.

currents kicked up by the dancers below. Guests spill up the stairs where the Dragon Ritual Drummers play in one suite and a line snakes out of another room set aside for psychic readings.

The costumes are definitely uptown: lots of Renaissance, Victorian, and French court. There's a fetish faction—all leather, vinyl, and six-inch heels—and styles from Buffy to *Twilight* to a solitary Merlin, who has to casually lift his fake beard to sip a glass of Cabernet. There are plenty of über-creative costumes, too. A woman labeled "Swim at Your Own Risk," for example, limps around the party on a leg half swallowed by a shark head.

Everything about the ball is elegant. But what makes it one of the most sought-after tickets in town is the witch part. Just before midnight, the music shuts off, drummers set up a beat, and Christian Day takes the stage to lead the initiation ritual. He's tall, half-masked, and wears a full cape and gorgeous boots. His voice booms, confident and seductive.

"Are you ready to confront death?"

In one hand, Day cradles a human skull, and in the other, a rattle in the shape of Anubis, Egyptian protector of the afterlife. Day has the crowd mesmerized as he talks about the veil between this world and the next, this night of Samhain, Halloween, this night of death. He invites the crowd to come to the stage and be initiated into the Black Veil—a covenant between people who share a magical bond. The initiates stash their beer bottles and line up to walk, one by one, onto the stage, where a priestess marks their foreheads with oil. When the last one is anointed, the ritual is finished and the crowd cheers. DJ Addam Bombb slides in with the Stones' "Sympathy for the Devil," and the dance floor goes crazy.

The altar at Hex, Christian Day's shop in Salem.

"We didn't do anything small, Shawn and I. We were like the Patsy and Edina of witchcraft—you know, from 'Absolutely Fabulous?' We did everything big and obnoxious." It's been weeks since the ball, and Christian Day is explaining how he and his business partner, Shawn Poirier, helped put the witchery back into Salem's Halloween during a time when the town's then mayor wished it would all just go away. In 2003, the two, both practicing witches, created the Festival of the Dead, a series of events that included upscale parties like the Witches' Ball as well as a bit of necromancy, such as their Halloween Dumb Supper and séances.

"I had to get into those crevices of power using every obnoxious trick I could—blood and bikinis—and now they'll throw me a bone just to shut me up." (Poirier and Day created an infamous Vampires' Ball poster, which featured a blood-drenched woman in a bikini. The image instantly landed them on the eleven o'clock news.) "If I became somewhat of a caricature, and I still am to a point— it's a tourism town—it's because I had to go full throttle. This city needed a shock treatment. They needed to get it full force that this Halloween thing is not only magical, but it's financially feasible."

You'd never mistake Day for an attorney, travel agent, or anything but what he is. In a black velvet, lace-up shirt and silver pentacle necklace, he is every inch a witch. Not a reverend (although he is, officially, a reverend in the state of Massachusetts), not a high priest, Wiccan, or Druid. "I'm a witch. People come up with grandiose titles to make them feel more important. But I can't think of a more delicious word than witch. We are the magical mafia—the ones you go to when you need to get things done. Witches carry a big can of magical whoop-ass."

A quick glance around Day's shop, Hex, on Essex Street in Salem, will tell you there are no cute fairies here. "I carry things the other shops don't. I even like Anton LaVey's *The Satanic Witch* because he teaches glamour magic—using your feminine wiles to get what you

want—and that is real witchcraft. I carry *Mastering Witchcraft* by Paul Huson. It's old school, it's bad-assed. The proof of the pudding is this: does it work for you?"

Hex stocks incense for every purpose from Gallows Hill (to honor those who died unjustly in 1692) to Exorcism (to eliminate unwanted spirits) to Come Back to Me. There are glass cases and shelves stocked with mojo bags, wolf hair, Orphic eggs, candles, oils, and charms—all aids for spell casting, hexing, and fortune-telling. "I'm an old world witch," says Day. "I believe in retribution. I believe in hexing my enemies, and those who harm humanity, as long as it's in the name of justice."

He shows me an altar crowded with skulls, incense, notes, and photos. "That's my uncle," he says of one worn black-and-white photograph, "and my mom, who passed away in September. Here are my Auntie Cathy's ashes. Here's my dog that died twenty-one years ago. And this!" Day taps a photograph he's pinned beneath a brick, surrounded with what looks like coal dust. "I don't want anybody to touch this house until I have the money to buy it, so I sprinkled black salt around the photo of the house to create a barrier, then some dirt from the front lawn of the Amityville Horror place on Long Island to make 'em a little scared when they go in, and then I put a hexing candle on the whole thing."

People leave notes on the altar for things they want, things they want to say. After the Halloween season, Day had four hundred notes crammed in among the urns and frames on his altar. Notes with messages like "Grandpa we miss you" and "My sister needs a new handbag."

"Not everybody writes to the dead," he says, smiling.

Day came to witchcraft as a teen. He was intrigued with his aunt's tarot cards, but she refused to teach him how to use them because she thought he was too young. He bought his own deck and taught himself, then started plowing through books on witchcraft and taking classes. "It started as more of a Wicca thing and grew into something very different. I don't look at witchcraft as a religion. I don't worship anything, I don't go to a church—I do magic and work with spirits. I look at what I do as a service. The witch answers to humanity."

And Day's specific work, he believes, is to help people confront their own mortality and their relationship to death.

"One of the reasons I created this Festival of the Dead is that I thought we as a culture had grown away from a respect for the dead. Each year I do a dumb supper (a silent meal to be shared with the spirit world), and each year someone will say, 'Oh, is this a haunted house?'"

In October 2008, Day held his dumb supper in the ballroom of a local hotel where he created the river Styx with a long red carpet symbolizing the blood of the dead. He strung a fifteen-foot-tall veil across the room to dramatize the separation from the world of the living.

"When you say ancestors, there is a connotation of 'out there,' the person that came before—it sounds kitschy or mysterious. You know something? The dead are your daughter that died of cancer, your sister that passed away of a liver disease, your brother or cousin that died in a car crash. I go right for the jugular. Yes, the ancestors are important. But how about your best friend?"

So I have to ask: do you ever hear from Shawn? I know that Day's dear friend and business partner passed away in 2007.

"I have definitely felt him there guiding me, and he has come through in dreams and in visions during ritual work. At first, it was a very angry energy. I think he was upset at some of the challenges I faced at his passing, and he kept encouraging me to fight harder . . . and I did! Now, on the rare occasion when he comes through to me, he seems much more at peace."

It's November, and the streets of Salem are damp after a rain. They're also empty. The throngs who flock here in October are back home, figuring out how they're going to deep-fry their turkeys. The residents of Salem breathe deeply, happy to get their parking spaces back. But for Day, and for many in both the pagan and tourism community, Halloween is hardly over. There's the work of setting up next year's events, of course, but there's also the witch work that keeps Salem the magical place so many find it to be. The city's been a mecca for pagans of all persuasions, healers, and esoteric groups since the "Official Witch of Salem," Laurie Cabot, first opened her shop in the early 1970s. Day believes that all these alternative practices help create the sense that Salem is magical. And that, Day has been trying to convince the town, is what draws people.

"Ninety-nine percent of the people who come into this shop are not witches and they're not looking to become one," Day states. Many, he says, just want candles for good luck at the casino. They come to Salem because they want magic in their lives.

It's accessible, this otherworldly gift, and we can all learn to do it, Day believes. He compares it to singing. All of us have some voice. But some of us were born with a better one, as in no amount of voice lessons will make Joe Cocker sound like Pavarotti. "What makes a witch different from an ordinary person who practices magic is that magic is our specialty. Want a four-star meal? Go to a good restaurant. Want help figuring out whether you should take a new job? Where to find a new boyfriend? Who's out to get you? Go to a witch.

"I don't believe that witchcraft was an ancient religion in Europe that everyone practiced in an unbroken line from the Stone Age. I don't think that witchcraft is that defined. Shawn used to say that the moment you nail down that word completely it loses its power. The power of the word 'witch' is in its mystery—that we don't fully know what witches are and we don't fully understand them—it's purposefully obscure, as both symbol and reality. And besides, how do you define 'witch'? The worlds we work in are not the worlds everybody lives in. We're talking to people's dead grandmothers, we're pondering spells and affecting the weather and doing things that are not everyday things. They're not easily quantifiable and not easily analyzed."

Day fusses through drawers, looking for a specific tarot card he promised to a customer a few minutes ago. Unlike lots of the little storefront museums and haunted houses of Salem, Hex will stay open year-round.

"They come for the witch," he says, still lost in his thread of thought. "But they stay for the magic."

WITCH

New York City, 1968. Picture Janis dallying with the ever-elegant Leonard Cohen at the Chelsea Hotel. *Hair* just opened on Broadway, and up at Columbia University, students have barricaded themselves inside the university president's office. It was a good year for revolution. A good year for a group of New York City radicals to release their first manifesto under the banner, Women's International Terrorist Conspiracy from Hell, or WITCH.[1] The manifesto—to be "female, untamed, angry, joyous, and immortal"[2]—is meant to provoke. They were more guerrilla theater artists than magic-makers and staged political media events, such as putting a curse on Wall Street on Halloween and on Halloween in 1969, demonstrating outside the building where the Chicago Seven were on trial.

The witch was a powerful symbol of second-wave feminism.[3] But the eruption of modern witchcraft that happened in the '60s and '70s had repercussions beyond politics. Until then, most of us thought the witch was a creature of children's Halloween, two-dimensional and decorative, a character from some storybook past.

If we pictured human witches at all, most of us imagined them as bonneted Puritans or maybe, vaguely British.

Imagine what people thought when they picked up the *New York Times* on Halloween, 1969, and read that Raymond Buckland and his wife, Rosemary, were meeting that very night with their coven in a Brentwood, Long Island basement—nude. That their neighbors—clerks, a barber, housewives—were with them, hopping on broomsticks, and that they regularly practiced magic in gatherings at each full moon. Buckland—with a gold earring and dark goatee (Wait! Doesn't Satan have a goatee?)—had even opened the first Museum of Witchcraft and Magic in the United States a year earlier, in 1968, which was the same year Roman Polanski's horror blockbuster *Rosemary's Baby* hit the big screen, conjuring a Satanic cult disguised as kindly old neighbors.[4]

In August 1969 came the Manson murders, which were tangled up with Satanism in our consciousness, and then this, from Sybil Leek, in the October 31 edition of the *New York Times:* "Almost 1,000 people tell me each week they want to be witches."[5]

Most Americans wouldn't differentiate the Bucklands' god-and-goddess, nature-based Wicca from Polanski's fictional "Hail Satan!" devil worship. All they knew was that witches now looked like insurance salesmen or elevator operators, and there were more of them than anyone ever imagined. As Buckland told a reporter when asked just how many covens there were in America in 1972, "It's probably closer to 2,000 than 20."[6]

The outing of witchcraft as a present-day, seemingly viral, spiritual movement with priestesses and a calendar of ritual celebrations that included Halloween changed the holiday in two ways.[7] First, it bound American Halloween to contemporary witchcraft in the public's imagination. (Although there are usually eight annual celebrations in the modern pagan calendar, Halloween was, and still is, the one most often described in news stories.) Secondly, it cast twentieth-century Halloween as a religious holiday. The more public the witch became about spirituality, the more controversial Halloween grew. Just what were we celebrating here?

Art, Magic, and How to Meet Johnny Depp

"They don't call it magic. They call it quantum physics."
—Ellie Schuster

Magic is a part of everyday life with Ellie Schuster, an artist who makes her home in suburban New Jersey. Magical-seeming things gravitate to her as a matter of course. Once, she found a lime green turkey in her yard. No explanation, just a turkey dyed green. There was a box turtle teetering on its hind legs knocking on her door one morning. And a hawk, perched outside her window, peering in at her. And, after she'd done a magic ritual under a tree in her yard one early spring, the grass grew lush and green there in the shape of a heart.

Schuster's a witch, of course, a Wiccan from way back when there were very few books and fewer fellow travelers. She used to make jewelry for Stevie Nicks, and she and her husband, Kurt, hung out every once in a while with the likes of Jimmy Page and Keith Richards. But when she became pregnant with her son and had to stay home, she discovered the books of first-generation practitioners such as Doreen Valiente. Her curiosity led her to a parapsychology class in an adult education center in New Jersey, where she met up with a woman who was a practicing witch.

"Little by little we got to know each other. . . . We started to work together. You go by the laws of the universe and eventually you are going to meet the people who are correct for your group. Like attracts like. We founded our own coven. We taught each other, supported each other, did a little healing."

She's a solitary practitioner now, going, as she says, into her crone aspect. With a vivacious personality and gorgeous red hair tumbling down her back, Schuster doesn't resemble what I imagine when I hear the word "crone."

I sought her out because she's unique—a Wiccan who creates original Halloween-themed artwork that features wise women, a witch imagining witches. And because her first Halloween sculpture was a skeleton in a black top hat inspired by Mick Jagger on the 1969 Rolling Stones tour.

"[My witches] show their wrinkles as a sign of wisdom and have a twinkle in their eye that I liken to a star to wish on. They always will wear the garb of a traditional witch, black, that represents the culmination of the entire color spectrum and all color energy and never evil. Her black hat is like a pyramid, receiving energy as well as projecting the power toward her focal point in a spell."

Modern-day witches can be touchy about how they are portrayed. They are so over green skin and cackles that witches have aggressively defined a more up-to-date image. Google the word "witch" on the Web and you can't miss it: there's more décolletage, less decomposition. Elvira, not Almira Gulch. However, Schuster's witches are old school.

The inspiration for Ellie Schuster's screen comes from German lanterns. (Photograph by Kurt Schuster)

"The kind of witch I use in my artwork, they're not the kind you would normally see on Hallmark cards. She may look haggish but that's alright; she represents the wisdom of elder. But I don't make her green, and she's not abusive to animals. All my artwork depicts the witch as a wise, nature-loving woman, the equal to the male, and part of the whole."

Schuster has a sensitive, porous relationship with the universe. She sees messages in license plates, does her magic timed to the phases of the moon, and even the word "coincidence" makes her smile. Her artwork is no different. "My mom passed away in 2001. Just afterwards, when I saw some Halloween art on eBay, it inspired me—it was almost a message from her.

"As a child I believed in vampires and ghosts, and nobody could tell me that they didn't exist. I was a big fan of [paranormal

Sculpture by Ellie Schuster. (Photograph by Kurt Schuster)

expert] Hans Holzer. I was fascinated by him, but in Clifton, New Jersey, no one knew who he was."

She eventually met Holzer, and because Schuster believes the universe provides for us what we wish for, she has also met Johnny Depp—three times.

Halloween, she insists, is not a celebration of *death*. "On Halloween I don't want to die. I'm celebrating the people who have gone on. For me, it's a time to connect with the spirit realm. It's easier. I actually feel them around me, ready to come out, around a week before. People I know. I'll get messages or indications that family members are saying hello, or other things I can't explain."

Death is part of the natural life cycle for Schuster, the dormant part. "At Halloween we're celebrating the sleeping time that we haven't yet experienced here on Earth. We get to connect with the darkness, a realm we don't know anything about. It's not macabre. Skeletons, skulls—they're mysterious, not macabre. To be connected to the unknown means you have a certain power or control that other people don't have. It's human nature to try to have at least some control over your surroundings."

And again, here we are, in the province of magic. Or is it science? Quick question: In what year did a group of wise men looking for the secrets of elemental forces immerse a gold-coated sphere in liquid and measure its attraction to a metallic plate? Answer: January 2009, when U.S. scientists discovered a way to levitate small objects using the forces of quantum mechanics.[8] OK, what about this one: In what century did science find a possible physical link between man and the divine? A) The twenty-first, when physiologist Vilayanur Ramachandran found that a specific part of the brain was associated with intense religious experience, and B) The sixteenth, when Leonardo da Vinci drew pictures of the brain that included a region for the soul (turns out da Vinci's locale wasn't far from Ramachandran's).[9] What, exactly, is magic in this world where scientists can levitate tiny mechanical parts and identify the source of spiritual passion?

"Magic is physics and metaphysics combined," says Schuster. "For myself, I love the romance, the folklore, the artistry, and the sensualness of what magic is about. But most people want to understand what magic is, how it works. Well, it's all based on the seven laws of the universe, like the law of attraction, which is what the book *The Secret* was about.[10] A teacher told me once that nothing is either/or; it's always both/and. Once you understand how it all works, you can create reality for yourself. And as you get older, you can just think it and it will happen. I think that's what the old magicians were up to, and the tools came about as symbolisms.

"There's a certain feeling I get when willfulness is stronger than anything else. Desire and visualization work hand in hand. Sometimes I feel, 'I want to see this.' Okay, but, 'I want to meet *Johnny Depp*.' That's a different willfulness. The universe always has a way—you just have to look."

Fascination with the occult and the rise of religious fundamentalism happened in tandem. This polarized us, and as a result, celebrations altered. Some schools dropped Halloween parties, for example, and new Halloween-like traditions rose up, such as trunk-or-treating, where kids go car to car in a church parking lot.[11] The fact that witches openly and aggressively trafficked in magic was unsettling to those who believed the world was pulsing with demons ready to rage through any portal available, be it the Ouija board, tarot card, unbaptized infant, or even Halloween, a holiday that is, after all, populated by monsters and celebrated at night.[12] On the other hand, the fact that Wiccans and other pagans were lambasted for their spiritual practices challenged the First Amendment, the very rock of religious freedom in America.[13]

Here's the good news. In the forty-odd years after the women of WITCH posted their manifesto and Polanski's Satanists sipped coffee in a New York penthouse waiting for the Antichrist, most people have come to accept that Halloween is not a religious holiday, but rather a holiday viewed as religious by some people, and therein lies the difference. We have made a certain peace with the iconic Halloween witch because we need her. First of all, she's the only feminine holiday icon in a year crowded with men: Santa, Rudolph, the New Year's Baby and Father Time, Punxsutawney Phil, St. Patrick, Uncle Sam, even Tom Turkey. But more than that, we need her power—be it real, symbolic, or pure fantasy.

Witches in Bikinis

"It would be interesting to try the effect [of projecting a magickal force] of one team [of witches] in the traditional nude and one in bikinis."

—Gerald Gardner, *Witchcraft Today*

August, Coney Island. Thousands of people pack the beach with umbrellas and coolers. New York's most famous Ferris wheel, Deno's Wonder Wheel, turns lazily, its cars barely swaying in a stupor of near-record heat. Out on the pier, Cambodian women fish for crabs, their babies sleeping in strollers. The boardwalk buzzes with boomboxes and kids, and there's a surf band thrumming guitars on a temporary stage. Above the din, a sideshow barker shouts his patter into a microphone.

"I'm gonna bring 'em out now, just a sneak peak, to show you what's inside. In a second, you're gonna see Elephant Girl, Fire-Eating Girl, and Elastic Girl, but I gotta tell you, Elephant Girl will be wearing a veil. You'll be able to see her feet and hands, but to see more and to hear her story you've got to go inside. Three dollars, and right now, everyone gets in for the kids' price. Three dollars."

I'm here to see a band, Witches in Bikinis, but they won't be on for at least an hour. Three dollars it is.

Inside, I'm delighted to find, for the third time in my life, a display that includes the "World's Only Feejee Mermaid"—part monkey head, part fish tail, part I really don't know what. A magician—who sullenly admits that his signature goes for $200 in Hollywood, where he's from (his second cousin, he drops, is the actor William Holden)—introduces Johnny Bizarre, the thick-skinned man. Johnny jumps up and down on broken glass with his bare feet. Fire-Eater Girl has a surgically forked tongue, piercings, and a tolerance for lighter fluid. Elephant Girl tells us the story of her debilitating skin disease. As William Holden's second cousin reaches for a few long nails and a hammer so he can bang them up his nostrils, I decide it's time to check out the band, curious to see if the witch mojo will work at the beach in the full glare of a summer's day.

"Pink, orange, red, blue . . . the witches are coming to entertain you!" croons the emcee. The guys in the band—guitar, drums, bass—peer down the boardwalk, and we, the crowd, follow their gaze. Four women in black hooded robes and spike-heeled boots snake through the audience, climb to the stage, and form a circle and undulate. Suddenly, everyone in the crowd has a camera.

The women are glamorously camp in a Pussycat Dolls way, if the Dolls wore cotton-candy-colored wigs and sang songs about zombie attacks, raising the dead, or horror films. (If you were born farther back, think Samantha Stevens meets *Laugh-In*'s Goldie Hawn.) The first number sets the tone: "I saw witches in bikinis / Flying through the air / Drinking black martinis / And throwing back their hair."

The ladies of Witches in Bikinis (WIB) are not witches any more than Snake Girl, in the sideshow not three hundred feet away, is half snake. They are performers, and, frankly, the crowd doesn't care what kind of spirituality they practice. The witch theme just adds an edge to the theatrics because witches, at least in the hazy August sun of Coney Island, are hot. As kites fly over the beach behind them, WIB goes through a clever set of Halloween-inspired songs written by guitarist and creator of the band Bill Rozar.

WIB singers at MusikFest in Bethlehem, Pennsylvania. Left to right: *Andrea Caron, Marcia Leigh, Melissa Bayern, Carrie Plew, Colleen Huley-Hart.* Not pictured: *Rori Nogee, Christina Johnson.* (Photograph by Steve McClellan)

"Joan was home alone relaxing in the bath
When through the cellar window climbed a deadly psychopath
Then she heard what sounded like a growl
So she went down to the cellar wearing nothing but a towel
Beautiful and brave but no brains in her head
Doesn't have a clue that any second she'll be dead
She's a horror flick chick

Dangerously thick
Misses every single trick
Cause she's a horror flick chick"

—"Horror Flick Chicks"

"When I first came up with Witches in Bikinis, I knew very little about witches and had never heard of Gerald Gardner," says Rozar, who counts the Beatles, They Might Be Giants, Jonathan Richman, and Alice Cooper among his musical influences. "I had been writing songs about Halloween, songs like 'Cemetery Boogie' and 'Zombie March,' and 'Witches in Bikinis' was just another song that kind of fit into the whole campy genre. It was years after writing the song that I decided to record an album and form a performance group."

He didn't know about Gardner's bikinis conjecture? I'm stunned. Two men, independently, imagining witches wearing bikinis?

"It's about being free to be yourself," says the aqua-haired witch Mila Greach (Marca Leigh) when I ask her what the witch in WIB means to her. "It's to be magical. And not just women. Everyone's free to be themselves."

The pink-haired Erimaya Snelbs (Melissa Bayern) is on the same good-vibes page. "What does witch mean? Power and magic, that's what it's about."

Fine, but it's also about bikinis. Try the act in baggy T-shirts and culottes.

Rozar says the group appeals to a diverse audience, from hardcore metal fans to young kids, and they play gigs that run the gamut from Goth parties to corporate events.

And the pagan community? What do witches think about Witches in Bikinis?

"Every pagan I've talked to could care less about what beliefs we are representing or not representing," says Rozar.

When WIB finishes their set, the crowd lunges forward to get autographs and closer snapshots of the women. I'm caught in a paparazzi moment as I pose for their manager with the singers in front of Deno's Wonder Wheel. As camera flashes pop all around us, the savvy gals smolder like pros and I blink out at the throng, bewildered, remembering only at the last second to take my reading glasses off. As I'm leaving, the show's host, Jordan Astier, hollers after me with a grin that lights up his sunburned face. "Hey! Write this! In the twenty-first century, witches started wearing bikinis!"

If Not Halloween, When?

Caveat: The following letter is being published anonymously. Normally I wouldn't include it, but frankly, given the circumstances, I'm afraid not to. It's the only piece of mail I've ever had delivered to me in the light of a full moon, through my kitchen window, clenched in the beak of a crow.

I'll come clean right up front. I'm a witch. The kind of witch who packs Turkish Delight, who's the Hansel-and-Gretel, all-in-good-time-my-pretty, buy-one-of-my-apples witch you remember from storybooks. Not an Odinist, Wiccan, or Druid, not hardly. I'm the pointed-hat, striped-socked, spell-casting, black-cat-loving, toad-and-snake-toting, cauldron-brewing witch. Halloween's my busy season, and you'd best not cross my path.

People are clamoring more than ever for money and revenge spells, curses, and love potions. I get so many requests for the evil eye now I can't keep up. And predictions? Jeez. There aren't enough hours in the day. (No, I don't know where you put your remote control/thumb drive/car keys.) Come Halloween, I'm out working 24/7 conjuring icy blasts, rusting gates, digging up old friends, tolling bells, switching street signs, and whispering the future in the wind to those who dare stand at the crossroads at midnight.

All this, despite your penchant for impaling my sisters on telephone poles and porches. Honestly. Could you be more juvenile?

It used to be easier. For centuries, we witches had a close bond with humans—love/hate to be sure, and, granted, we're not the best with kids—but a kinship just the same. Now you insist on trying to eviscerate us, remake us into cute characters on paper napkins, and give us bobble-y bosoms and kind faces on window stickers and lunch boxes. You sell "sexy witch" costumes to grown-ups. Sexy witch? Get real.

We haven't changed. You have.

It started with the great whimpering of the last few decades, when the Secret Council of the Aggressively Tolerant (SCAT) decreed that Halloween witches frighten children and urged the market to push pumpkins instead. Puh-lease! Never send a squash to do a witch's job. The pumpkin is froufrou. A witch, a force to be reckoned with. You're not likely to find us sitting around on a stoop, grinning like a gutted, lobotomized idiot. We actually do things—imprison girls with long hair, set scarecrows on fire, fence in our homes with the bones of our victims. And on Halloween, the gloves and girdle come off completely.

That tug on the sleeve of your costume Halloween night? That's me. The sudden loss of moon, deep shadows gathering under the bushes? Me. Someone has to put the boo in Halloween. It's that old shoe, duality: Without fear, no courage. Without shock, no thrill. Without a dark night, the candy's too easy.

Admit it. You love us. We remind you of the freedom you had as a kid on Halloween, when you could get away with wearing a cape and tights. A tiara. A tail. Every year, grown women drive by me in cars and yell, "Where do you work that they let you dress like that?" You wish.

Darken the moon, stir the wind, chill the air. There's a delicious, frightening magic afoot. If not witches, who? If not Halloween, when?

Witches' market, La Paz. High up in the Bolivian Andes, they set up in the early morning in a four-block by four-block warren of shops. Dried llama fetuses dangle from the doorways. Makeshift shelves are packed with feathers, bones, and ceramic statues of Pachamama, the Earth goddess, wrapped in colorfully dyed wool. Frankincense wafts through the narrow streets as men tell fortunes with coca leaves placed on a board etched with squares. If you move to a new house, you'll need that llama fetus to bury near the front step for good fortune. If your wife no longer loves you, you'll need a witch to fill a bowl with the right elements to burn—herbs, tokens, papers—so you can bring her back. Witches are an important part of modern life here and in many parts of the world. They're uncontroversial, existing side by side with Catholicism and native Aymara beliefs, such as the conviction that spirits inhabit the mountains, skies, and lightning and that tributes must be made to Pachamama to ensure the fertility of soil.

Ritual magic, which exists in most cultures, is something that's come to us from ancient times as a way to deal with loss and fear and to give expression to hope. The things we know now seem more fearsome than ever. Banks fail. Towers fall. Levees crack. Maybe the biggest boogeyman of our time is the sense that we're under assault, but we can't put our hands on the assailant. There's a helplessness afoot; so much is out of our control. It's no wonder we seek out a bit of magic now and again.

Samhain Ritual, 2008

They don't call it Halloween, but rather Samhain, and on this night, some pagan communities open their rituals to the rest of us. If you believe there is one God, you won't find him here. Nor will you find the Bible, or prophets of the Judeo-Christian tradition. However, paganism is not godless.

The goddesses and gods invoked here are mythological—Hecate, Greek goddess of the crossroads; Cerridwen, Celtic mother of the underworld. Spirituality manifests in metaphor and ritual. Modern witchcraft is focused on the cycles of the Earth, and on a balance of god and goddess, myth and ritual action, on using the power of the mind and heart to focus on truth. On this night, it's especially focused on helping us build a pathway between this world and the next. The word "hell" won't come up. Or "Satan," or "devil," or "sin." Samhain is very much about the dark, but it is a transient darkness.

If you've never been to a Samhain ritual gathering, here's a peek inside the Earthspirit community celebration.

One by one, you enter a darkened room lit only with the flickering of candles. There is an altar along the wall decorated with autumn leaves, twinkling lights, and photographs of friends and family who have passed away. A kind-faced woman greets you, tells you to take off your shoes to go to the altar to pay your respects, and that, if you like, you can leave a photo of someone you've lost. You're then greeted by a child, who takes you by the hand and leads you to a figure robed in black. The figure leans close and makes a low, whooshing sound—encouraging you to exhale, listen, be wary of the season of shadows, of wind. Faintly, in the background, a drum marks time passing. My young guide asks in a whisper, "Can you go on by yourself now?" I think I can, but I like being with him so much I say no. He's wearing a bowler hat and glasses and reminds me of my ten-year-old nephew.

There are about forty of us here tonight. We stand in a circle and listen to readings about winter, the earth going dormant. We hear a story—a good one—about a man trying to communicate with his wife after he'd died. A chant begins. "Hecate, Cerridwen / Dark Mother, take us in / Hecate, Cerridwen / Let us be reborn."

The chanting quickens as we hold onto each other's waists, swaying, then it gentles and goes silent. We speak aloud the names of our dead—who they were to us, their cause of death. Rose, my mother, of dementia. Patricia, my friend, of cancer. Bill, my swim coach; Elena, my sister. The names multiply and tumble over each other until they are all out. One woman had cremated her mother just two days before and tears pour down her face.

Another chant begins:

"Hold me, hold me, never let me go.
Hold me like the leaves on the ends of the branches.

And when I die, let me fly, let me fly,
Through the air like the leaves when they're falling."

We are blindfolded, guided to sit, and asked to think of those who have passed on before us and to listen to them, to try and hear a message from them. We wait. When we lift our blindfolds, there is a white path made of glowing plastic bones that leads to a cauldron. If we heard anything, or imagined anything, we are to write it down on a maple leaf and one by one drop our messages in the cauldron. I can read some: "Be strong," "Recover," "I love you."

The singers chant quietly, "For those who've gone before us / And those who've gone before them / We raise this cup in honor of your lives."

Suddenly the mood lifts. We are out of the dark now, coming back to life. We pass apples around a circle and sing, louder and louder, faster and faster, "Cauldron of change / Blossom of bone / Arc of eternity / Hole in the stone." The drums beat. We hold hands and run in zigzagging S-curves, faster and faster, around the room until everyone is smiling and singing and, finally, cheering.

It's odd to be among strangers, thinking such private thoughts, sharing the names of lost friends and parents. Sorrow is such a private matter. And yet it's not. The Samhain ritual doesn't feel familiar to me—I've been to less than a dozen—but it feels right. I'm thinking that it's not actually death that's so terrifying; it's the fear of being alone. And here, the dead can help. Our deepest shared culture includes them, in the way their stories become the story of our nation or of our families. They help us see that we are not alone in some relentless march of generations, that we are part of those who came before and those yet to be born.

What harm is it to celebrate their lives, our lives together, on this stunning blue planet?

Insider Info: A Witch's Wishing Spell
Christian Day, cocreator, Festival of the Dead, and owner, Hex

For a basic ritual that can apply to a variety of different goals and aspirations, I would use elements that can work in any number of different intentions. You will need:

A white candle to send out the energy (a votive or taper will do, available from any supermarket)

A piece of fine paper (velum or parchment or linen style from any stationery store)

A pen (any will do, but one that you use all the time is better)

A black or white lighter (Try to find one without advertisements. "Eat at Joe's" won't help your magic!)

Sit in a comfortable chair with a table in front of you. Place a candle in a candleholder on the table. Relax yourself in the chair as you gaze into the flame of the candle. Close your eyes and count backwards from one hundred to one as you breathe deeply, in through the nose and out through the mouth, to create a circuit of air. This is a great way to calm your mind into a relaxed, meditative state.

Once you reach the number one, say aloud or to yourself, "I am now in the perfect level of mind for working magic. May the spirits guide my every thought and deed. So mote it be!" (You may substitute God, gods, saints, or guardian spirits for the word "spirit." It's important you work with the energies that you're comfortable with.) Now, open your eyes and gaze again into the flame of the candle. Take your pen and write the goal you wish to achieve nine times onto the paper and then write, "So mote it be!" This is a term witches use; it means, "Let it be done!" Keep the paper with the spell on it under your mattress, near your pillow, so that your dreams lend power to the spell as you sleep. When you reach your goal, remove the spell and bury it in your yard (or somewhere in nature) so that the magic may feed the land!

Chapter Four
Pumpkin Obsessions

They've been exploded, catapulted, gutted with a blow torch, filled with pudding, and frozen with liquid nitrogen. They've been carved underwater; carved in 24.03 seconds; carved at the rate of one ton in three hours, thirty-three minutes; and grown to the weight of 1,725 pounds.[1] They're targeted at autumn "shoots" where riflemen line up to blast a head-sized pumpkin to smithereens. In perhaps their most unorthodox use, a hollowed-out pumpkin was used to stash two rolls of 35 mm film that became key evidence against accused Soviet spy Alger Hiss.

There are those who wear them, sculpt them, hurl them, smash them, sail them, and turn them into beer and cheesecake. It's safe to say that there is an army of people for whom pumpkins are an obsession. But why? What is it about this fruit that inspires people to go to such extremes?

To understand the fascination with the pumpkin and its nighttime cousin, the jack-o'-lantern, what better way than to go straight to the obsessed? In this case, to those who live and breathe pumpkins, be they fermented, carved, glass, giant, or papier-mâché.

So What *Is* It About Pumpkins?

Hoppy Halloween

"I really think there's an unconscious connection people have to squash in general but especially to pumpkins."

This is Will Meyers talking. He's brewmaster at the Cambridge Brewing Company (CBC) in Massachusetts, and the go-to guy for

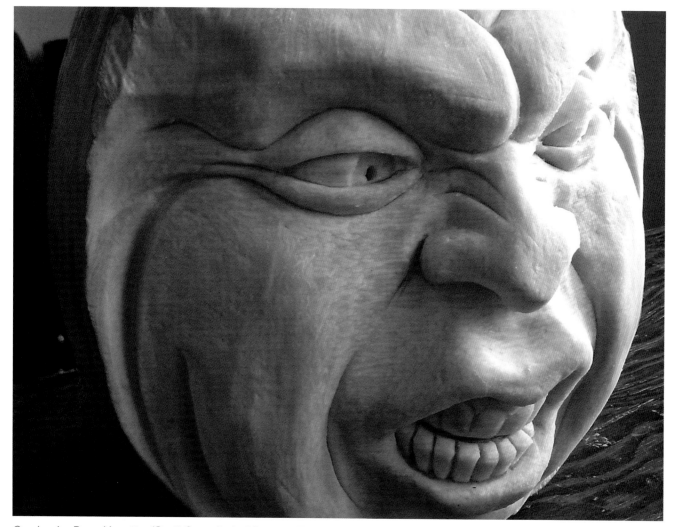

Carving by Pumpkingutter (Scott Cummins) of Perryton, Texas.
He lights his carvings with a thirty-watt bulb on a droplight.

information about its pumpkin ale. And you should know this: while we chat, Meyers is whacking pumpkins with a meat cleaver the size of Paul Bunyan's axe. Thwack! The happy orange orb cracks in two. Thwack! Its pulpy guts are scraped out and the flesh is tossed into an industrial shredder, then dumped into a 150-gallon, stainless-steel-and-copper tank.

"Maybe it's the name 'pumpkin' that's just more fun to say than squash," offers Meyers. Thwack! Another fat, rounded pumpkin chunk rolls across the table like Marie Antoinette's head.

The microbrewery will use four thousand pounds of pumpkins to make twenty-five batches of beer: three hundred gallons. All

Brewmaster Will Meyers guts and chops around thirteen hundred pumpkins to make Cambridge Brewing Company's Pumpkin Ale.

CBC "monks" with an ale-filled pumpkin. The pumpkin is created for their annual Halloween party, where it is paraded and tapped with great fanfare.

of it will sell. (Full disclosure: my brother, Phil, better known as Brewdaddy Bannatyne, owns the Cambridge Brewing Company, and he came up with the pumpkin ale recipe eighteen years ago. And even though as kids we pricked our fingers and touched them together to become blood brothers for life, he won't tell me what secret spices make his ale so popular.)

"The guts go into the tub, the rinds into the box," Will calls out to a new volunteer.

Thwack.

The CBC hauls in friends and family to help with the process because, frankly—and the brewers are first to admit this—pumpkin ale is a boatload of grief. And it's the pumpkins, not the beer, that make it so. Four thousand pounds is a tsunami of pumpkin. If you figure that they're each about three pounds, that's over thirteen hundred little pumpkins that have to be washed, cut, scooped, and shredded—pretty much all by hand—even before the beer science starts.

"The volunteers usually volunteer only once," my brother chuckles.

Despite the pain pumpkins can cause, CBC's ale is one of their most popular.

"Pumpkins are part of the greater social subconscious," theorizes Meyers. "People imagine a happy family time—like Thanksgiving, pumpkin pie. It does something in your brain that makes everyone say, 'Oh, PUMPKINS!'"

And with this theory, Meyers has happened on one of the reasons we seem to love pumpkins so much, at least for men. The experiments of smellandtaste.org researcher Dr. Alan Hirsch found that males were most "stimulated" by the smell of pumpkin pie combined with lavender. Doughnuts and black licorice were second, and buttered popcorn, believe it or not, was down near the bottom. (Even more intriguing, roasting meat and cheese pizza were tied with parsley for a tepid response, and chocolate had essentially the same effect as pink grapefruit.) Women, by the way, responded most to Good & Plenty and baby powder, but the combination of pumpkin pie and lavender was a pretty close second.[2]

But there are other reasons people go crazy for pumpkins. Like their size.

Training the Next Generation of Pumpkin Kings

"They're substantial enough to have a presence," says Ryan Wickstrand of the Internet business zombiepumpkins.com. "The fact that they're hollow is interesting. So is the idea that they rot and keep coming back." (As in seeds, not reanimated pumpkin beasts, although that intrigues him too.)

Wickstrand creates pumpkin-carving patterns featuring the likenesses of horror and pop culture icons, such as characters from *Shaun of the Dead*, Gollum, Jack Torrance, Jack Sparrow, Jack Skellington, and lots of monsters. His "Eye of the Beholder" is a guy who's plucked out his own eye and is looking at it. His "Tooth Fairy" wields oversized pliers and grins, showing a mouthful of crooked, rotting teeth.

"If you told me ten years ago I would be this involved with pumpkins I wouldn't have believed it," he laughs. "Orange was my least favorite color in art school. Now everything I see looks like a pumpkin. If I see a car go by and it's orange—I see a pumpkin."

Since Wickstrand lives pumpkins 24/7, I figure he's got to have a sense of what drives the obsession. And by pumpkin, I mean carved. And real, not artificial.

"It has to do with the fact that someone would take the time to do an intricate design in something that's temporary," Wickstrand explains. "Like a sandcastle. You can make a perfect sandcastle out of clay, but the ones made out of sand are more appreciated because one wave and they're gone."

Wickstrand looks around his office, eyeing the storage boxes stacked all the way up to his ceiling. He likes it that real pumpkins rot and go away.

Like many start-ups, zombiepumpkins.com began with one serendipitous act. Wickstrand, who always carved a pumpkin to go with his Halloween costumes, posted a pumpkin carving he'd done of musician and horror film director Rob Zombie on his personal Web site. People found it, loved it, asked where they could get something like it, and off he went. That was 2001. Now he's got more than two hundred patterns posted and over a million visitors drop by zombiepumpkins.com each fall. Sometimes they request things, odd things—a pattern in the shape of sausages or a tractor—or personal things. A member once wrote him to say, "My grandfather just passed away. He loved Halloween, would you make a tribute pumpkin?"

"I couldn't resist that one," Wickstrand admits. "I think as modernized as Halloween has become—even pumpkin carving as an art, how it's changed and gotten more elaborate—and as commercial as some aspects have become, at the core it's about tradition, it's about sharing time with friends and family. Plus, it's inclusive. People can make their own jack-o'-lantern. You don't say, 'Oh it's

Above and opposite: *"Rotting Ryan" Wickstrand and his creation "Undead Ted."* (Photographs by Ryan Wickstrand, zombiepumpkins.com)

Halloween, let's construct a witch. I love that I can help people raise the next generation of pumpkin kings."

Raising a Glass Pumpkin Patch

"I've thought and thought and thought about why people love pumpkins. But it's a mystery," admits Peter Houk, director of the Glass Lab at Massachusetts Institute of Technology (MIT) and the prime mover behind the lab's wildly popular glass pumpkins. "I know that people love groups of them—they usually don't buy just one."

It's early on a Sunday morning in August, and we've met in a suffocatingly hot MIT basement to talk about pumpkins and Halloween. The Glass Lab's furnace glowers at us from its industrial casing, its belly full of four hundred pounds of molten glass. "Such a benign and beautiful material at room temperature, but a universal solvent when molten," murmurs Houk. "It's very Halloween-ish in a way."

He hoists a one-hundred-pound bag of ground glass up to a counter and starts preparations for today's pumpkin-making. Houk and a team of volunteers create more than one thousand glass pumpkins each year to be sold during the four-hour frenzy that is the lab's annual fundraiser, the Great Glass Pumpkin Patch. This means that at almost any given time during the year there are people at MIT rolling molten blobs of liquid glass on the end of 4½-foot-long blow sticks to create pumpkins for the event.

One man brings a van from Cleveland, Ohio, buys $8,000 worth of pumpkins, and drives back. Others camp out for hours with baskets to be first in line and snap up the cheaper ones. A few call Houk six months in advance to beg him for the date. They're planning their vacation to Boston around the sale and need to know exactly when it will be.

"We pretty much sell out," Houk tells me. "You get down to the last few and everyone just stands and looks at them like they are sick patients."

So what makes the patch so popular?

"I can tell you that it's kind of like Filene's Basement in that there's a limited commodity and we only do it once a year, and that feeds the mentality, the scarcity thing, that's part of human nature. But what is the basic appeal of pumpkins? It really is a mystery. There's something magical about them."

Is it the happy orange color? Sure, it's great. But there are other great-colored fruits and vegetables, like eggplant. Is it the winsome,

A blob of molten glass is repeatedly rolled in colored glass, shaped, blown, then set briefly in a mold to give it pumpkinlike ridges. A smaller piece of melted glass is attached and stretched to form the stem.

More than a thousand glass pumpkins are displayed on the grass at the annual Great Glass Pumpkin Patch fundraiser at MIT.

headlike appeal of their shape? Or the pumpkin's anthropomorphic potential? Maybe that's not so wrong. Scientist Michael C. LaBarbera of the University of Chicago says that we're hardwired to adore anything with a large head and big eyes; it says "baby" to us and pulls on all the nurturing parts of our brain.[3] Jack-o'-lanterns, if nothing else, have large heads and big eyes.

And pumpkins almost have personalities—witness the care most people take when choosing the right one to take home and carve. They're not quite like pets, but people seem to have an affection for them well beyond that which they feel for other fruit.

If pumpkins inspire such strong feelings, I wondered, do giant pumpkins inspire even stronger ones? I packed my camera and headed out to Topsfield, Massachusetts, for the New England Giant Pumpkin Grower's Association's weigh-off to see if what's true about a normal-sized pumpkin is gigantically true of a big one.

They Must Be Giants

"Bad people don't grow giant pumpkins."
—John Doucet, New England Giant Pumpkin
Growers Association (NEGPGA)

Sixty-five giant pumpkins rest in what can only be called herds: the three hundred pounders, the five hundreds, the eight hundreds, and then the real divas—giant pumpkins estimated to weigh more than one thousand pounds—lounging like a tent full of Jabba the Hutts on thick padded blankets as they wait for their turn on the scale.

A dim light leaks into the Topsfield Fair arena early in the morning, but as the sun cuts higher and higher through the windows, you can see that most everyone inside is wearing some sort of orange sweater or sweatshirt under their coats in solidarity with the contestants of the Great Pumpkin Commonwealth's 2008 NEGPGA weigh-off.

"Rob Hardy come on up!" the emcee shouts. "This first time grower weighs in at . . . 335.5 pounds!"

Muffled, mittened hands applaud. It's only October, but mornings in New England have already turned frigid.

"These giant pumpkins are ninety days old, on average," announces the emcee. "Pollinated the first week of July. They'll grow thirty-five to forty pounds a day if they're doing well."

Forty pounds a day? That's like growing a six-year-old over the weekend.

"It's all about the weight," he banters. "This is not a beauty contest."

I'll say. They look like deformed invalids or sleeping, overweight cats, if the cats were the size of an industrial dryer. Eight men wearing "Giant Pumpkin Lift Team" sweatshirts take a specially designed blanket with custom hand holes and slide it under a pumpkin. "On my count. One, two, three!" They lift it onto a forklift, which then hauls it to a flatbed scale. Above, an electronic scoreboard keeps track of the current winner and the weight of his or her pumpkin. By 9:30 A.M., it's 832 pounds.

The emcee stokes up the crowd. "Will we see a fifteen hundred-pound pumpkin today? I think so!" In between weight

The Camp Sunshine Pumpkin Festival at City Hall Plaza, Boston, 2008. The festival raises money to support a retreat for children with life-threatening illnesses and currently holds the world record for the greatest number of carved pumpkins (30,128, in 2006).

Giant pumpkins waiting their turn on the scale at the Topsfield Fair weigh-off.

announcements, he fills in with trivia: "If it's green or gray it's a squash. Any other color, it's a pumpkin. Splits and soft spots disqualify the pumpkin. Pale pumpkins weigh heavy."

Nurturing a one-thousand-plus-pound pumpkin takes time—up to five hours a day during the peak growing season—and constant attention. They can drink a lot, like around one hundred gallons of water a day. And the vines grow about three feet each day so there's a lot of trimming, weeding, and debugging to be done. Then there's the obsession—growers build sheds, windbreakers, and tents for their pumpkins. They sing to them; hug them; shine high-wattage bulbs on them; feed them kelp, liquid fish, worm casings, and rabbit manure; wrap them in warm blankets; cool them with fans; surround them with mousetraps; shoot woodchucks that try to eat them; and, occasionally, protect them from prying eyes with sensors, cameras, and fences.

Joe Jutras watches as they lower his entry onto the scale. A buzz goes around the arena. Jutras won last year's weigh-off with a 1,689-pound specimen, clinching the Guinness World Record in 2007. The seeds were dubbed "1,689 Jutras," and he grew this year's entry from them. But the pumpkin goes shockingly light—1,055 pounds. Jutras glances over his shoulder at the electronic scoreboard as he leaves the weighing area, double-checking the weight. He won't win Topsfield this year, but, so far, he's still got the world record.

Pumpkins that don't make the leader board try to keep their dignity as they're shuffled off to the back of the staging area. When a 1,180-pounder knocks the rest out of competition, the crowd roars, and the pumpkin glides through the arena on the forklift like a plus-sized beauty queen on a parade float.

The stands begin to fill. This may be the slowest, but nonetheless thrilling, race in the world. And it's personal. As one of the heavy hitters—growers who break the one-thousand-pound barrier—walks across the dirt floor, a woman behind me whispers sadly, "All of his died but one."

The weigh-off suddenly gets serious—a 1,398.9-pound giant takes the lead. The emcee is exhilarated: "Didn't we tell you we were going to take you to the next level?"

And then there were two.

Forklifts move the giants to the scale.

Wes Dwelly's lumpen monster weighs in at 1,464. As the last pumpkin is hoisted onto the forklift, the the crowd quiets. The officials carefully inspect the front, rear, sides, and bottom. They give a thumbs up, and the giant is lowered slowly onto the scale.

The grand dame, the last giant, comes up light.

Like the end of *Saturday Night Live* when the sax hits those goodbye notes, Dwelly stands in the midst of a crowd of growers, grinning and slapping high fives. Within seconds, the camera lights come on and he's cut from his pals, surrounded by boom microphones and camera cords as he gives his first interview. "How does it feel to win Topsfield?"

As any grower can tell you, it feels good. But to pinpoint what draws them to pumpkins, say, rather than zucchini or pigs, that's harder.

"You ask the toughest question there is," John Doucet tells me outright. He grows his pumpkins in Ipswich, Massachusetts, and is one of the directors of the NEGPGA. "I feel it breaks down to this single virtue: you hardly ever meet a pumpkin grower that is

HALLOWEEN NATION   💀

not in general a nice human being. And we are all *extremely* competitive. I guess a big pumpkin that weighs over one thousand pounds just looks better than a three-pound tomato."

But let's not underplay the fame and fortune. Record-busting giants can become celebrities when they're exploded on *The Late Show with David Letterman,* which was the fate of Wes Dwelly's pumpkin. (For Letterman's 2008 Halloween show, the pumpkin was trucked to Coney Island, filled with dynamite, and blown to pieces.) Growers get calls from Leno and Regis, and the record-breaking giants are bought by Las Vegas casinos and restaurants where top-dog carvers line up for a chance to work on them. The seeds can be very valuable—those proven to produce heavy pumpkins can sell for north of $500 per seed, and sometimes way north. There's the prize money too. Wes Dwelly walked away with $5,500 for his 1,464-pounder at Topsfield in 2008. But more than any of these incentives, growing the heaviest pumpkin in the world comes with the most coveted prize of all—bragging rights.

Halloween pumpkins and jack-o'-lanterns go straight to the smell-and-instinct parts of our brains. They invoke all the good associations of fire—hearth, warmth, protection, roaring flames against the primitive night. (Christmas, by comparison, is also about chasing away darkness, but the colors of Christmas are celestial—the twinkle of stars, the greens, reds, blues of the Northern Lights.) We all seem to have a special place for pumpkins in our hearts. But for some of us, pumpkins can become an obsession.

Painter Hugh Luck is well respected around Philadelphia for his exquisite, high-end faux-finish work. But in the Halloween world, he's known as the guy who bought a house with the money he made selling his collection of vintage decorations.

The House That Pumpkins Bought

He was just seven, at his parent's home in the Shenandoah Valley of Virginia, when he piled half a dozen pumpkins onto a wagon and pulled it up the hill to the road. He lined up two cinderblocks and balanced a wooden plank on top to make his pumpkin stand. Maybe someone came along and bought one, he doesn't remember.

And he didn't buy his Philadelphia-area house outright, Hugh Luck says, correcting the mythology about the sale of his vintage Halloween pumpkin collection. "I put 20 percent down on the house, bought a car, and didn't work much for a year." The sale netted more than $200,000 for four hundred items and more than five hundred postcards he'd amassed picking through the antique stores of rural Pennsylvania with an eye for the rarest and most wonderful Halloween decorations.

The house is gorgeous. And the pumpkin collection is growing again.

"That's a Mr. Bony," Luck says, pointing out a motorized, bobble-headed jack-o'-lantern. "They say Mr. Bony is in an insane asylum, and he makes things from the stuff he finds around the grounds. His nurse Linda sells them for him on eBay."

A quick sweep of any room in this house is a joy. I spy a photograph of Luck standing with Buffalo Bob at an antique booth in Atlantic City; a green devil's head from New Jersey's Asbury Park Pier funhouse; a hymn rack from a Baptist church decorated with Halloween ephemera; a pirate—life-sized with two vivid glass eyes—made by the Disney artist who created most of the original *Pirates of the Caribbean* figures for the California park; and a motion-activated witch's face from K-Mart that unrolls a long Pepto Bismol-pink tongue and shrieks, "You STINK!"

"I do like scary decorations," grins Luck, "just not the kind where they're chewing people's faces off."

Rarely have I ever seen someone's love affair with objects—with color, texture, and character—manifest like this. The things Luck loves take shape and hang on walls or gather on shelves. In one smallish glass case sits about $12,000 in Halloween collectibles. Dominating the case is a blue-eyed, red-nosed jack-o'-lantern with two perfect rows of white teeth.

"That's my favorite—it's the biggest German-composition jack-o'-lantern I've ever seen," confides Luck.

Vintage Halloween decorations were meant to be discarded, so their value lies in the fact that they're still here. The rarest and most coveted are the German-made favors created between the turn of the century and the 1930s.

Every Saturday for years, Luck drove seventy miles to the heart of Amish country to scour the five thousand booths and antique shops clustered around Adamstown, Pennsylvania. "The Pennsylvania Dutch save everything!" he says. "A lot of the great German Halloween stuff ended up in Adamstown."

He'd hunt for treasures all day, then get up at 4:00 A.M. the next morning, grab a flashlight and go out again. "[The outdoor antique market] Renningers was bustling by then, and everybody would save things for me. Most antique dealers were collectors and still are—and they know once you get somebody that's

Opposite: Hugh Luck with a few of his favorite things: a hand-painted bowl by Carolee Clark, papier-mâché jack-o'-lantern by Scott Smith of Rucus Studio, witch by Mr. Bony, and shadow boxes, black cat, raven circus figures by Paul Gordon, among others. The painting is Luck's work.

obsessed, that person will come back. The dealers will keep you in debt. I always owe somebody something."

Luck started buying Halloween ephemera because it was cheap, but more than that, because it took him back. Spotting a 1960s jointed cardboard skeleton in an antique booth shot him straight to childhood friend Bill Clark's basement in Waynesboro, Virginia, on Halloween. "We'd string the Beistle skeletons across the rafters and the strings would come back down to a control panel, and you could pull them so everything would move throughout the room. We'd turn out the lights and bring little girls in and shake their hands with wet sponges. Then we'd move the decorations."

The pumpkin, especially, is pure childhood for him. "I spent three weeks every summer on a farm with my cousins, milking cows and swimming with the water moccasins in the creek. We grew pumpkins. My grandmother had jack-o'-lanterns. So every year at Halloween it's like déjà vu. It's just a feeling I get."

First he started buying Halloween collectibles, then he opened a few booths and started selling them, all the while upgrading his own collection. By 1997, Luck could say something even the most rabid Halloween fan only dreams of, "Every penny I had was in Halloween decorations.

"Sell my collection? The thought never crossed my mind. But I was living in a rental apartment, feeling kind of like a vagrant with lots of punkins. I thought it would be nice, by the time I was forty-five, to have my own house. It was time to become responsible. Not that I ever did. But I do have a house. And I bought my first vehicle—a Mitsubishi Montero Sport. Loved that car."

There were three auctions held for Luck's collection. The auctions closed at midnight, but in the wee hours of the morning, hardcore collectors were still on the phone, fighting for the last few pieces. He sold it all.

Like an ex, Luck bumps into his things here and there. Pieces from his collection, for example, can pop up on segments of Martha Stewart's show around Halloween or in a magazine spread. He still buys and sells a bit. But Halloween collectibles are expensive now, and Luck more temperate. "You could spend $5,000 on a pumpkin, and I could get a whole couch for that." On the other hand, Luck loves his new artisan-made Halloween things, his Mr. Bony creatures, Paul Gordon's circus-costumed ravens, Rucus Studio's oversized, monster-headed jack-o'-lantern. "Antique collectors used to shun them, but now they're buying top-of-the-line, new Halloween stuff."

Again, I have to ask. What is it about Halloween—and about pumpkins and jack-o'-lanterns specifically—that people love so

Opposite: An assortment of collectibles including Luck's favorite pumpkin lantern.

much that they're willing to buy and sell enough to finance a house and a Mitsubishi Montero Sport?

"The imagery of Halloween is much better than Christmas imagery. And the color is vivid. You put a whole room full of this stuff together and it's a vivid, hot room. There's more imagination. And I think the jack-o'-lantern is the quintessential image of Halloween. It's taking something inanimate and giving it a spirit."

Given the real terrors we live with day to day, our traditional Halloween creatures—ghosts, witches, jack-o'-lanterns—can seem almost quaint. But driving the crises about the environment, nation, and survival is the big one, the one that's the most essentially down-to-the-bone human fear there is: fear of death, the dead, the unknown. The one thing that has shaped Halloween for centuries still does. It's all about the end.

Chapter Five
Dead Man Rising

Corpses for Sale

A box arrives at your house. It's big—the largest size UPS offers. Delighted, you slice through the tape and open the flaps. Inside, curled into a fetal position, is a full-size corpse. You lift it out and unbend the torso, the legs, and marvel at that nicely decaying head. Is it just what you wanted? Do you know exactly where you'll put it?

Every year about a dozen of these get packed on trucks for delivery to independent filmmakers or to guys who are into old cars; they like to strap one in the passenger seat and drive around for kicks. A few go to radio stations, one or two to military bases. Once, a corpse was delivered to One Microsoft Way.

You do have to make a few choices when you order one: male or female? Blue eyes or brown? Hair color? And what level of decay?

"There's light or heavy decay," explains Jaime Di Stefano, the proprietor and creator of corpsesforsale.com. "For light decay I leave a bit more of the eyelid, build up the nose. With heavy decay, the eye sockets are more hollow, the nose is deteriorated—more like a flat nose—and the neck is thinner. The mouth shows more teeth, almost like it's smiling. Every body decays differently," he adds, "so I have some artistic liberty."

Since 1991, Di Stefano has created around 150 corpses, crafted from chicken wire, wood, latex, and cotton. He thinks of them as art projects, not stiffs. He made the first for a Halloween decoration, then posted it on eBay, sold it, and got orders for three more. Di Stefano describes his customers as "normal, average people . . . who are into that kind of thing. I think everybody's a little bit fascinated with death. Normally you'd think it would be morbid, but

Jenifer Michel Schultz organized this zombie walk in Jacksonville, Florida, in 2008.
(Photograph by Max Michaels, movementmagazine.com)

I think people like morbid things. We like to flirt with death a little bit. You're close, but you're not there."

And there's the elephant in the room: most of us are afraid of dead people. And Halloween, always associated with the creepy dead (as opposed to Memorial Day that honors better-behaved, military dead), is when they most often appear. For more than one thousand years, the dead have been close by around Halloween. We see it in the ghosts that inhabit the holiday, we see it in the way modern witches commemorate the spirit world on Samhain, or the Catholic Church on All Souls' Day.

From the sheer volume of eviscerated-body props, blood-soaked costumes, and zombie-attack movies alone, it's clear our biggest fears and fascinations of the twenty-first century are still focused around dying, dying badly, and not staying dead.[1] Why is a dead body so frightening? And why is the world littered with corpses at Halloween?

Dancing With Death

Inside the New England Institute at Mount Ida College in Newton, Massachusetts, someone has tossed a notebook on a chair, and where "U Tech" should be is the word "Mortuary." The glass trophy case in the hallway contains a wax head with a plaque reading, "Best in Show, Spring 2008 Restorative Art Class." On the bulletin board nearby, a post reads, "Position available. Crematory in Central Vermont."

Jacquelyn Taylor runs the Institute at Mount Ida College, one of six private colleges in the country with a baccalaureate program in mortuary science. If anyone would know why we're frightened of corpses it would be Taylor. Thanatology is her business.

The director's office sits a few floors above the school's morgue. A small statue of Anubis, the jackal-headed god of embalming, decorates one corner of the room; in another, there's Rodin's *The Thinker* rendered in bones. I'm eager to chat with Taylor because she has thirty years experience in and around the death business. (Although you'd never know it to look at her. She has energy more akin to an adventure tour guide than a funeral home director.) She is also a licensed embalmer, certified thanatologist, and expert witness in her field. Taylor is happy to talk, because when it comes to mortuary science, so many people have it wrong.

"I told the Mystery Writers convention in Marin County, 'I don't care if you're sensational about this, but at least get this right. We don't drain the blood and then put in the embalming fluid, we put in the embalming fluid and that pushes the blood out.'"

So then, I ask right off, let me get this first thing straight: Why are we so afraid of dead bodies? Why are they cast as monsters in horror films and fiction, in Halloween haunted houses, and in our own nightmares?

"We're Neanderthals sitting around the cave," she explains, "and John's not looking so good. He hasn't been contributing, hasn't been hunting. And we sense that something's different about John. Back then, if we left John in the cave, pretty soon he would become malodorous and his appearance would change, and I really think that it began there. I think we have this cognitive, innate ability to say, 'That's different than us, and it's not good.'

"A lot of the fear of the dead comes from pragmatism [like staying away from contagious plague victims]. It's a little leap to go from dead to bad to fear to monster. We had to separate ourselves from death, and therefore, it must not be right. People have always felt the emotion of separation and the pain of loss, and when all of that mixes together, I don't think it's hard to get to the idea that the dead are somehow evil."

Taylor is talking only about North American attitudes toward death. The rest of world, she says, sees death very differently.

This innate fear of something different—them vs. us—makes a lot of evolutionary sense. I wouldn't want to spend a lot of time in the cave with John either. But it seems like recently there are corpses everywhere. They are not just in the aisles of Halloween stores and in haunted houses, but appear regularly in all the muck and ooze that splays across our TV screens every night. Corpses even turn up in science-oriented touring exhibits like Body Worlds, where collections of skinned human "plastinates" are posed, flayed, in glass cases for families to admire. Are we becoming *more* fascinated with dead bodies? Or is all this carnage simply a way to get our attention?

"Do we need to set the bar higher to shock? Yes," Taylor agrees. "You have to sensationalize everything to get our bandwidth. But I don't see us getting any more used to death. I'm concerned there's more detachment. We're now dealing with a generation of kids for whom school shootings or 9/11 are ordinary events. There's an overload of information, sensory information, and they become detached from it."

By way of illustrating this, Taylor laughs and mentions that the students in her program use the school's mortuary science equipment to stage a haunted house in her building each Halloween.

Come again?

"The honor society has to do a public service event, and we let them do it here."

Apparently, it's an over-the-top, crazy-scary haunted house staged for about three hundred to four hundred people who come from the campus community. Students not enrolled in the mortuary program hover at the entryway because they know this is the building where the dead people are, and they're not sure how much of it they're going to see.

No kidding. I'd hover too.

But Taylor's point is that the students who create these scenes of horror make absolutely no connection to the bodies they work with in the classroom and morgue. They're detached.

"They can compartmentalize things. The haunted house can be as outrageous as we can make it, and then we can sit in funeral directing class and talk about respect for the dead."

Halloween is play, death is real, and where they overlap is where the fear-as-entertainment lives. I make a note in large letters: "Do NOT miss Institute mortuary haunt."

This detachment, though, is troubling for Taylor. "The generation before us grew up understanding death—it was common. It's not unusual now for a person in their forties to not have experienced the death of someone close to them. And yet they are inundated with images of death. There's some sort of dissonance. Because we have now institutionalized death and put it 'over there,' we have a culture in which death is optional. When you're cremated and scattered, the people around you never see you dead. They can imagine you out there somewhere."

In other words, there's no body, no tangible, undeniably absent, loved one.

"The first reason to have a viewing of the body is reality; as in, there is no denying this. A death fractures our conceptions of how life is supposed to go. Even people who work in oncology or the medical examiner's office—people who see dead bodies all the time—when it happens to them, it's incomprehensible. It turns us upside down.

"One of the reasons monsters have to appear so horrific is that in some ways we *want* to disturb our mind that way," explains Taylor. "I've always thought Halloween gives us this chance to flirt with death, a way to look at ghastly bodies, a way to practice dealing with death. You know, we're not very good at teaching our kids how to do this. So maybe, with Halloween, they're just finding their own way."

Confronting corpses also connects us to our most essential curiosities. A dead body is above all a cipher, a mysterious husk. The dead go where the secrets are and slam the door shut behind them. As Taylor says pretty emphatically, "There is no question about the difference between a live person and a dead person. If you believe in anything—energy, soul, spirit—*something's* changed."

Encounters with fake dead bodies help us prepare for our lives in the dark, kind of like a Sweet Hereafter boot camp. No wonder corpses sink into our subconscious. Maybe the frights of Halloween really are part of the cure for what Taylor sees as a cultural dissonance. We used to be physically with the dead, and now we're not. Maybe we miss that. And Halloween's corpse-soaked horror, zombie pub crawls, and hearse rallies—all things we think of as fun and unserious—could be a modern version of sitting with the dead, a way to go head to head, without pain or danger, with malodorous John. To dance, as Taylor says, with death.

It can come like a deep, welcome sleep, or it can come like a cat clawing its way down your throat, but it comes. The Danse Macabre, Dance of Death, has been with us since images of skeletons leading hapless humans in their last waltz first appeared in the fifteenth century.[2] The theme emerged all over late-medieval Europe to remind people death is always waiting, no matter who you are and how many gold coins are hidden under your floor boards. It's been a part of Day of the Dead festivals in Europe and the Americas for centuries, and the idea lives on in the still-jitterbugging bones of Halloween.

Here's the paradox: although images of death seem more pervasive than ever, the actual deaths of those close to us are hidden and under the jurisdiction of specialists we sometimes never meet. What scares us now about death in the twenty-first century may be unique to our lifetimes.

Human death-fears change based on real threats. Consider 1830s Britain—the only legal source of corpses for the study of anatomy was a scant supply from the gallows. Enterprising criminals stole bodies from unmarked graves in potter's fields, and, understandably, the poor became terrified of dying and having their bodies skinned and dissected. (Wealthier families were also concerned, precipitating a run on iron coffins with sturdy locks.)

A few decades later, people were less afraid of grave robbers and more afraid of doctors who couldn't tell the difference between a corpse and an unconscious person. Being buried alive became an obsession, so much so that a report of an exhumed female corpse with lacerations on her arms—as if she had tried to claw her way out of the ground—caused public panic. People pleaded to have their throats cut after death to be absolutely sure they wouldn't wake up in a coffin under six feet of damp earth. Promoters of "safe burial" weighed in with other sure-fire methods, such as decapitation, which was a comforting certainty. So was a steel needle through the heart or an injection of strychnine. Embalmers recommended injecting the chemical fluorescein into corpses; they knew if the blood was still flowing, the substance would make the eyes glow an otherworldly emerald.[3]

New, twentieth-century standards opened a different vein of death-fear. Defining death in terms of brain activity (rather than cold-to-the-touch bodily death) meant that you could be declared dead while your heart was still beating, which is critical for successful organ transplant surgery.[4] But now we suffer visions of waking to find surgeons with scalpels poised over our chests, an icy cooler waiting nearby for our eyes or kidneys. Or the opposite—having our hair curled and nails painted by well-meaning hospital aides when we've been brain dead for months.

No wonder the dead are such potent symbols of terror; cadres of vivisected, ragged, pieced-together once-humans stagger through

Vampire Mischief. (Illustration by Chad Savage)

HALLOWEEN NATION

our collective imaginations, caught on the snag of modern science—neither dead nor alive. That zombies would be so popular now is a no-brainer.

Zombie Science?

"This brain is tender, juicy, and full of all the neurotransmitters a young, growing, bloodthirsty zombie needs. The frontal and occipital lobes are particularly tender, making for an excellent roast, or diced for a quick snack."

—brains4zombies.com

"Corpses are the worst, foulest kind of trash—potentially full of disease." This is Dr. Kim Paffenroth, one of the few scholars who is both a professor of religious studies and a writer of zombie horror, which meant there was a better chance he'd take my questions about the living dead more seriously than, say, the principal of my neighborhood parochial school. "They remind us of mortality and pain, and of our own limited, finite existence as a physical, corporeal being. Yet, for most of us, they point on to something beyond, that the person who used to be these remains is now *not* just these ashes or this corpse—the vital flame or spirit or soul or atman [universal life principle] is now gone—usually, we imagine, gone somewhere better."

So if remains are dangerous trash and, at the same time, point toward a better beyond, then wouldn't reanimated remains—zombies—be trash without any of the redemption? Is that part of what makes them horrible to us? That to be both dead and alive at the same time is just wrong?

"Exactly. Zombies violate the natural order, and they threaten to make us (the living) share in that eternal liminal state—not passing on, but being consumed by never-ending hunger. Which, by the way, is exactly the insight Dante has into the damned in *Inferno*—eternal, insatiable hunger is the essence of sin, for him and for George Romero."[5]

"Please date responsibly, bring a baseball bat or crowbar."
—zombieharmony.com, a zombie-only Internet dating site

It's 7:00 P.M. on a Monday night in April, and I'm stuffed cheek to jowl with several hundred other audience members in the plush seats of the Coolidge Corner Theatre in Brookline, a Boston suburb. To my right, a girl tells her friend how unpleasant it is to fall

Zombies shouldn't be capable of higher-order functions, like texting, according to Dr. Schlozman.

on the floor of a mosh pit. He tells her about a haunted house in New Hampshire that starts with a ski lift ride. Definitely feels like a Halloween crowd.

By 7:05 P.M., there's not a single seat left. What's the draw? The theater's screening George Romero's 1968 *Night of the Living Dead,* and who doesn't like that? But what's really brought us out is the academic preshow. Psychiatry professor Steven C. Schlozman is introducing the film with his lecture "The Neurobiology, Psychology, and Cultural Overtones of the Zombie Film Genre" (subtitled "A Way Cool Tax Deal for a Bunch of Cool Books, Action Figures, and a Movie").

He's greeted like a rock star.

We listen raptly as Schlozman describes how zombies, which lack most of their frontal lobe function, run pretty much on impulses sent from what scientists call the crocodile brain. Zombies aren't able to make higher-order decisions, which is why they stand at closed doors and can't seem to figure out how to open them. (These are the Romero-type zombies, Schlozman notes, as opposed to the *28 Days Later*-type zombies, which, first of all, aren't dead—they're infected—and, secondly, show group hunting skills, indicating more sophisticated brain activity.) Without higher brain function, base emotions such as aggression, lust, and fear arise, uncensored, out of the limbic region. Zombies have a dysfunctional ventromedial hypothalamus (they're always hungry), and they stagger because their cerebellum is also probably dysfunctional, as are their basal ganglia. In other words, states Schlozman, you really can't get mad at a zombie because it's just a clumsy crocodile.

Schlozman sails through PowerPoint slides of sections of the brain with names that sound like galaxies—anterior cingulate cortex, amygdalae—he's our Kirk. No, cooler, he's Spock. Science as the new sci-fi? When he asks the audience how many have heard of mirror neuron theory, a third raise their hands. Do I need any more proof that science, especially brain science, is *cool?*

Zombies, more than any other monster right now, hit all our buttons: horror, fear, fantasy, and the fun of guiltless violence. Being a zombie—shambling en masse on World Zombie Day or lurching your leaden limbs at a Halloween Zombie Ball—is a way to flirt with some of the things that scare us to death about living in the twenty-first century. There's the dead/alive conundrum to be sure, but there are plenty others.

Are zombies a way to vent our paranoia about infectious disease? Germ warfare and epidemics often play across the front pages of our newspapers and the fears seem justified. *Newsweek* recently reported that "the planet contains an estimated 1,415 pathogens . . . that we know about: 217 viruses, 307 fungi, 538 bacteria, 66 protozoa, and 287 types of worms. Nearly ⅔ of these pathogens live among nonhuman species, but they are not staying put." [6] It's a small step to see how real-world fears could slip into zombie culture, how easy it would be to imagine that the monsters are already inside us, laying eggs. [7]

Or are we afraid of battling an enemy that has no fear? Is the popular zombie annihilation of humankind a way to deal with the horror of being the last human left? Maybe it's the idea that when it really, really matters, you can't trust *anyone?* Identifying with zombies becomes a way of protecting ourselves, as in, "You can't hurt me. I'm already dead." For lots of very good reasons, zombies really grab us.

Shamblin' On

Two lobes in the skull.
I eat the bloodier one—
not much difference.

—Ryan Mecum, "Zombie Haiku by Robert Frost"

"Many cultures have their own end of the world, archetypal avatars," says Dan Burrello, an Asheville, North Carolina, horror writer and zombiephile with master's degrees in psychology and writing. "The pagan cultures believed in a constant death and renewal. With the advent of the Christian, linear view of time, we have a beginning and an end. The Enlightenment gave us escape from a particular vision of damnation; science destroyed the old gods, but we retained the linear paradigm. We are still aching for the end. . . . [W]e are aching for the death of our fake culture and a renewal into something else. If a god cannot manage it, and science has put too many safeguards in place, then perhaps our ancestors, perhaps our own dead—set to walk among us, free of any illusions—can hit the reset switch."

I like this. Zombie infestation as a let's-get-this-right-next-time, biblical-sized flood spilling its way through our downtowns like a bizarro-world public service. I like even more the way Burrello relishes the chance to zombie up and trudge through Asheville with seven hundred other zombies, which he did in 2008 as leader of a World Zombie Day crawl.

"So much of it is about actually fooling myself into the idea, just for the moment, that this is actually happening," says Burrello. "That the dead are returning and the tired, ridiculous, hypocritical, consumerist culture has ended. Put lovingly to bed with the rotting jaws of an army of those we know and love. . . . [Zombie culture] is the entrance by which the cynical hipster can access the land of the Jungian archetypes and still remain relevant."

Although zombie crawls can happen at any time of the year (Valentine's Day seems a favorite), World Zombie Day (WZD)—usually held on a weekend near Halloween—unites zombie lovers around the world. The word goes out via Internet sites, and just like, in Burello's words, "a flash mob gone very, very dead," dozens to hundreds converge at a certain time and place and zom their way down the main streets of towns as far-flung as Fairbanks, Alaska; Middletown, Rhode Island; Stockton, California; and Kansas City, Missouri. In 2008, for example, six thousand zombies marched in forty-six cities worldwide on WZD.

Opposite: Dan Burrello and his deadwedded bride, Tara Watts. Burrello's Asheville Zombie Walk 2008 came under scrutiny by the Secret Service when they learned that the walk would accidentally coincide with a Sarah Palin rally. (Photograph by Peter M. Lorenz)

"The line of people stretched four blocks long. There was a football game that day, and the police actually stopped traffic to let all 267 of us cross."
—Jenifer Michel Schultz, WZD organizer, Jacksonville, Florida

"We have a Brain Eating Contest where we place Jell-O in zombified mannequin heads. The participants have to eat the "brains" as fast as they can without using their hands."
—Bridgette Fish, WZD organizer, Ybor City, Florida

"My first year I had an older woman in her sixties come out dressed as an undead Mickey Mouse. Her husband dropped her off and wanted nothing to do with the event, but she was excited. She said it sounded different and fun and wanted to give it a try."
—Bambi Braun, WZD organizer, Ann Arbor, Michigan

"As someone who is pretty shy in real life, dressing up and playing a part—albeit of a brain stem—is freeing for me because I can cut loose a little. I take off my glasses and I cover myself in make-up and suddenly I'm not so shy or worried about what others think of me. It's a nice feeling."
—Jo Finlay, WZD organizer, London, England

Right now, I'm looking at a photograph of a little boy, maybe eleven months, in a stroller with darkened eyes and dribbles of fake blood on his chubby cheeks. I have to ask Dan Burrello about this. I've seen lots of babies dressed as pumpkins and kittens and purple dragons at Halloween, but baby gore is new to me.

"I believe that the gory aspect is an initiatory gate through which those who get the joke may enter and those who do not cannot," he answers.

Aha! It's about real versus fake, the same terrain as the real death/fake death we tread at Halloween. It's about irony and distance, about things that heal (community, expression, humor) as opposed to things that corrode (real violence). There's a level of irony in zombie love that is understood only by those inside the circle. Like getting the word "abomination" tattooed on your back, you can literally be it and comment on it at the same time. Irony suits the outsider—it definitely works in zombie culture.

"[*Dawn of the Dead* makeup artist] Tom Savini said that after Vietnam, he couldn't be around any kind of actual dead bodies, but it was fun creating fake ones," Burrello says. "Now, as a psychology instructor, I must add that the idea of granting life, even to the most mangled of the dead, is an act of a god. We are powerless in the face of death. When we walk right up to it . . . right up

Opposite: *Elvis hands out beef jerky at a Jacksonville, Florida, zombie walk.* (Photograph by Max Michaels, movementmagazine.com)

to the most horrific endings, accept them, and revel in that power . . . death loses its hold over us. A Zen philosopher once said something to the effect of, 'Die, and be truly dead to yourself, and be free of its power.'"

Zombies are stacking up as actually good for us. Good for the soul, our health (Hey! walking is exercise), and the family (inclusive of even the stroller bound). And in his prefilm lecture for *Night of the Living Dead*, Dr. Schlozman had concluded with the idea that zombies help us process all the scary stuff of the twenty-first century with humor, which, again, is a healthy response.

They even seem to bring people together. I mean, you don't have Vampire Fly-ins or Mummy Shuffles (yet). How is it that the nonverbal, putrid, and generally bad-mannered zombie has become the monster of choice for huge social gatherings?

"What better way to break the ice than to not have to break it?" says Burrello. "Wandering up to a couple of hot zombie chicks and having no other pressure than to moan rather well is pretty empowering for someone who may spend hours watching zombie flicks and trying to level at W.O.W. [World of Warcraft] in his parent's basement. Right?"

Yes, Dan's right. Zombie culture, and Halloween overall, is pretty darn geek friendly.

"Man-eating is virtually never a nutritional practice."
—David Gilmore, anthropologist

The zombie is a cannibal, and anthropologists say that cannibalism is universally man's prime phobia, possibly originating in our collective memory of predators.[8] Fear of cannibalism is from way *before,* as in prehistoric and still living in our DNA, or as in when we were babies, vulnerable and powerless. Plain and simple, the zombie represents the absolute worst it can get.

Is that why zombies are way too much fun to kill? Is it because they're ruined humans—their mortality drenched with worm-infested mud, their predatory nature so vividly clear—that it becomes a guiltless pleasure to blast a bullet into their reptile brains?

"There's a very potent male fantasy to the genre," says Eric S. Brown, prolific zombie fiction author. "There's a deeply rooted alpha-male, military appeal—the 'only the strong survive' aspect. It's hard to find a truly well done end-of-the-world zombie book where you don't have cops running around with AR-15s or Soviet soldiers using rocket launchers to attack zombies marching on Stalingrad."

(Photograph by Max Michaels, movementmagazine.com)

HALLOWEEN NATION

All the games, books, comics, and movies play to some extent on the joy of zombie annihilation, as if there's catharsis to be had in fighting back against the monsters of Armageddon. We love killing them. But if the avalanche of zombie crawls is any indication, we also love being them and for lots of good reasons.

First off, zombies are WYSIWYG (what you see is what you get), and you can see all the way down to the bone. The romance and complexity of nocturnal creatures, say, vampires or werewolves, have given way to single-minded, monosyllabic zombies. Braaaiiiins. Pure instinct is refreshing in a monster. Then there's the group glee, the mob factor. Dressing up as a zombie and hanging around in a horde is unifying, a bloody, tribal thing. There are no leaders, no lines to memorize (well, there's one), and the actions are easy to perform—show up and shuffle. Rip your clothes, put dark circles under your eyes, and growl. And the zombie's appeal is panpolitical as well, as Professor Paffenroth puts it: "Lefties enjoy the critique of modern American consumerist society while a right-winger looks at the movies and says, 'Hell yeah! They would've survived better if they had more GUNS!'"[9]

But here's my own theory for why zombies are the current superstar of the monster world: all is dark within. They're mindless; there's no conscience, no moral or social pressure. The zombie is an aggressive anti-intellectual, something that might appeal to anyone who occasionally feels overwhelmed. No thoughts, no responsibility, no feelings. They don't have to do well at school or make money. Sure, they need humans, like lots of other monsters, for food, but they require nothing more than that—no sympathy, compassion, or loyalty. They are human (as opposed to alien or supernatural), spawned by disease or industrial accident, ravenous, and morally rudderless. For better or worse, they're a twenty-first-century monster we can understand.

World Zombie Day at the Monroeville Mall, 2009

"Heya Tom, it's Bob from the office down the hall
Good to see ya buddy, how've you been?
Things have been OK for me except I'm a zombie now
I really wish you'd let us in . . ."
—Jonathan Coulton, "Re: Your Brains"

I should have paid more attention to the blood.
When I pulled into the parking lot of the Monroeville Mall,

there were just a few of them. College kids, I thought, playing around in torn, bloody clothing, chugging V-8 bottles full of red sticky stuff that dribbled down their beards and pigtails. Really, there were only a few clusters of them hanging out between the parked cars, like some kind of "Thriller" tailgate party.

I should have paid more attention.

In my defense, it didn't look like the Apocalypse. It was a sleepy Sunday afternoon in Pittsburgh. The University of Pittsburgh had beaten the University of Connecticut with a field goal in the final three seconds of last night's game, and everyone on the streets was smiling. Even the highway through nearby Monroeville, with its string of fast-food chains and endless red lights, seemed normal. Happy. Good.

As I locked my car, a zombie dad walked by with eight-year-old twins dressed as cheerleaders. Cute, I thought. But their eyes were dead-fish eyes.

I should have paid more attention to the eyes.

George Romero shot *Dawn of the Dead* here in 1977-78, and once I made my way inside the mall, things started to feel familiar—the potted plants, buffed floor, the old skylights, hordes of shoppers, the escalator—too familiar. I mean, we know how the movie goes.

A few zombies had stumbled inside the mall. Teen zombies texted their friends while they stood in line at Orange Julius, and pregnant zombies shopped at Victoria's Secret. There were zombies with giant syringes embedded in their chests, zombies in garter belts, zombies with tennis rackets, alien zombies, and a zombie Billy Mays lumbering down the escalator, dragging an OxiClean jug. Teeth and noses bloodied, staggering and dripping, they dotted the mall like a rabid infection.

The mall cops? Useless. They were taking pictures.

I clung to the walls, edging my way back out toward the daylight, through the glass doors. The parking lot had turned into a full-out zombie bait ball. A thousand of them piled up around a patch of asphalt, watching a javelin toss (the javelin—someone's leg—looked fresh).

"This is about style, not strength," growled the ragged master of ceremonies, zombie Mark Menold.

The winner stood dumb, drooling, unaware.

"Hang the gold medal around his goiter," grumbled Menold.

The zombies were agitated. "Brains . . ." they mumbled. "Braaaaaaiiiins . . ."

"Fishhhh tacosssss," growled a schoolgirl zombie right into my ear. There was a deep, nasty sore where her belly button should have been.

A zombie accordion player stationed himself at the mall's entrance

World Zombie Day at the Monroeville Mall, Monroeville, Pennsylvania. Nearly two thousand zombies shuffled through the site of George Romero's 1978 film Dawn of the Dead.

and sang a little ditty, "One day this will all come crashing down / We will bring you down." Zombies from the crowd tossed balled-up tissues into the instrument case the accordion player had set up for donations. I peeked inside. There was a foot in there.

Behind me someone muttered, "What's more amazing—playing the accordion in public or doing it in zombie makeup?"

Makeup? I don't think so.

Things were getting out of control. The pavement was slick with blood, and the creatures looked starved. A kid passed by, sucking on a human finger. Up on stage, the band, Deathmobile, laid down an angry bass beat. The mosh pit was thrashing with the undead pumping severed arms into the air, their heads wagging on limp necks, their backbones exposed.

"Aaarrrggghhh," moaned the leather-throated Menold. "Rise! Open your eyes and rise!"

"Aaarrrggghhh," they screamed back at him. Zombies in curlers, in kilts, in golf pants, with pencils jammed into their eye sockets. Zombie computer geeks, professors, moms in aqua leisure suits.

World Zombie Day at the Monroeville Mall. Sponsored by the It's Alive Show in Pittsburgh, WZD is now celebrated in cities across America.

Zombies with zippers in their skulls, zombies in pizza delivery uniforms.

"Pizzaaaaaaaaaaaa . . ."

A woman standing too close to me chewed on an intestine. "It's only pantyhose stuffed with paper towels soaked in liquid cherry Jell-O," she hissed.

I didn't believe it for a second.

"There're two things you think about when you're a zombie," growled Menold, as his band kicked it up into head-banging mode.

"Kill . . . Feed . . . Kill . . . Feed . . . Do it with me now. . . . Kill . . . Feed . . . Rise, my minions. . . . My lifeless . . . Rise!"

The din was inhuman. The zombies lurched toward the mall entrance and pawed at the doors, leaving smears of blood on the plate glass. When the doors slid open, the throng flowed in, two thousand strong, transforming the Monroeville Mall into an unholy temple of the decayed. They rattled the locked grates of Macy's and stumbled down the escalators, leaving ooze and bloody hand prints on banisters and benches.

"What do we want?"

"Braaaaaaiiiins!"

"When do we want them?"

"Nowwwwwwwww!"

The sound of screaming echoed off floors and walls like a monkey house at feeding time. Shambling, shuffling, limping, lumbering, and dragging, they filled the mall like a fetid wave of stink, all the time gnawing on severed hands, ears, furniture legs, and each other.

I struggled past them toward the mall doors, past the zombies with utility mops swabbing the mall entrance, out into the twilight across the empty lot toward my car. The sun was a bloody thumbprint in the sky; night was coming.

Did they notice me?

I huddled down in the back seat of my car, chest thumping, trying for all the world to disappear, to not breathe or move. Waiting. For it to be over, for it to have been a bad dream, for the sun to rise and everything to go back to normal. Or to die, slowly, in the rotted jaws of an undead maintenance worker from the suburbs of Pittsburgh.[10]

Insider Info: Top of the Heap Zombie Films
Geoff Bough, creator, *Revenant: The Premiere Zombie Magazine*

Bough sponsors the Revenant Film Festival in Seattle and has pegged the following classic and cult zombie movies as his current top five favorites:

1. *Night of the Living Dead*, 1968, directed by George Romero

The beauty of this subgenre is that it has encouraged anyone with a camera to make a film. That's really how the whole modern zombie movie movement was started—with hordes of backyard filmmakers attempting to emulate George Romero after *Night of the Living Dead.* This is the classic zombie tale of a group of people holed up in a house fighting to survive against a relentless wave of undead attackers. There's also a lot of psychological tension, which at times in the film is much more dangerous than the undead.

2. *Cemetery Man* (or *Dellamorte Dellamore*), 1994, directed by Michele Soavi

I was captivated by this film because of its arthouse cinematography and styling very reminiscent of Italian filmmaker Dario Argento's style. As with the more interesting zombie films, there is so much more going on in this film than the undead.

3. *Dawn of the Dead*, 1978, directed by George Romero

One of my favorites because of the sly social commentary about anticonsumerism and the amazing special effects by Tom Savini.

4. *The Living Dead at Manchester Morgue* (or *Let Sleeping Corpses Lie*), 1974, directed by Jorge Grau

Amazing contrasts of emerald green in the English countryside with the pale faces of the dead; it also had some incredible special effects!

5. *Zombi 2* (or *Zombie*), 1979, directed by Lucio Fulci

An epic tale of a zombie outbreak on a Caribbean island with some of the most memorable scenes in any zombie film. No one will ever forget the eye-gouge scene!

Chapter Six
CAUTION:
FOR HALLOWEEN WONKS ONLY

The Jack-o'-Lantern Story: Uncut and Uncensored

In the more than two decades I've been writing about Halloween, I've been asked this question more than any other: where do jack-o'-lanterns come from? For those of you who love the historical bits of Halloween, this is for you. Sit back. Most explanations for Halloween jack-o'-lanterns start with a story.

Jack is a mean bully of a blacksmith who tricks the devil out of capturing his soul time after time, until, at last, Jack finds himself a tired old man and dies. He's too much of a sinner to go to heaven, but hell won't have him either; when Jack approaches, the devil bolts the gates shut, throws him a lump of burning coal, and tells him to get lost. Jack wanders forever in the dark with only this light to guide him. And there it is—Jack-of-the-lantern, or jack-o'-lantern.

There are just two problems: it has nothing to do with a pumpkin or Halloween. So how do we get from Jack-of-the-lantern, the crusty blacksmith with a hellfire lamp, to jack-o'-lantern, the Halloween icon?

Long story short—the jack-o'-lantern erupted out of swamp gas, worked its way through religion and came out the other side into superstition, materialized as an early-nineteenth-century children's prank in America, and landed on Halloween through the course of about five hundred years. Here's how it happened.

"Unctuous Vapor, which the Night Condenses."

—John Milton, *Paradise Lost*

The first jack-o'-lanterns were not carved pumpkins or lanterns of any kind. "Inflammable air," wrote the science editors of the February 1832 issue of *Atkinson's Casket,* "which is continually exhaling hydrogen gas, phosphorus, carbonic acid gas, and occasionally sulphurous vapours." Jack-o'-lanterns were "marshy meteors" that flared up when they came in contact with electricity or heat generated by the decomposition of animal or vegetable materials. Or, more basely, according to the 1637 book *Curiosities, or the Cabinet of Nature,* an "[e]xhalation . . . bred near execution places, or Church Yards, or great Kitchens, where viscous and slimy matters and vapours abound in great quantity."[1] The Latin name given to the lights was *ignis fatuus,* which means foolish or false fire, but the phenomenon was called by many different names: Kit, Meg, Willy, Jenny, corpse candle, fairy light, spunkie or punkie, to name just a few. Will-o'-the-wisp and jack-o'-lantern are the two you've most likely heard of.

No matter how it was scientifically explained, and it was explained often (in magazines and newspapers but also in at least one book, titled, Edward Gorey-like, *A Wonderful History of all the Storms, Hurricanes, Earthquakes, & etc., & lights that lead people out of their way at night,* published in 1704), the bluish, first-you-see-'em, now-you-don't lights were pretty much viewed by everyone as eerie. It was sneaky, the way they seemed to drift out of another dimension to give us a fright. Seductive, the way they'd beckon like a lantern in a distant window, then vanish, not of this world, not of the next. As if they came from a place that could leak spirits like fireflies: purgatory.[2]

Early-eighteenth-century foreign travelers to Ireland reported that the Irish believed the lights were linked to dead souls. Not surprising, given that Cluniac abbot Peter the Venerable (who we should thank for writing the very first collection of ghost stories) called the lights "lanterns of the dead" some six hundred years before in the twelfth century.[3]

The sight of a sudden, unexplainable fire instinctively strikes us as otherworldly. Tolkien felt it. Lights flicker above the Dead Marshes outside Mordor in *The Two Towers,* and Gollum warns Frodo and Sam, "Very carefully! Or Hobbits go down to join the Dead ones and light little candles. Follow Sméagol! Don't look at the lights!" Contemporary author Poppy Z. Brite writes of their power in her short story "Lantern Marsh," about a boy who is transfixed by the elusive lights floating above a beloved marshland and eventually slips away with them one Halloween night.[4]

Today, unexplainable lights set us wondering about visitors from another world, either extraterrestrial or from some unfinished historical past, like the restless spirits of Native Americans killed in battle that are featured in so many regional ghost stories. On the other hand, they are also rumored to be markers for hidden treasure or even, in the case of the Marfa Lights in Texas, the phosphorescent fur of jackrabbits.

The Man with the Lantern

For centuries, people told each other stories to explain these lights, but increasingly they told a tale not about the light, but about the man who carried it. And if you've spent even ten minutes on the Internet searching "jack-o'-lantern," you've seen the one that starts this chapter—the story of Jack, the devil, and his light from hell. Our Jack.

It's usually described as an Irish folktale, and it is. It's also Slavic, Russian, Chinese, Argentinean, and Norwegian, to just scratch the surface of how widespread this little tale is. It's no big wonder the story travels; facing mortality and escaping hell are as essential a plotline as you can get.

The Irish version was set in literary form by novelist William Carleton (1794-1869), who took what was already a popular tale in Ireland, fleshed it out, and published it as "The Three Wishes."[5] This is the story of Billy Duffy, a cretinous but quick-thinking, clever man. He worked as a blacksmith, but as little as possible, and he married a woman, Judy, in every way his equal. By chance, St. Moroky (Moroky? Hey, this is a story) came to Billy's blacksmith shop in disguise, and Billy offered him the warmth of his bellows. For this one act of kindness, Billy is granted three wishes. He wishes that anyone who picks up his sledgehammer won't be able to put it down until he says so; anyone who sits in his chair will be stuck there until he lets them go; and no one can open Billy's purse but him. Billy has tons of fun with his neighbors until no one will go near him, and he becomes so destitute he sells his soul to the devil, Old Nick.

Here's where the cleverness comes in. Three times the devil comes for Billy's soul, and three times Billy tricks him with the gifts from St. Moroky. In one particularly raucous scene, the devil tries to intervene in a fistfight between Judy and Bill, and Judy slams Old Nick into the magic chair. He's trapped. Delighted, Judy and Bill heat up a pair of blacksmith's tongs in the fire until they're red hot, grab hold of the devil's nose, and

Jack, the devil, and his hellfire lamp. (Illustration by Skot Olsen,
www.skotolsen.com)

Billy and Judy grab the devil's nose with hot tongs in William Carleton's story "The Three Wishes."

stretch it all the way through the house, over the hearth, and out the chimney. Ouch.

Needless to say, when Billy finally dies and makes his way to hell, the devil bangs the gate closed, grabs Bill's nose through the bars and jams a hot coal up a nostril. Let that, says the devil, light your way, you miserable creep.

Carleton's tale—used to explain the origin of the will-o'-the-wisp (hence the name Billy or William)—is but one variation of a well-traveled tale.[6] Bill Duffy is more widely known as Jack or John and St. Moroky as St. Peter, Jesus, or the Virgin Mary. In South America, he's Juan Pobrezo from the pampas of Argentina; in Spain, he's Pedro de Ordimalas. Sometimes the devil works alone, often he has his children with him (and in one American version, Elvis), and in Latin America or Italy, it's not the devil, but death, a woman, who comes for our antihero.

This is one of the details, says the founder of the *Journal of American Folklore*, William Wells Newell, that indicates how old the tale is. Newell believes the story originated in medieval Britain, and he has found several versions (including one in which death wears out seven hundred pairs of shoes pursuing his prey) that go as far back as 1551.[7] Parts of the story are even older. The idea of being stuck to the chair, for example, can be found in stories from twelfth-century Irish saga literature or even farther back in Hebrew tales. Tricking the devil into a bag goes back to tricking a demon into a bottle from Muslim legend, and the blacksmith can be seen as a direct descendent of the divine blacksmith of Celtic mythology, Lugh. Pulling the devil's nose with hot tongs is found in the hagiography of St. Dunstan, tenth-century archbishop of Canterbury. Moreover, cheating death is the reason Sisyphus, of Greek mythology, was forced to roll a stone up a hill for eternity.[8]

So the tale we've got here is a Frankenstein's monster. It's made up of parts, some of which were sewn together in antiquity. It's elegant to the extent that each storyteller has made it so and is as travel-worn as the tellers who gave it legs.

"Bar the Door, Boys, Bar the Door."

—Satan to his sons when he spies the blacksmith heading for the gates of hell in Richard Chase's "Wicked John and the Devil"

The jack-o'-lantern in the early nineteenth century is both a character in a folktale and a fiery quirk of nature. In his fictional form, Jack is the kind of guy you'd expect to have an angry tattoo or to train his pit bull to attack. In its incarnation as a bluish flame, the jack-o'-lantern is either a light that comes out of the darkness and scares the bejeesus out of you, or one that seduces you into following, only to dart off and leave you sinking into the black water hidden under rotting sphagnum moss. Neither incarnation is Hallmark material.

The story that explains the jack-o'-lantern's origin immigrated to America; met with tellers from Africa, the Caribbean, and beyond; and was retold in hybrid versions. The earliest I could locate, "Jacky-ma-lantern," was put in the mouth of a well-known character created by Georgia newsman Joel Chandler Harris—Uncle Remus. The blacksmith we recognize as a lazy drunk. And the plot goes along pretty much the same until the devil gets tempted by food and the prospect of stealing souls at a Fourth of July picnic. He stuffs Jacky into a bag. The smith escapes, leaves a bulldog in his place, and when the devil gets home and magnanimously opens the bag to show his kids, the bulldog bursts out, locks its jaws around their scrawny legs, and shakes them half to death. Jacky's banished from hell for eternity so he "shines out" on dark nights, and the story explains the rootless light African Americans called jacky-ma-lantern.[9]

Once it hit Appalachia and the American South, the story was likely more often told aloud than read. It had to relate to the listening audience, and it took on the quirks and cadences of the teller. Richard Chase, who told the jack-o'-lantern story often, says, "No two individuals . . . ever tell the same story exactly alike; nor does the same man ever tell any one tale quite the same twice over."[10] Storytellers held onto "Jack and the Devil" so tightly and for so long that the patched-together tale hardened into a diamond of American folklore told repeatedly, published, and performed live at storytelling festivals well into the twentieth century.[11]

But we still have the same two problems. No pumpkins. And no Halloween.

Lanterns with Legs

You should smell the toasted pumpkin seeds you can buy on the street in Mexico City, or see the piles of pale *calabazas* sold in the markets of Guatemala. Pumpkin growing is not exclusive to the United States. And carving faces in food—say, turnips and beets—was part of many holiday celebrations in the Old World.[12] But there came, between the Revolution and the Civil War, a perfect storm that created the uniquely American pumpkin jack-o'-lantern.

Illustration for the story "A Halloween Wraith," by William Black, that appeared in Harper's Magazine, *November 1890. Note the Scotsman—most Victorians came to know Halloween as an ethnic holiday celebrated by rural Scots.*

It involved three things: darkness, a surfeit of pumpkins, and a generations-old tradition of hell-raising.

Imagine no electricity, no moon. You know about this time of year—people whisper that it's when the witches are out, when the spirits of the dead might rise up from their graves and hover behind a hedge, waiting for you. Overhead, the wind kicks up, and branches click like finger bones. You make it home, run into the house, wedge a chair against the door, and strain to listen. Footsteps? Have you been followed? There's a sudden rap at the window, and it's leering at you—a glowing, disembodied head with a deep black hole where its mouth should be. You scream bloody murder. When you look again, it's gone.

This carved pumpkin trick was one of an arsenal of nineteenth-century kids' pranks that included anything from freeing a neighbor's pigs to stuffing newspaper into their chimney and lighting it on fire. Cut the top off the pumpkin, scoop out the guts, carve a face, and wait for dark. Light the beast from the inside with the butt of a candle and then . . . Well, there were many delicious possibilities. You could hang it from the end of a stick in front of somebody's window until they screamed and then run away into the night. Or you could pop up from behind a wall and scare the daylights out of whoever was coming by. Or you could even mount the head on a stick, cover yourself up with a sheet, and go out terrorizing smaller kids.

The trick was common enough for John Greenleaf Whittier (1807-1892) to memorialize it in the poem "The Pumpkin," and it remained popular for about one hundred years afterwards.[13] But why? Why pick a pumpkin, carve it, light it up, and take to the streets looking for victims?

The folklorist Newell theorized that the American pumpkin trick was derived from the carved, candlelit turnips associated with November 5, Guy Fawkes Day, in England.[14] Other factors could be equally important. The early nineteenth century in American history is known as "The Era of Good Feelings" (ca. 1817-1825), which was a period of relative unity and prosperity. There were candle stubs to spare, pumpkins not needed for cattle feed or pies, and maybe even enough breathing room in the national consciousness to allow for humor and mischief. My guess is that pranksters concocted the pumpkin trick not just because their cousins may or may not have been doing something like it in Britain, but because they had the means (pumpkins and candles), the method (under cover of darkness), and the motive (really good fun). In addition, pumpkins were in the air at this time, literally and literarily. The story chronicling the mother of all pumpkin tricks, Washington Irving's "The Legend of Sleepy Hollow," was an instant success when it was published in 1820.

The Pumpkin Jack-o'-Lantern

You could thumb through the pages of newspapers as early as 1805 and find occasional science pieces on jack-o'-lantern lights[15] or the word "jack-o'-lantern" used metaphorically to mean something illusory or misleading.[16] But starting around the 1840s, something new cropped up. Writers occasionally referred to the childrens' carved pumpkin as a jack-o'-lantern. After all, it appeared suddenly out of the ink black night, glowed briefly, and then disappeared.[17]

Here is the start of the jack-o'-lantern we recognize. Once people began to use the name "jack-o'-lantern" to describe the pumpkin trick, we finally had a *pumpkin* jack-o'-lantern. Within a few short decades, this jack-o'-lantern would become better known as a stationary Halloween party decoration, grounded and tamed.

Be My Guest

The mayor of Atlanta and his wife, Mr. and Mrs. Hemphill, threw a Halloween bash in 1892, notable especially for the inclusion of possum on the menu (before you blanch, consider that a standard seventeenth-century menu for All Hallows included marinated carp). The next day's *Atlanta Constitution* described the decorations: "As the guests entered the hospitable mansion they were greeted by all manner of smiling lanterns made of pumpkins, cleverly carved with faces."

These pumpkins weren't popping out from behind a wall or riding on top of a stick. They were posed and smiling. It was the hostess that finally lopped the legs off our jack-o'-lantern.

Halloween parties became popular late in the nineteenth century, and decorations were pulled from the outdoors to set a rustic atmosphere—cornstalks, apples, pumpkins, and even wild turkeys and pigs in crates. It wasn't long before the rural jack-o'-lantern was co-opted by the imaginative party-giver, and then, eventually, American business, as jack-o'-lantern-themed party favors grew more and more popular.[18]

At last, the Halloween jack-o'-lantern! But now we have the opposite problem. His origin story—how Jack came to be a wandering light—is the origin story for the *wrong* jack-o'-lantern. Once "jack-o'-lantern" meant a carved pumpkin decoration instead of a rootless light, the tale of Jack and the devil no longer fit.[19] Modern writers had to bend the tale to make it conform to what they knew about Halloween.

William H. Hooks (*Mean Jake and the Devils*, 1981) says he heard the story in North Carolina from his mom and aunt, who built tales for him, including one called "Jake-o-My-Lantern." After Jake tricks the devil and is given a fireball and told to "go find a hell of your own," he ends up imprisoned in the Great Dismal Swamp. In return for a day on dry land each Halloween, Jake leaves one half of his fireball in a pumpkin for the devil.

Contemporary witch Silver Ravenwolf puts the light in a turnip, not a pumpkin, Old World-style. Jack becomes a good-hearted, friendly sort with a "lop-sided smile and missing tooth," but he cuts a bargain with you-know-who and begins the slippery slide into drink and sin. This Jack is banned from eternal rest unless he can find some poor soul to trade places with him—but it's too dark to find someone. The devil throws Jack a coal, and Jack makes a lantern out of a turnip. "On Halloween night, when the veil between the worlds is thin, you kin see Jack and his little light, across the field and in the woods, roamin' in the night, seachin' for someone to take his place."[20]

To make the jack-o'-lantern story relevant, writers fit a pumpkin around the light and set the story on October 31.

Soft Spots

"For jack-o'-lantern faces
Are charms 'gainst things unseen
And they will keep their owners safe
The night of Hallowe'en."
    —Solveig Paulson Russell, "Halloween," *Children's Activities*,
October 1944[21]

While jack-o'-lantern lights were used by adults to explain some pretty serious topics—souls stranded in purgatory or the restless dead—the jack-o'-lantern trick belonged to children. Even more, it belonged to country children. Anyone who's grown a pumpkin knows it takes a lot of earth to nurture a vine, and it's hard to imagine too many snaking up the crowded stoops of turn-of-the-century American tenements. Kids in Brooklyn, Chicago, Washington, D.C., and elsewhere disguised themselves on Halloween and ran wild in the streets, begging for coins or sweets, and whacking people on the back with socks filled with flour or soot. It was mostly kids in America's rural towns who terrorized with jack-o'-lanterns, and nobody really seemed to mind. The trick didn't show up on police blotters the way other Halloween pranks did. It was portrayed—even in the very first mentions—as nostalgic, a trick for a young child, more charming than dangerous.

Something was happening to the jack-o'-lantern and Halloween as the twentieth century unfolded. A general sweetness washed over our culture when it came to children, and Halloween celebrations were focused more and more around them. The jack-o'-lantern softened. (Take a look at the Halloween postcards of the early twentieth century and you'll see how adorable, how childlike they became—plump, almost rosy-cheeked.) In fact, within fifty years of its debut as a Halloween symbol, the jack-o'-lantern had become a comfort rather than a fright. Once it became porch-bound and legless, the jack-o'-lantern lost its menace. Certainly, the marketing of whimsical jack-o'-lantern favors and cards had something to do with it, as did the trends of the times. But truth to tell, the kids themselves eventually jettisoned trick in favor of treat. There just wasn't time to sneak around, trying to scare the little kids with a pumpkin when there were parties and parades and—eventually—house after house with bowls of Mars bars inside. Not only did the jack-o'-lantern become a ubiquitous decoration, but it was now stationed on private property, moving from instrument of terror to object of vandalism. Ironic, yes. But priorities had changed. Jack bought the severance package and retired to the front steps.

Or did he?

Postmodern Jack

"The eyes had sagged, although the slitted pupils were still narrow and mean. The nose was bubbling with some vile mucus. . . . In the orange light that streamed out between them, the hooked fangs appeared to have been transformed from points of pumpkin rind into hard, sharp protuberances of bone."

—Dean Koontz, "The Black Pumpkin," *October Dreams*

The original trailer of John Carpenter's *Halloween* (1978) went like this: Medium shot of a smiling jack-o'-lantern next to bold letters spelling "Halloween." Midway through is a shot of the same jack-o'-lantern, grinning happily on a nightstand next to a bed where a splayed body lies murdered. Final image is the

Opposite: Phantom Jack, *watercolor.* (Illustration by Chad Savage)

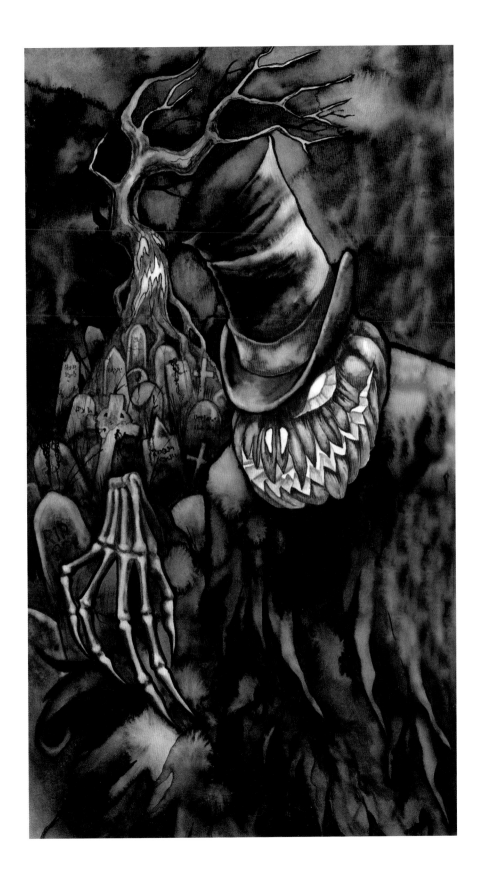

jack-o'-lantern, the boldface "Halloween," and that creepy, ¾-time theme music that gets under your skin. *Halloween* took what had become the most innocuous of symbols, the most childlike and innocent, and subverted it to horrify. If the suburbs—symbolized by the lit pumpkin—could breed unmitigated evil, if jack-o'-lanterns could seem monstrous, even by association, was anything safe anymore? *Halloween* played on the same sense of fear that the myth of the psycho who puts razor blades in apples did—something dangerous and evil is lurking under the ordinary.[22]

But let's go back even farther, to 1963, when Marvel comics introduced a new enemy for Spider-Man. Flames licked out of the cut features in his pumpkin head. His body was lizard green, his fingers ended in creepy-looking tendrils. Dubbed Jack O'Lantern, he was a killer for hire, and he's been lobbing flaming pumpkins at Spider-Man for more than forty years now. He's a second-tier villain and he knows it. This Jack's got attitude. He's not confined to Halloween or to a porch for that matter.

All along, it was the jack-o'-lantern's unpredictability that made it scary. That it could suddenly appear out of nowhere gave it a certain sort of fearsomeness; that you weren't sure what it was, what it could do, or where it came from made it unsettling.[23] And remember that Jack, the character, was always a bit of a thug; he does a deal with the devil for goodness sake.

Right next to the friendly jack-o'-lantern that graces children's books and party napkins has reemerged the jack-o'-lantern that can terrorize, hurt, confuse, or chase you. Jack-o'-lanterns, says much of our contemporary iconography, are not as innocent as you think. They never were.

Part III. Creating Halloween: Frights of Fantasy

Preparing for the Village Halloween Parade, 2008.

Chapter Seven
Kindred Spirits

To celebrate Halloween is to dabble in deviance, says Global Halloween Alliance founder Rochelle Santopoalo. And we don't outgrow the need for creative play. In fact, she argues, our common desire for play—especially at Halloween—leads us to form the communities we're losing in other avenues of our lives.[1]

It's no secret that over the last five decades much of America has suffered a breakdown of community in the traditional sense—church, school, neighborhood—but it's also clear that alternative communities have flooded the void. Some of the strongest, most enduring, intensely loyal Halloween communities are made of nothing more than affinity. Of the joy of being in the same place at the same time with people who love the same things you do. At Halloween, we're united by common rituals, and in a pluralistic, fractured, and fractious culture—a culture that romanticizes independence and lauds individuality—this is exciting. A neighborhood comes alive for one night. A whole town throws a party. City streets fill with people in costume. Where other holidays cocoon in dining rooms or backyards, Halloween spills out into the streets, expressive and egalitarian, bound not by family ties or even friendship, but by a dark aesthetic and a love for a certain kind of anarchy. It makes us part of something bigger, deeper than just you and me.

Samhain. All Hallows. Halloween. Toussaint. The old stories tell us that this was a time for the gathering of the tribes. We instinctively find our people, light a fire, make a little noise, and dare each other to go out alone into the night. But what kind of community does twenty-first-century Halloween create? What draws the tribes to the fire?

Village Halloween Parade: America's Largest Halloween Night Celebration

"Festivity—like bread or freedom—can be a social good worth fighting for."
—Barbara Ehrenreich, *Dancing in the Streets*

Journalist and activist Barbara Ehrenreich has a theory: when the people of Catholic Europe stopped dancing in the graveyards, when they lost their opportunities for group ecstasy (like carnival), that's when widespread human depression set in. She says that we've been without this for around four hundred years now, and we really need it back.[2] If ever there were a place to start, it's the Village Halloween Parade in New York City. Each year on October 31, some sixty thousand costumed marchers and two million spectators throng Sixth Avenue to be a part of the parade. If you've never seen it, you really, really should. It's listed in the book *100 Things to Do Before You Die*, and it remains the nation's largest public Halloween night celebration, period.

Rokeby, 2008

The Village parade begins every year in a tiny office in producer and artistic director Jeanne Fleming's home on the historic Rokeby estate in Red Hook, New York, about an hour up the Hudson from Manhattan. She thinks of it as a public artwork.

"I run the whole parade with this," Fleming says, holding up an ordinary sheet of paper, crammed with neatly printed notes on both sides. Today—in early October 2008—she's huddled around a wooden kitchen table with the event's main organizers, trying to nail down the hundreds of details that will make this year's parade unique.

"We've got bubble machines, that prizewinning port-o-potty, ghost mermaids, an inflatable snake, the *Buffy the Vampire Slayer* sing-along, and the Tahitians. Oh, and the 'Thriller' group is coming back. Peter, how many purple witches are coming?"

"Three hundred."

"Matthew, what are you going to do with the ukulele band?"

Some participants need tending to, such as the hot rod Rodzilla ("Last time, Rodzilla broke down in front of the TV cameras and there was grease on the street," Fleming explains, "and then the stilters came and the whole road was filled with grease."), and some require double-checking ("They told me they'd bring a small bus with one hundred zombies, but they arrived with a large bus

Opposite: "Thriller" dancers (including a mock Michael Jackson), 2008 Village Halloween Parade.

Opposite: Richard Simmonses pose on the streets of Greenwich Village before the parade takes off.

and no zombies."), but most parade elements will get the organizers' full-bore support. Acey Slade of the glam/horror rock band Murderdolls and Anne Lindfjeld, MTV host in Denmark, want to be married during this year's parade on a wedding float. Fleming will figure out how to make it happen.

"My role is to make it possible for everyone to design their own parade. You completely create a reality for yourself that night that has nothing to do with me. It's kind of a courageous choice to decide to step in front of a couple million people—where else does something like that happen?"

Fleming is an artist, a smart, energetic woman with a grown son who creates several large-scale events each year. She's run the Village Halloween Parade since 1979. "Most of the things I do are based on stories, creating a story that everyone enacts together. The Halloween parade is different in that there's a larger story to it, which is about being in this incredible, huge, urban, diverse, modern city doing this ancient rite. Sometimes I really do believe when I look down at the parade that these are the same people who have always been doing this. They're ancient spirits, just the latest reincarnation of them. They feel familiar to me."

The Village parade is more performance than parade. There are no waving politicians, no Shriners on tricycles, or armies of Revolutionary War reenactors. The only restriction is on noise, because Fleming doesn't want to field calls from every mother on Sixth Avenue complaining that the parade woke their children. But that doesn't mean by any stretch of the imagination that it's tame.

Anyone with a costume can march in the parade, which stretches more than twenty blocks.

The word the organizers use again and again to describe the parade is "chaotic."

"We'll build this amazing thing and we'll involve a lot of people in it, but that's not the key for me," says Fleming. "The key has always been the people who show up. [Anyone with a costume can march, and forty to sixty thousand join in over the course of the route.] I organize a certain amount of it, but after that, you have no idea. And it's New York! So you get amazing people doing amazing things. Things I couldn't think of."

Like the thirty Richard Simmonses who jumping-jacked and high-kicked their way down the parade route. Or the Imperial Stormtroopers who simply showed up to help keep the paraders in line.

With more than two million loosely organized people in one place, the potential for disaster is huge, but, miraculously, trouble is rare. Things happen of course—in 1989 a woman dressed as Medusa went into labor—but crime has never been a problem. The squadrons of cops every few blocks help. The

HALLOWEEN NATION   💀

police, says Fleming, are key. "They are full collaborators."

"Is this your first time?" Peter, the purple-witch wrangler, asks a parade volunteer from Australia.

"Yeah."

"Wear double socks."

The parade has not missed a year since artist Ralph Lee first created it in the early 1970s, including Halloween 2001. As among any group of New Yorkers, the conversation can turn to 9/11 in a heartbeat.

"I was sitting at my desk and I saw the shadow of the plane," says Fleming. "It went across the field and we all saw the shadow of this big, low-flying jet flying down the river."

"After 9/11," adds Peter, "the people in the city were zombies. The parade that Halloween, I'll never forget it. There was an outcry because they were saying, 'Why are you creating this public spectacle right at this point, right after?' People thought it made us a target."

"When the parade started you could hear a pin drop," Fleming recounts. "You could see the fire [at Ground Zero] still burning from where we started. We had made a baby phoenix puppet to begin the parade, and you could see the smoke down the street behind it. We played 'New York, New York' like a dirge, then we sped up as we went along. It was as if no one had breathed since the towers were hit. You could feel people start to breathe again.

"The parade is cathartic. The year Joseph Papp died, we stopped in front of the Public Theater and everyone lay down. After Katrina, we built a coffin, but there was a light in it. We got bands from New Orleans back together and got instruments for them. The crowd went crazy when they went by—they wouldn't let them stop playing."

Ghost!

"The ghost was an obvious choice for a thirty-fifth-anniversary parade, looking back, taking stock," Alex Kahn tells me. He's standing in the middle of a huge barn on the Rokeby grounds, surrounded by pieces of what will—in three short weeks—become a centerpiece of the 2008 Village Halloween Parade. The pieces are the beginnings of a séance scene starring eighteen-foot-tall ghost puppets and a glowing table set in a Victorian drawing room, all of which will move up Sixth Avenue. The parade uses two enormous barns at Rokeby. One is packed with puppets and props from past parades. In this one, I count twenty volunteers hammering, cutting, sewing, and gluing together "Ghost."

Victorian windows lie prone in various stages of construction. Kahn and his partner Sophia Michahelles, both of Superior Concept

Most of the larger parade puppets are created in this Red Hook, New York, workshop. Here, volunteers put together "Ghost" under the direction of Alex Kahn and Sophia Michahelles of Superior Concept Monsters.

Monsters, will project early Edison film images on them. Chandeliers made of recycled plastic are being dressed with decorative leaves, twisted carefully to catch the light. One of the eighteen-foot-tall ghosts leans against the barn's beams, idly staring into the middle distance, its fabric billowing. Below, workers construct giant forks, knives, and a teapot that will fly off the séance table when it begins to rise.

"It's like moving underwater; you just can't go fast with these," says Kahn about the giant ghosts.

The volunteers who will perform the séance sequence get just one day of rehearsal. They'll go through the movements using the two-hundred-year-old driveway leading to the Rokeby mansion as a stand-in for Sixth Avenue. Fleming will watch from the front steps. This is the only chance she'll get to see the pageant, and

Opposite: *Murderdolls guitarist Acey Slade married Danish MTV host Anne Lindfjeld during the parade in 2008.* (Courtesy Steve Prue, teamrockstarimages.com)

here—looking out across the estate fields in the twilight of late October—she'll mark her own, private Halloween.

The Village, Halloween Night

Before kickoff, the parade is like an amoeba; no one in it knows where the head is. It shimmers with the sequins and LED lights of fabulous costumes, and the streets are teeming with giant puppets, bands, floats, stilters, and New York City police. The park near the parade's takeoff point pops with camera flashes against the hypnotic beats of drum circles and the acrid scent of incense. Fleming keeps a close eye on her watch between television interviews. Right at 7:00 P.M., a group of men and women dressed in white are released up Sixth Avenue to purify the route. Then Fleming steps off, kicking her feet in the air like a chorine, and the parade officially begins.

Jeanne Fleming, artistic director and producer, kicks off the 2008 parade.

From Spring Street to Twenty-second, the Village Halloween Parade honks and creeps along, as spectators stand twenty-deep behind barricades on each side of the street, smiling and hollering. Marchers stride down the middle of the street: dead brides, aliens, Chippendale dancers, rats, mimes, a photo booth, stove (with witch inside), G3 computer, Lite-Brite game, Pacman, Thing 1 and Thing 2, Colonel Sanders and a chicken, French maids, St. Pauli Girls, pilgrims, people in underwear, topless women with painted torsos, Victorian women in mourning, Marie Antoinette, Heath Ledger-style Jokers, parachutists, twins, dogs, wolves, giraffes, cats, Marilyn, all four members of Kiss, robots, Groucho, the gingerbread man, Smurfs (thirty), the Manhattan Bridge (twelve), a decapitated Ronald McDonald, bananas, chickens, swimmers, babies, pirates, Power Rangers, Dorothys, Red Riding Hoods, a Dracula on roller skates, and a trio costumed as Alaska, Russia and the "Narrow Maritime Border."

That's just the first few minutes of the parade.

Bats attached to long, flexible poles swoop down over the heads of shrieking spectators. A snake puppet, manipulated by a dozen or more runners, coils and strikes across the width of the street. The parade route darkens enough to make out that there are people up above, in the Gothic clock tower of the Jefferson Market Library. Puppeteers. From the top of the tower, Basil Twist's giant white spider picks its way down toward the street, seemingly supported by a ghost web that stretches across the whole city.

Bats swoop over spectators piled twenty-people-deep on both sides of Sixth Avenue.

Come midnight, the last buses will be packed and sent home, the barricades will be stacked and stored, and Twist's spider will go back to sleep in the library tower. But now, on Halloween night in Greenwich Village, a beautiful chaos reigns.

Imagining Halloween

On the other coast, in a parallel but wildly different Halloween universe, people gather in the misty predawn outside Hermann Sons Hall in Petaluma, California, north of San Francisco, to be first in line for the folk art show, Halloween and Vine.

At 9:00 A.M., the doors open and the crowd pours into the hall like sugared-up kids at a theme park, wanting to be everywhere and see everything all at once. By 9:05, there's a line at Johanna Parker's table of pumpkin-headed candy boxes. By 9:30, Allen W. Cunningham's eerie Halloween dolls are sold out. By ten o'clock, the din has softened and there are fewer people in line, and more of them clutching big shopping bags. The serious collectors are sated.

It's called Halloween and Vine because the show started in 1996 at Madonna Estate Winery, in the Carneros region of Napa, with a handful of artists showing their work atop oak wine barrels in a cozy tasting room.[3]

"When we were at the winery, there were maybe two hundred visitors," Scott Smith of Rucus Studio recounts, as the crowd buzzes under the orange-and-black paper lanterns decorating the hall. "Then a *Better Homes and Gardens* article came out [in 2004] and there were five hundred to seven hundred. These people are dedicated. They're not coming to spend $20. They're coming to spend $2,000. People are hungry for this."

Twenty-five artists' displays are stacked cheek to jowl in a room about the size of a church hall. There are lots of bobble-headed moons and cats in collars, but there's edgy stuff too: dolls with two heads, slinky stilettos with witch buckles, Katherine Webber's shrouded pumpkin-turned-hungry-nightmare creature. At Edgar and Edgar, there's a black gumball machine filled with small, glittery skulls. Charles Batte has brought a series of elongated, exquisitely costumed figures of Poe, a dead bride, and Lucifer, who's on sale today for $560. Will Bezek's got only one unsold piece left, a painted gray fortune teller with clawlike fingers, for $550. Two thousand dollars? Gone in a New York minute.

"Until twenty years ago, everyone was doing repros of the old German stuff," says Ginny Betourne, one of the show's organizers and artists. "But buyers are more sophisticated now. They want something really unique."[4]

Vergie Lightfoot picks up one of her ravens. "There's only one of him," she agrees. "I might use the same pattern, but then turn the head, quilt the wings, move the tongue. I make my own cat's eyes. There are eighteen different colors in those eyes."

"Do you do commissions?" shouts a woman from across the table.

"Oh, yeah!" Lightfoot shouts back, smiling. "Prepaid. No refunds."

What strikes me about the way Halloween is imagined here is this: 99 percent of the objects in this room have eyes. Look around and you can almost feel it; everything's looking back at you—even the carrots. Moons have eyes, hats have eyes, clocks, shoes, and geraniums have eyes. There's a human-head-sized pumpkin at Lightfoot's table that (I swear!) tracks you as you walk by. It's not a decoration; it's a presence.

"I used to collect postcards," George Parola tells me as he browses the display tables. Parola is famous in the collecting world as the guy who built an addition onto his house to display his Halloween stuff. "But you have to keep them in books. I can't enjoy them. These," and here he jerks his head toward a group of Lightfoot's sculpted black ravens, "I can leave out where I can see them."

The creatures at Halloween and Vine have the playfulness of Day of the Dead figures, but it's not death being represented here. Rather, it's some sort of secret, mythical dimension accessed only through the imagination. Take a long look into one of these quixotic faces and off you go into another world. Dismiss them as just cute or silly, and the faces harden into painted papier-mâché—they're dead to you. And although the room is overflowing with demons, claws, fangs, and fury, there's no danger here. These pieces evoke a gentler, more wonder-filled time.

These Halloween creations construct a bridge back. We dig our nails deeper into the past to slow the accelerating speed of time, to get back to that feeling of delicious foreboding that Halloween could bring. And it's not just the folk art collectors who are drawn to Halloween's powerful nostalgia. Even the most nihilistic-looking, tattooed-and-pierced haunters go soft when they think about their childhood Halloweens. Consider this: when the editors of the horror fiction anthology *October Dreams* asked all twenty-eight contributors to describe their favorite Halloween memory, more than half went back to when they were kids. And not to the flayed flesh and the pits of evil that normally fill their stories, but to more-or-less happy memories. Our childhood Halloweens can live like tiny beasts inside us, coiled and ready to deliver their emotional charge at the slightest prod.

Moreover, because Halloween starts in the imagination and moves out into the world, there's a freedom you won't find in other holidays.

"Halloween is more open-minded with its characters," Smith believes. "There's no preconceived notion, like Santa has to be red."

"I love the fact that a pumpkin figure could look hundreds of

Halloween Party Queen, *by artist Virgie Lightfoot.*

Will Bezek's undead doll, Ezra Samuel Collins, who comes complete with a death certificate: November 12, 1888, of heart failure.

ways," agrees Laurie Hardin of Monkey-Cats Studio. "Sweet, spooky, scary, gory, whimsical, bewildered. Unlike a snowman, bunny, Uncle Sam, or other figures that are expected to look a certain way."

But in all truth, you *could* make a bunny who looks irritated or a snowman who glowers like he's after your soul, but people don't. It's Halloween that gives artists the license to create pumpkins with teeth or angry turnips. Other days are buttoned down. This one isn't. Halloween lets its iconography go wild.

Then too, there's the affinity aspect.

"There's a real camaraderie among all these people who love Halloween—they get it," says Smith.

This, you can feel every time someone enters the hall. People walk through the door; look at that sea of orange, pointy party hats; and smile. They can't help it. And they keep smiling at the art, the artists, each other. The people here *get* Halloween the same way the people at the Village Halloween Parade do. They understand fantasy, the need to connect, to create, to play. The color palette may be more toward orange than black, but the obsession with Halloween is just as strong. Less blood, more sparkles.

"It's good I'm not rich," says a woman with a wry smile as she plops down next to me to rest. "Imagine all the money you'd be spending, all the stuff you'd have to bring home, all the places you'd have to find to put it."

So what brought you here if you're not buying? I ask her.

"I don't have this kind of imagination. Did you see that white bat? I would never have thought of that. It doesn't cost me tons of money just to look."

If You Build It

The room is unseasonably dark for an afternoon in August. Inside, several dozen people sit rapt, watching a demo on how to animate a fake arm so that it plunges a spike into a disembodied head. I'm visiting the East Coast Haunt Club's annual gathering on the outskirts of Salem, Massachusetts. The rented hall is really an Irish social club function room, but today the room's been transformed into the kind of glowing orange-and-black cave that warms the hearts of even the most blood-splatter-loving Halloween fan.

As my eyes get used to the dimness, the crowd comes into focus. I can make out a clown with shiny plastic pants and a madras jacket. Someone else has a rapier discreetly tucked under her arm. There's a pirate in the back row, and next to him is a woman poured into a leather bustier. All of them are mesmerized by a

PowerPoint presentation on a tiny screen at the front of the room. I peer at the title of the talk, "How to Give Your Prop Some Brains."

The largest gathering of Halloween lovers—by far—doesn't exist. Well, it does exist, just not in the sense of what you think of as a gathering. It exists on the Internet.

The East Coast Haunt Club emerged ten years ago from a cyber-group of Halloween enthusiasts who wanted to meet in the real world to share ideas and expertise. It's one of many. Every single day of the year and nearly every single hour of those days, there are people posting their thoughts and inventions to listservs, forums, YouTube, and message boards on MySpace or Yahoo and Facebook groups devoted specifically to Halloween. The burgeoning cyber-community may be the closest we'll ever get to a permanent, year-round, Tim Burton-esque Halloween town.[5]

"Decayed Corpse Skin. Worn once. Pants not included."
"Can you use Day-Glo paint on latex-molded yeti feet?"
"Three dozen Wow Wee chimp heads. Make me an offer."

The most popular topic? Prop building. On Halloweenforum.com under the category "Halloween props," you could browse—say on a spring afternoon in 2009—any of 10,419 topic threads, a total of 110,469 posts. On that same warm, April day, the social networking site hauntspace.com was showing two thousand topics and eight thousand posts, and its moderator, Pete Henderson, told me the site can log sixty thousand user sessions (from search engine visits, lurkers, and members) in a *day*. On *the* day, October 31, 2008, there were 2,443 people logged onto Halloweenforum.com at one o' clock in the afternoon.

"Zombie head putting a strain on the nod servo. Help."

Outside the lists, you could mention Danny Elfman or Tom Savini and people might ask, "Who?" But on the Halloween lists, people accept you for the horror-monster god you are.

"In my opinion," says David Lindblom, moderator of the 2,600-plus-member hauntforum.com, "haunting is what Halloween has become for a lot of people, myself included. . . . [P]rop building and setting up a mini-haunted attraction offer a lot of creative wiggle room. I think a lot of us kids who were products of the '70s and '80s and who have fond memories of 'that house'—the one that did the crazy Halloween decorations—wish to re-create those fond memories. Now that we are all adults and own homes of our own and we have the means to haunt, we do."

Again, the wheel turns. The torch—terrorizing one's neighbors with a pop-up pneumatic zombie-in-a-trash-can—is passed.

"Anyone already built a low profile pop-up with a scissor-fit mechanism?"
"How low?"
"Probably 3-ft. at the apex."
"Got an old coffin-banger Druid that might work."

Cybergroups have personalities. The Garage of Evil, a 650-member, prop-building community created by Steve O'Connor and Geoff Varosky, offers a good amount of tech tips. Hauntworld.com's Fright Forum has threads in its "Trading Post" discussing everything from how to run a pumpkin-patch hayride to where to find a prebuilt trebuchet.

The most storied of lists, though, is the Halloween L.

"Don Bertino started Halloween L around 1995," says Chuck Rice, the man who's kept the list on a series of Apple computers for more than a decade.[6] When Rice, a computer programmer, moved away from Silicon Valley, he loaded the Halloween L server onto an Apple PowerBook laptop; flew to Houston, drove to his new home in Katy, Texas; plugged the computer back in; and downloaded. Those were the only six hours the four-thousand-or-so member list has ever been down on purpose.

"Pre-Internet each of us thought we were the only guy who did this full-bore, all year round." I'm talking on the phone with Paul Venturella, now sixty years old, of Provo, Utah, moderator of the Halloweenpropmaster.com list since 2005. I ask him how active the list is now. "Let's see," he says, clicking through his screens. "Oh, I've got 7,099 messages stored in my inbox."

When Venturella discovered Halloween on the net, he was thrilled. "I thought, 'You can make a fence out of pvc pipe?! You can actually buy a skeleton for $70!?' It was an amazing thing to see. Some of us are programmers, and some are electrical wizards, and some can't do anything with electricity but are artists and creators. If one hundred people come together and they all bring their own little piece—the sum total is more than the parts."

Right now, early in the spring, I e-mail Venturella to see what he's working on. He's putting together a ground-breaker pneumatic zombie. "Ground breaker is the generic term for a prop that appears to be coming out of the ground. It's not something you see at Wal-Mart. LOL."

What's the result of all this posting/crafting/programming/trading/wiring? If you build it, they will come. Venturella gets up to 1,200 trick-or-treaters each Halloween, *and* he hands out full-sized candy bars. "That's about $400 to $500 I spend on candy every year," he sighs.

It's not just a sheet over a Pepsi bottle anymore," agreed Garage of Evil's O'Connor. "When I look at my yard, I think, 'I wish I'd been to this guy's house when I was a kid.'"

What it's really about is passion. You build and collect props to create displays, maybe just inside your living room at first or as party decorations. Maybe you leave a few up year-round. You collect more stuff, you forage through clearance bins the day after Halloween, and your friends start giving you Halloween decorations. The collection grows so large your display spills out of your house across the porch, down the steps, and into the yard. And before you know it, you've got taloned creatures crawling through the grass, wraiths drifting through your trees, and bones springing from shallow graves you've dug in the side yard.

Halloween transcends mass-market merchandising when it is created by individuals; it's a bottom-up holiday at heart (pranking, begging for food, and scaring people—none of these are really top-down activities). Halloween celebrations are more exciting these days not just because there are people sitting in a room trying to figure out what we'll buy, but because there are people sitting in their basements trying to figure out how to make something no one's ever seen before. Something really cool.

"Re: Halloween centerpieces. Must fit on table. Be creative. No fire."
"Medieval torture rack, cheap. Takers?"
"Laser-eye pumpkin works! Very cool."

List members are each other's eyes and ears, hands and feet. Someone in St. Louis knows how to wire a pair of eyeballs to move side-to-side; a guy in Corpus Christi has a line on cheap linear activators; a woman in Ann Arbor knows how to build fake arms from foam pool noodles. Once the Internet became PC-friendly in the mid-1990s, Halloween prop building exploded. More props meant more decorated houses, which meant more trick-or-treaters, which meant more fun Halloweens for everyone. List members decorate their yards and porches because they like to, not because it strengthens the communities they live in. Yet, it does.

The lists have generated friendships, businesses, even a marriage or two.[7] And why not? Cybercommunication is expressive. You can wink, flirt, thumbs-up, and high-five in cyberspace (albeit metaphorically or with goofy-looking icons). And you can joke around, no problem.

"Anyone been to Scary, West Virginia?"
"No, but drove through Toad Suck, Arkansas."
"Boar Tusk, Alabama?"
"Bone Gap, Illinois?"
"ROTFLMAO" [rolling on the floor laughing my ass off].

In some ways, the cyber-Halloween community is utopian. The lists render people genderless and ageless, forcing us to use different antennae to "suss" each other out. We'll never know that "Dracul" is a woman who works for the school board of a Midwestern town or that "Cereal Killer" imports wine for a living unless they decide to tell us. Instead, we get to know a person by their wit, rather than by their looks, or by their spelling, for goodness sake. What's missing is the obvious. There's no connection to real flesh; you can't dance. Which is why so many listers agitate to create real-world Halloween gatherings.

HAuNTcon, Haunted Attraction National Tradeshow and Convention, Milwaukee, Wisconsin, 2009

Day One: 2:00 P.M., trade show floor

There are thousands of ways to die, and here they are, all of them, splayed out across the trade show floor: asphyxiation, electrocution, pox, gangrene, drowning, dismemberment, decapitation, and disembowelment. I'm taking my first loop around the displays, where there are around sixty booths filled with objects that bleed, chatter, burn, dart, drool, shake, and slither.

Say you run a haunted house. The trade show is full of goodies you can buy to create new effects: video projections, fake castle walls, femurs, foam latex masks, sea hags, man-eating plants, theatrical fluids, and buckets of very realistic-looking maggots. Say you create thermoplastic webbing guns, mist-spewing evil worms, or piles of butchered pig parts. Here's where you come to show them off and sell your stock. Or say you are a home haunter (you decorate your yard to the max). You might come to HAuNTcon to learn how to bump it up a notch at an entire week's worth of workshops, including "Creating Gaping Wounds and Pustulant Sores with Liquid Latex," "Styrofoam Masonry V," or "All about Servos."

At the fringe, there are films, an art show, a costume ball, and celebrities. (Want to meet Ari Lehman? He played *Friday the 13th*'s boy-in-the-lake, Jason Voorhees. He's here in leather gloves, wearing a T-shirt that says "Camp Counselor.")

I stand at one end of the room and try to take in the whole scene, a convention floor awash in black T-shirts and jeans. Out of nowhere, a girl runs past me in stiletto-heeled boots, a green top hat, and whip. Like Alice after the rabbit, I follow.

4:00 P.M., trade show floor (still)

It is never silent here. A garbage can suddenly slams side to side, banging like a hopped-up drummer. It's LOUD. (By the eighteenth time, you learn to pause your conversation, smile, and then continue). Displays of animatronic figures mumble as you walk past. The click and hiss of air-powered cylinders permeate every conversation.

"Why all the butcher-shop props?" I ask Michael Chaille, president of Ghost Ride Productions, Inc.

I'm looking at a pile of fake chicken feet, a goat's head sliced in half, and maybe two dozen pig ears glommed together in a pile. They're popular I know; I've seen folks wandering around the hotel with big plastic bags full of them.

"When I go to a haunted house, I'm thinking to myself, 'Something's missing,'" Chaille says. "'There's all this blood, but where is it coming from?'"

Ah! He makes the things that bleed. So where would you put this pile of pig parts, for example?

"You can use them in lots of scenes . . . a freezer scene, *Texas Chainsaw Massacre* scene."

As we talk, a full-sized body jerks sporadically, trying to wiggle its way out of a plastic bag in a nearby booth. Next to us, a mannequin rises up in a tattered lace smock and hacks repeatedly at the air with a bloody ax, her toes creepily distended, her limp, black hair hanging in her face. It's amazing how quickly you get used to all this.

Across the aisle, a laptop slideshow of young women in colorful costumes catches my eye. I go a little closer. No, not quite costumes. They're airbrushed. I stare at one, a model-pretty woman with a pumpkin painted on each naked breast. Of course, I think to myself, pumpkins are the obvious choice.

In another booth, I marvel at a shockingly realistic man's forearm. The proprietor mentions that the arms are made in Asia. I imagine a sixty-year-old Korean woman inserting fine hairs one by one into a man's arm cast in latex. At some point, she has to wonder, Why? For whom?

People who don't get Halloween, who think it's just a holiday for kids, and not a great one at that, probably aren't fans

Evilusions booth at HAuNTcon 2009. (Photograph by Pam Tole)

of fantasy or horror either. They probably didn't watch a lot of monster movies when they were young, weren't crazy about trick-or-treating, and missed the Haunted Mansion on their family vacation to Disneyland. (I've never talked with anyone in the haunt business whose eyes don't mist over when I mention the original Haunted Mansion.) There is a certain . . . aesthetic . . . you have to appreciate to love a place like HAuNTcon. Almost everything here is dark, deformed, and demented. There are very few happy orange pumpkins, and most of those are tattooed on people's calves or painted on . . . well, I told you already.

7:00 P.M.

This I know: if someone asks you if you'd like to ride the Zombie Army bus to the nighttime haunted house tour, say, "Absolutely I do."

10 P.M., Wisconsin Feargrounds, Waukesha Expo Center Grounds

Tim and Anne Marie Gavinski have fired up three of their haunted houses for conventioneers. I'm in the second one, Morgana's Torment, in a room where the ceiling is low and the walls are inflated so that you have to literally push your way through them. There's no light. I'm lost for many, many, long minutes, feeling my way in the dark. I can sense someone in front of me—no idea who—so I slip my finger through his belt loop and hang on for dear life. Outside, in the light, we decide not to mention it.

Day Two: 12:00 P.M., trade show floor

At the Haunted Enterprises booth sits the Last Ride, a polished wooden casket that's really a simulated-motion ride that haunted attractions can buy to entertain their crowds. Its lid is open, and the ivory satin interior looks inviting. Somehow, I had missed this.

"Would you like to get inside?" asks proprietor Randy Grigg.

Absolutely I would.

Grigg helps me into the coffin, which he assures me is real. He mentions an emergency shut-off button, gives me a quick smile, and closes the lid.

It's deep-water black. The pillow and padding are smooth and luxurious, and I'm thinking I could almost fall asleep when I hear voices on either side of my head. Two Cockney gravediggers—the accents take me back to the grave robbers in *Mr. Magoo's Christmas Carol*—talk about lifting the coffin into the hearse, and bumpedy-bump, the coffin lurches and the ride begins. The hearse careens through the streets. The coffin bangs around, gets unloaded at the cemetery—bump, bang, tilt, thud—and the diggers decide to take off for a pint. In case you ever get to take the Last Ride, I won't say what happens next.

When the ride is over, everything goes still and quiet for a few seconds. Just as I begin to wonder if Grigg has forgotten I'm stuck in his coffin, the lid opens and I see his friendly smile. I ask if a lot of people enjoy this.

Yes, they do, he assures me, helping me hoist myself out. They're curious about it. In life, he says, "People only get into a coffin once, and they're never going to get back out."

2:00 P.M., trade show floor (again)

It's congenial, this community of haunters. Outside the convention hall, the smokers gab, looking just like any other cluster of pals, except that one has a skull tattooed onto the back of his bald head and another's skin is painted entirely red. The hotel staff looks as if they've gotten used to assisting guests who have open sores on their hands and odd growths sprouting from their ears. In the front office, most of the stored baggage has a skull pattern on it.

If a time traveler from the Middle Ages were to drop down at HAuNTcon, she'd think she had landed smack in the middle of a very active cult of the dead. That thought might have crossed the minds of the hotel's other non-HAuNTcon guests as well; they seem to be growing a little testy.

The horns, pointed ears, boils, and scars are signs of the tribe. But subtler clues also identify members of the haunted house community, such as black T-shirts with a skull, clown, vicious jack-o'-lantern, or anything dead printed on the front. (Sweaters, for example, don't belong here.) The crowd is united by a love of all things fanged and oozing, but more than that, by memory.

"I can remember the smell of those early costumes," says Rodney Geffert of NightScream Studios about his first Halloweens. "I can remember opening that box—it was the smell of plastic. It's the best smell in the world. Since you were a kid, you've loved that one night a year."

"People don't go to a haunted house to be scared." As we talk, I watch a five-foot-long, nasty-looking worm lunge forward and spew a fine mist at a family walking by. "People argue with me all the time, but I say you're not paying to be scared. No, you're paying for the thrill and fun. People just want to see cool stuff— stuff they don't normally see. You gotta do something you don't normally do."

Pushing the edges. What your imagination can do in the dark. That's what we remember. That's what we're after.

11:00 P.M., *Haunted Attraction Magazine* Costume Ball, convention center ballroom

A beautiful young woman from a Goth radio station told me earlier that she'd come from California with only one bag and couldn't fit a costume in it. Ingenuity prevails. She enters the ball with an intricate green design airbrushed on the naked top half of her body.

There is a contingent here from Hong Kong looking to bring ideas back to their Ocean Park Halloween Bash, something I've heard described as a Chinese Sea World. Really? Halloween in China? Oh, yes, a member of the group shouts to me over the music. But because our two cultures are so different, they need to find local angles to make their haunted attractions scarier to the Chinese. The Chinese, I'm told, are terrified of a man with an umbrella where his head should be.

A pair of pigs and red devil Rebecca Rose (opposite page) *at the the Haunted Attraction Magazine costume ball at HAuNTcon, 2009.* (Rose photograph by Pam Tole)

HALLOWEEN NATION

Purgatori is a 1968 Cadillac Superior hearse owned by Kevin and Teri Giebel of Neenah, Wisconsin. Every hearse is unique, says Teri, and most people in the hearse community name them. The hearse detail is part of Mordecai, owned by Jim and Amy Germain of Chilton, Wisconsin.

The DJ plays Michael Jackson's "Thriller" and there's a mad rush to the dance floor. Just about everyone in the room seems to know the choreography by heart. How is that?[8]

Day Three: 2:00 P.M., hearse rally, convention center parking lot
Twenty beautifully kept hearses are lined up with doors and hoods open for viewing. From one rearview mirror hangs an air freshener in the shape of Chewbacca. From another dangles a full-sized, human head. The phrase "The eyes see only what the mind is prepared to understand" is stenciled on the side of another vehicle.

6:00 P.M., hotel pub
The hotel bar and hospitality suites are humming with haunt industry people; many of whom have been huddling all weekend, talking through the haunted house rooms they're planning this year.

"Who's for getting the polka dot room? Okay. What about the stalkers? You guys sure?"

These haunt conventioneers and vendors are connected by commerce, no question. But they're also connected, in many cases, by a common obsession. Although some sellers do very well, thank you, many of them run mom-and-pop businesses that are driven by a love for Halloween.

"These trade shows make me giddy," says the copper-haired Dawn Emanuele, who's staffing the MoonHowler Productions booth. "I see a werewolf eating half a leg and it's new, interesting, creative. It's like the circus is for other people."

In the hotel bar, a man wearing a blood-stained jumpsuit and a Hannibal Lecter-style restraint mask happily drinks a bottle of Stella Artois through a straw. This convention is like a trip to another planet—a planet where everyone truly and deeply understands you.

Chapter Eight
Terrortainment

Haunting Outside the Box

A liability waiver and a $1 whiskey shot gets you through the door. Then a surgical mask, a weak flashlight, and instructions: just follow the white line till the end. Say goodbye to your friends; you're completely alone for this one. Pitch black. The soundtrack's concocted from distorted Peking opera, the music of an ice cream truck, and constant pounding. Disorientation is the point. Of everything. Walk forty feet down a completely dark hallway that's only two-feet wide. Nothing happens, but that's what you'll remember most when you come out. We create our own fear. The scenarios are eighteen-plus: medieval gynecology, a toilet teeming with snakes. There's one part you have to crawl through. The room's filled with ordinary garbage bags stuffed with balloons but still, you panic. Remember, it's dark. You're alone. The soundtrack is hammering. You don't know what's next, but you do know it will be bloody. Nine minutes. You made it. Outside on Eleventh Avenue, the sun shines.

Midsummer Nightmare was created by Josh Randall and Kris Thor (produced by Vortex Theater Company in New York City during May and June 2009) because they wanted to create an intense haunted house experience. It was innovative and relatively low-tech—for example, kids' water toys kept the toilet water thrashing around the rubber snakes for the snakes-in-the-bowl scene. But can you have a haunted house in late spring?

"You can see horror movies anytime," Randall offered. "Why not haunted houses?"

People did come, and Randall deemed the springtime haunt a

success. But did they get the same response that Halloween season haunts do? No. The *sun* was shining outside for goodness sake.

People in the haunted house business talk a lot about having to constantly up the ante for more shocking effects or to think outside the box—like staging a haunt in May or building fifteen-foot-tall monsters that can run. For the most part, it takes a lot more vivid imagining to create scares for a generation raised on *Hellraiser* as opposed to, say, *Betty Boop's Halloween Party.*[1]

For the first time in history, the planet is populated with people raised on film—jittery images of increasingly more realistic horror, driven by soundtracks that coax our emotions along dark pathways and then pound us with sudden shocks. Is it any wonder we're looking for more thrills, more grit, more extreme *everything* in our Halloween entertainment? Audiences want to live inside the horror movies they love, to be *Halloween*'s Laurie Strode for a few, very intense minutes. And haunted houses deliver thrills straight up your spine because, unlike movies, they're real. These monsters and psychos are right there, breathing down your neck, eye to bloodshot eye.

If it seems like there are a lot more seriously terrifying haunted houses out there, you're right. First off, there are now somewhere in the neighborhood of four thousand haunted attraction events in the U.S. each October, not to mention the thousands of home-grown haunts you find in garages or front lawns.[2] And yes, there's pressure to raise the bar each year, to be more graphic, detailed, and fantastic.

Who sets that bar? How? And what does it take to scare us in a way that makes us come back and beg for more?

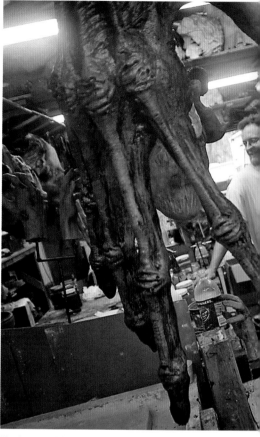

"I always think of it like Willy Wonka's Zombie Factory. The building looks small from the outside but when you open the doors it appears to go on forever," says Kevin Alvey (right, with Jake Rich) about Gore Galore's workshop.

Come Up to the Lab . . .

"If it can chase you, it's more real."

—Jake Rich, Gore Galore

The two-lane highway lays flat for miles between acres of field corn with leaves burnt brown in the southern Indiana sun. Go past the Feed Mill with its sign for an "All You Can Eat" frog legs festival, past the churches in prefab trailers and the Masonic Lodge, and you'll come to an ordinary white house with an enormous, former chicken coop behind it. This is the headquarters of Gore Galore, Inc., a business that supplies the haunted house industry with disemboweled corpses, monsters, music, and oversized costumes, every single one of which live up to the company's name.

("Thank you for your interest and intestinal fortitude," reads the Gore Galore Web site.)

"Ah," says owner Kevin Alvey, as we walk toward the long, low shed behind his house—"The Chicken Coop of Doom." He unlocks the wooden doors and swings them open.

This, for a Halloween lover, is akin to being a kid transported magically to the North Pole where Santa stands at the toyshop door and asks, "Hey, do you want to see what we've been working on this year?"

Yes, please.

As we talk, one of Alvey's colleagues, artist Jake Rich, lifts a female, three-breasted torso out of the trunk of his car and carries it into the shop—something he's working on for a burlesque show.

One hundred forty feet long, just about the width of a football field, the shop is crammed floor to ceiling with scary stuff. Monster heads and feet, draggers (a half-zombie that comes with eight feet of free-hanging intestines), and one-hundred-count boxes of toes are packed up in the rafters. A skull half the size of a Volkswagen sits, waiting to be boxed and shipped. A severed gargoyle's head hangs from wires that will eventually make the eyes glow. Six-foot-long bony hands are strung from the ceiling, and on shelves, there are neat piles of thighbones and stashes of horns and teeth. The worktables are littered with dead hands and fingernails, and there's a solitary jar filled to the brim with ears.

"Whenever we have extra latex," Alvey explains, "We pour a little in the ear mold, and throw them in the jar."

At my quizzical look, he adds, "Accessories. Accessories are a big deal now."

I'm trying to imagine what exactly you accessorize with ears.

"*Severed* ears. People like them for trophy necklaces."

Oh, right! *Severed* ears.

Gore Galore's work has an unsettling realism to it. Even mythical beasts are pockmarked and ravaged in a way that makes them seem blood-pumpingly real. Put it this way: if pumpkin lawn inflatables are on one end of the Halloween décor spectrum, Gore Galore's stuff is on the other—and then some.

Back in the shop, I ask Alvey if the scenes people build in their haunts have any relation to what's going on in the world.

After 9/11, he responds, "I noticed a severe decrease in gore in haunted houses. They thought people were going to be more sensitive about that. But now, in 2009, it's trending back in the opposite direction. People can't get enough."

Why do you think? Is it because the flood of images of torture and terror are sinking deeper into our psyches?

"For many, I do think it brings reality a little closer, and just try to tell me reality isn't scarier than anything else. Blood is a reminder of reality. But for me, I find over-the-top blood and gore to be tongue-and-cheek kind of funny."

In Alvey's opinion, though, gore is a detail, a starting point. It's not the main event. "Gore is easy. A story line is much harder to develop. Story lines help to make the haunted attraction more believable because all the scenes are at least loosely based on the story line. It all comes back to getting your customers to have a suspension of disbelief. If they believe what they see is real, they will be more entertained."

Just like movies. The special effects leaps the movie industry has recently made are sneaking into haunt design, too.

"Haunted house people are using video techniques, professional audio design. The quality of materials going into a house improves all the time," explains Alvey. "Audiences are smarter now. You can't get away with black plastic in a haunted house anymore."

We're standing in front of the zombie-head storage room; nearby, a row of butcher knives hang drying on a line like laundered socks. It seems to me that zombies and butcher knives are everywhere this year.

Do haunted house folks follow each other's leads? I wonder.

"Some do," says Rich. "They can be competitive. Our Grim Reaper costume, for example, would sell only one or two a year. Then this year, twelve. We're not sure why."

Really? With all the new vampire TV and apocalyptic zombie fiction out there now, you wouldn't think the old death's head would be so popular.

Alvey shrugs and looks a bit wistfully at a prop they've named Botulism Buffet. It's a corpse of a man with open body cavities that you can fill with finger food. "I made it for a Halloween party. I put dip in the head. Then we offered it through Gore Galore the next year, but we didn't even sell one."

Rich jumps in. "[Making monsters] is an unpredictable beast in a way. You've got to feel it out and listen to people and use your imagination."

Truth to tell, you've also got to be a bit prescient. Gore Galore starts to develop new products in November for the following Halloween, so they need to have a decent idea of what people will find terrifying. The classics, say Alvey and Rich, have to do with our most common fears: clowns, butcher shops, torture rooms, "dark rooms" (meaning sensory deprivation), and haunted

Gore Galore zombie bodies waiting to be shipped.

Gore Galore's "Goblin" costume stands over nine feet tall. (Photograph by Gore Galore)

forests or swamps. For whatever reason, severed heads are in high demand these days.

Do you build things that scare you, or things that you think will scare other people? I asked Alvey.

"I would say both. If something really strikes me, I will use that to inspire a creation that captures a feeling. I first look to my intuition, and then see where that leads. And don't forget that everyone in the shop also contributes to development sessions, where most of the new ideas are born."

Are people more afraid of mythical beasts or real beasts?

Rich thinks either can work. "But I gotta say it's more effective if it looks real. A severed head prop is a great prop, and you'll get some people with it, but the main thing is how lifelike it looks. An animatronic is only going to shoot at you for a couple of feet, but if there's something running at you for twenty to fifty feet—or if it doesn't stop—it seems to make people more afraid."

He's referring to the oversized costumes that are Gore Galore's bread and butter—seven- to fifteen-foot-tall puppet-beasts that you wear like you'd wear a backpack, if your backpack were connected to a ten-foot rod that carried a sculpted monster. A helmet connects you to the costume's head so that when you look to the side, it looks to the side. You can manipulate the arms with rods, and the whole thing, with you inside it, is covered in yards and yards of moldy-looking costume shroud.

Rich pokes under the fabric to show me the structure. "My brother [Ben Rich] did praying-mantis-type arms so you could get them to shoot out and grab people. The trick is you've got to keep it simple enough so that you don't trip. If people are falling down in your costume at trade shows, no one's going to buy your stuff."

There are nearly thirty styles of creatures, and right now, they're stored upright on stands, an unholy collection of hags, goblins, and giant crustaceans, patiently waiting their turn for a ride on the UPS truck. Business is brisk in spite of the current recession. "There are at least six haunted houses in each major American city now," Alvey says. "And that doesn't include smaller haunts and yard haunts."

He'll sell five to ten of each of the thirty styles this year, at around $2,500 per costume.

All this carnage, I ask Rich, does it ever get to you? Do you ever come home and wish you could just hold onto something soft for a while? I don't know, a kitten maybe? Something that doesn't bite?

Rich laughs outright. "I'm into gory movies. I'm a metal kid and whatnot. I used to watch *Star Wars, Predator,* and *Alien.* Those three franchises wrecked me."

We walk past a bay full of men's shoes nailed to square platforms, as if the office workers at Morgan Stanley had been suddenly vaporized, leaving behind only their dress oxfords.

"Zombie stands," explains Alvey. "Waiting for bodies."

Industrial fans throw a breeze over a row of metal armatures waiting to slide into life-sized, fully costumed zombie forms ("Do you need medical [scrubs, lab coats, gowns, robes], sanitarium [straight jackets], religious [priests], or anything else to fit your theme?" asks the company's catalogue copy). It's not always this pleasant in the shop. In the summer, temperatures can reach the upper nineties. Come winter, Alvey says, they only heat one small storage room so, he sighs, "You can find a layer of ice on any standing water."

Outside the shop, stored in an old silo, are all the original costume creatures, the templates for the others. Alvey and I climb through the silo door and stand amongst the jumble of claws and jaws.

"That's the grandfather of everything here," Alvey tells me quietly, as if not to disturb him. We're looking up at a fifteen-foot-tall, yellowish-green puppet costume called Spooky Ernie, one of Alvey's very first creations. Alvey has decades of experience with puppetry, and he built Ernie with a friend, Eric Ridenour, for a local haunted house. They took the beast to the mother lode of Halloween trade shows, Transworld, in 1998, to draw attention to their exhibit booth. It worked. Gore Galore started doing business in a one-hundred-square-foot room in a house in Evansville, Indiana. Eleven years later, they were able to buy the shop, silo, and house in Cynthiana.

"I learned enough from building Ernie—it's seventy-five pounds—that these newer ones," Alvey points to a huge clown head, "are only thirty-five pounds. Essentially, it's all about solving problems."

Alvey stands in the doorway of the silo and looks off across the cornfields. "I can feel it coming. Fall. I can smell it. It's kind of sad. It means the season is almost over."

He squints up into the peak of the silo. "I want to make a rig up there so I can hang all the big costumes from the top and use the space down here for parties. Wouldn't it be great to have parties with those monsters hanging all around?"

It's a torture scene. A man's got a grip on a young girl's hand, pulling her toward an industrial-sized fan. The lights go out; she screams. You

Nightmare, a haunted attraction in New York City directed by Timothy Haskell. (Photograph by jasonsmith.com)

hear the sound of her fingers hitting the fan. Warm, wet liquid sprays your face. You move on. The Buried Alive Room is only four-feet high. You're stooped, your face pressed against a Plexiglas ceiling, a gravedigger standing on top of the Plexi. He shovels, and you feel the sickening thud of each mound of dirt. More dirt, less and less light. Keep moving, oh please, keep moving. Surprised, cut off from the group, you're alone. A long hallway, bright light at the end. You hold onto the walls, keep walking. Where is everybody? Suddenly, footsteps and an angry clank of chains are coming toward you. You drop to the floor and hope he never sees you. In the distance, you hear the screams of your friends.

Bad Dreams Come True was the 2008 offering of Nightmare, a New York haunted house produced by Art Meets Commerce and directed by Timothy Haskell. The show was packed into a thirty-five-hundred-square-foot space on the Lower East Side and had around forty-five thousand visitors over its six-week run.

Haskell's an off-Broadway theater director by trade, and what his haunts lack in size he makes up for with audacity and performers—performers both with and without bones.

Haskell once mail-ordered one thousand cockroaches to create a wall-of-bugs set piece. It should have been audaciously disgusting, but it wasn't. "When you order one thousand cockroaches, you think that should do it. It really didn't," he told me. "They're just too small." Eels are trouble; there are too many regulations. "It just looked like they were floating around in a big aquarium." Even rats can be a problem. "They sleep a lot," sighed Haskell. "I put a little Red Bull in their water, but I don't think it worked. They really were boring."

Sometimes, you really need a human.

They're Watching You

"I stalk," says haunt actor Bruce Millet of New England's haunted attraction SpookyWorld. "I try to isolate a single person. I scan the crowd, and the first person who cringes, that's the person I walk towards and I fixate on. And they freak out, and then I turn to the next person who's scared. I could do that all night."

Most haunt designers will say that adding a real human to an attraction increases the scare more than any other element. And yes, when people pop out at you, it does work. Especially when they drop like raptors from above, suspended on bungee cords, or roll along the floor, snapping at your ankles. But serious haunt actors are after more than a quick scare.

I'm in Millet's kitchen, looking at a picture of his character, Lobo. Lobo's black-smudged eyes stare out from behind a pale mask that looks as if it's made of filthy, cracked porcelain. The face is reminiscent of a child's, but haunted, swollen, hating. Lobo's overalls are spattered with blood, and there, growing out of his gut, is a freakish part-fetus/part-chicken.

I sneak a glance up at Millet, six foot, two inches of gentleness with a Buddhist deity tattooed on his arm. He's talking about his childhood Halloweens, which were pretty much nonexistent. "I was raised a really strict Christian, kind of sheltered, a Seventh-Day Adventist. I think what attracted me to a lot of things in life [was] when I was told, 'No.'"

On the table between us sit four severed fingers strung on a rawhide cord that Millet found on eBay. I lift them gingerly; they're gut-twistingly realistic. "I'm always looking for props," he says. "When I chase people, I want stuff to look real."

Bruce Millet's Lobo character. Lobo doll by Morbid Creations.
(Photograph by Bruce Millet)

Millet's been building his arsenal of horror characters for twenty years, and he creates them based on his own fears. "What scares me personally is not so much ghosts and the supernatural, but serial killers," he says. "Killers who kill for no reason. A lot of the characters I've done over the past twenty years or so have been like that."

Lunatics, murderers, and cannibals are all unpredictable, unfathomable. Millet knows that the modern monster is not a creature, but a person unhinged, brimming with rage, a perverse hunger, or some deep disturbance way beyond normal.

He taps a finger on an image of Lobo glaring at the camera. "When you see a three-hundred-pound guy coming at you looking like this, it's reality. Coming face to face with a real flesh-and-blood killer, a killer right in front of you, staring you down, wanting you dead—that's the menace I try to bring."

Millet's Lobo will chase people for as long as ten minutes, and he'll pursue some out of the park, then track them down to where they're hiding in their cars, balled up and shaking like strawberry Jell-O. He'll sneak up to the car and then WHAM!—bang both hands on the hood and peer in through the windshield.

"I just want them to get their money's worth," he explains.

When do you back off?

"When they cry."

After all, it's really just entertainment.

"Real fear and entertaining," Millet says carefully, because this is important, "people confuse the two."

He tells me the story—I recognize it from newspaper reports a few years ago—of a murder at the regional high school where Millet works as building foreman. "I had to stay there all night with the murder scene," recalls Millet. "I was in shock. It was surreal, somber, and nothing like any of this," he says, his fingers sweeping across the table full of scary posters and rubber horror props. "And I had a few people say to me, 'Oh, you must not mind because you work at SpookyWorld, you like horror and gore.' And I say . . . *what?* SpookyWorld is not *real.*"

He looks back down at the photos of Lobo and his haunt park pals—a green-skinned demon, an Elvira look-alike, a stringy-haired ghoul drooling bluish blood.

"It's fantasy. I'm trying to create something fearful to *entertain* you."

I look from Millet, a forty-eight-year-old man in a sunny farm-house kitchen with a fridge door plastered with happy family photos, down to the severed fingers on the table. They look real, but they're not. Millet's characters are about illusion, not actual

Punch the Clown (Brian Chamberlin). (Photograph by Kerri Ann Crau)

horror. Sometimes, he tells me, he's giggling under the Lobo mask.

Driving away from Millet's home, past the soccer nets and farm stands, the world is summer-bright and full of flowers. But damn. I've still got the image of those fingers in my head.

"There's nothing funny about a clown in the moonlight."
—Lon Chaney

In the Musée Mécanique on Pier 45 in San Francisco, there are a handful of early twentieth-century coin-operated dioramas. Slip a quarter in a slot and the shoe-box-sized scene called "Opium Den" comes to life. A dead-eyed addict lies prone with his pipe, and cardboard dragons lurch at him from a closet. A plaster skeleton peeks out of a grave in "Drunkard's Dream." "English Execution" depicts the slowest hanging of a two-inch-tall criminal I've ever seen.

One hundred years ago, these twisted baby steps of terrortainment titillated horror-greedy carnival crowds. The roots of haunted houses, too, come from this same weirdness. Carnivals metamorphosed into fairgrounds with freak shows, roller coasters, and ghost rides. When you look at the canon of haunted house scenarios—insane asylums, freaks, disorienting funhouse floors, walls, and tunnels—it's so very carnival-like, isn't it? No wonder this netherworld is inhabited by so many clowns.

"One out of every seven people in America has a fear of clowns," says Brian Chamberlin, aka Punch the Clown, a longtime New England haunt actor. "Coulrophobia. It's one of the most irrational fears there is. Most people say it's because of media. They either saw Pennywise in [Stephen King's] *It* when they were young or *Killer Klowns from Outer Space*, which is a hilarious movie, and I don't see how anyone can be scared of it, or *Poltergeist*, with that clown doll that pulled the little boy under the bed. But the true, hard-core coulrophobes—the ones who will cry when they see a clown—that's childhood-induced trauma."

Chamberlin had sent me a photo of himself so I'd be able to recognize him when we met, but I didn't need it. There was only one guy in the restaurant with a T-shirt reading, "Your powers are useless. The clowns are on my side."

He leans forward quickly, and as he speaks, his eyes somehow grow darker.

"Ever feel like you want to scream at the top of your lungs?"

Oh, yeah.

"Want to get paid for it?"

He sits back and smiles widely. "Haunting is the funnest, hardest job you'll ever have."

Here's something you really should know. The sudden banging and flashes of light in a haunted attraction are there to get your attention. Once you're distracted, that's when the actors strike. Like magic, haunting is about misdirection. Three sarcophagi stand in a dim room with three mummies inside them. You know one of them's going to pop out. But which one? While you sneak by, the actor watches and waits in the shadows. All three were dummies? How lame. You relax, and look for the next room. BANG. That's when he gets you from behind. You whip around and stumble back against the wall, which feels like it's collapsing under your weight. You're starting to freak out, you grab onto a sarcophagus for balance. THEN the mummy pops out.

Whenever you think you're safe, you're not. The actors are constantly scanning the crowd, looking for you, their next mark. Cross your arms and hug them tight to your chest and you might as well be screaming, "Me! Me! Me next!" Pull your hood down over your face and you've just sent up a beacon that says "Fresh kill. Come and get it." They know it's human nature to keep the scaredy-cat of your group in the middle, so don't hide there.

In Chamberlin's experience, some people actually like being chased, and some hate it so much they'll instantly drop to the ground in a fetal position, which is dumb, he patiently explains, "Because we'll stand over you like you're just a piece of meat."

The performers I talked with said they rarely go after vulnerable kids or try to make victims of those who don't deserve it. They take special delight, though, in terrorizing the ones who do.

"Ninety percent of haunters won't go after the big guy," states Chamberlin. "I've been hit by the big guy. It hurts. But if I get him to scream like a girl it's going to be so worth it."

Chamberlin is a self-described in-your-face kind of actor, but like Millet, there are lines he won't cross. "Making someone feel threatened without actually threatening them is something you have to work at. Actually threatening them is not cool. You've got to give someone an escape route."

Then he confides the ultimate proof of a haunt actor's mettle: the number of people who are scared so badly that they pee themselves, or "wetters." Wetters are the stuff of legend; at the very least, their stories are fodder for 1:00 A.M. postshow gatherings at IHOP. Believe me, actors keep count.

"I treasure my time in the Clown House," Chamberlin says

Haunted Overload headless horseman. Says Lowther, "Even if they are not scared in my haunt (and most times, they are) I want them to come out saying 'that was cool-looking,' or 'beautiful,' or 'I have never seen anything like it before.'" (Photograph by Dan and Suzanne Plumpton of Artifact Images)

with a warm, light-up-the-room smile. "It helped me become a more social person."

Colored light streams from the mouths of huge creatures—two stories, three stories high. Here, the trees howl. Here, hundreds of candle-lit jack-o-lanterns line a path toward the witch's bonfire. Skeletal "soul takers" rise on ten-foot-tall frames and bare their teeth. Across the pasture, a solitary ghost figure beckons. Hoof-beats pound, first in the distance, then louder and louder, closer and closer, until a headless horseman gallops across the fields, a pumpkin head cradled in his arm.

Haunted Overload, staged every year in rural Lee, New Hampshire, erupts from the cornfields and pastures as if it grew there. And in a way, it did. The natural world has risen up and given shape to this haunt. Creator Eric Lowther simply follows its lead. The lumber for all the constructions—and by constructions I mean the twenty- to forty-foot-tall monsters Lowther refers to as "giant

luminaries"—was rescued from the burn pile of a local sawmill. ("Damaged by lightning strikes," Lowther tells me. "Bad for the sawyer, but good for a prop.") The creatures that line the pathway into the haunt are actual trees, sunk into the ground and carved with chainsaws. The hundreds of pumpkins that frame the entrance walkway are from a local farm, and the fences that guide patrons from scene to scene are made from boughs of trees shaken down in winter ice storms. Spiders spin webs in the nostrils of skeletons left out in makeshift storage sheds between Halloweens.

"Everyone's so inundated with technology and video games that we wanted it to be like stepping back in time when they came here," says Lowther.

No intestines, no blood, just creatures. Murderous pigs and birds in tuxedos erupt out of a miasma of fog and wood smoke in a setting so detailed that you feel like a visitor to another world.

Good Halloween is good theater. It excites the imagination, transports you to another time and place, and provides the kind of catharsis only a real, bloodcurdling scream can give. However, a good fright choreographer doesn't stop with visuals. The best haunted attractions play on as many other senses as they can, including smell, touch, and, of course, sound.

Sound Scares

Old radio shows such as "Lights Out" used sizzling bacon to simulate the sound of electrocution or had the sound effects guy crack a sparerib with a pipe wrench when they wanted the snap of a breaking bone.[3] Today's haunters also use sounds—sirens, whispering, even retching—to get under your skin.[4] But few things work as well as music to deliver the deliciously dark atmosphere that heightens fear. In the realm of terror delivery, Midnight Syndicate goes in through the ears.

Edward Douglas had just finished work on a concept CD, an eclectic film-soundscape-without-the-film project he dubbed "cinefusion." To promote it, he put together a show of original films, computer animation, live actors, and a band. The CD, which he called *Midnight Syndicate* after an image he had in his head of shrouded people gathering secretly in the dead of night, was an amalgam of horror-film-inspired instrumentals, hard rock, techno, and country. In the audience sat musician Gavin Goszka, becoming more and more convinced that he and Douglas shared a strong aesthetic, especially when it came to horror films. When Douglas started work on the next Midnight Syndicate CD, *Born of*

Gavin Goszka (seated) and Edward Douglas (standing). The ghostly images are Douglas's daughter Mary Kate and musician Lily Lane, who did the female vocals on The 13th Hour. (Photograph by Anthony Gray, courtesy Midnight Syndicate)

Opposite: *Giant luminary, Haunted Overload.* (Photograph by Dan and Suzanne Plumpton of Artifact Images)

the Night, Goszka signed on as cowriter. Since then, the two men have created "soundtracks for the imagination," the dramatic, richly textured music you hear in haunts from Universal Studios and Six Flags to hundreds of attractions across the United States and abroad.

"When we started this back in 1997 or so, there were no really good Halloween music CDs out there," says Douglas. "There were only 'Monster Mash' compilations and the proverbial screams and howls, and so one of the driving pushes at the time was to put together a Halloween CD and make it more about the music. What this meant was that once we hit with that CD [*Born of the Night*] people were like, 'Wow! This is what I've been looking for.'"

The music's incredibly evocative. Just play a track and see if you can't help but feel like you're being chased through a forest, castle, cathedral tower, or the gritty streets of some vaguely fascist state. And each disc has a specific theme. *Realm of Shadows* is set in an abandoned seaside village, *Gates of Delirium* in a haunted asylum, and *The 13th Hour* in a Victorian mansion. It's how Midnight Syndicate develops song ideas.

"When I have a deadline coming up," says Douglas, "I center myself by sitting alone in a room for two days watching back-to-back horror films. It's about being in the zone. Sometimes it's a really dark and creepy, nasty place. The whole time we're writing, we're keeping this world, this place, in our heads, and that's just pushing the music deeper into these places."

Goszka plays organ, drums, bass guitar, and piano. Douglas has played guitar since he was seven. Their composing is often done at the piano, but once they start the process of creating a piece, it's a mix of live and synthesized elements put together in the studio. The percussion and sound effects are done live. The creaky floors and doors on *The 13th Hour,* for example, are the creaky floors and doors of the house where Goszka's studio is located (Apothecary Nine Studios). Douglas has his own studio a few miles away.

"The first time I remember getting really interested in horror was when I saw the original *Salem's Lot,*" states Goszka. "I remember being terrified by it for two or three days. After that I thought, 'Oooh that was cool. I want more.' I used to do these haunted houses in my basement in high school, and I played *Dungeons & Dragons.* I'm surprised my parents put up with it."

For Douglas, it was the library that kick-started his aesthetic. "They had books in the kids' section about Universal Studios monsters—Dracula, Wolfman. I must have gotten those books out over a million times. There was also a 33 record you could take out that had Vincent Price doing Edgar Allan Poe stories like "The Telltale Heart." I loved closing my eyes and just listening to that record."

"Yeah," says Goszka. "And when Disney put out—was it called *The Haunted Mansion?*—I remember taking that out of the library."

"That's the granddaddy of what we do!" exclaims Douglas. "The very first haunted house that started it all, and certainly the soundtrack that started it all for what we do, the first Halloween music. It was awesome. Even now when we go to Disney, and we go once every other year, I just go on [The Haunted Mansion] ride over and over. You can lose yourself in it."

Midnight Syndicate has released ten CDs, including scores to the feature films *The Rage* and *The Dead Matter.* They have to have favorites, right?

"For me," says Douglas, "it's *13th Hour.* It's like our tour de force. Some of my favorite tracks are on that disc. When I close my eyes, I'm taken into that house. The sound design we did on that one pushed us as musicians and sound designers."

Goszka agrees. "Before *13th Hour,* it was *Gates of Delirium* for me, particularly because of the songs, but even more so because the sound design was miles ahead of the preceding disc. We did a lot of intricate mixing things. If you have headphones on when you're listening, it's really intense."

Psycho Haunting

We're born with two insuppressible terrors: fear of falling and fear of loud noises. All others are either learned or prepared. Learned fears come from the memory of a repeated danger, and prepared fears are the ones important for survival, such as a fear of snakes, heights, deep water, enclosed spaces, tunnels, or death.[5]

According to recent research, we also share fears based on how we live today: modern neuroses for our modern world. Flying, for example, or others you may not suspect, like math, elbows, "German things," and capital letters. We now fear success, rejection, intimacy, and even other people.[6]

What if a haunted house capitalized on these? If the dark creatures we found there were us? The Los Angeles Cacophony Society's Halloween haunts hack deep down inside our psyches to fish for fear.[7]

"There are still survivors of 1994's Museum of Mental Decay who relate in quavering tones tales of dodging fireballs, tripping on chocolate-smeared bodies, being groped by transvestite nuns and vacuum-cleaned

by rabid Klowns. Notorious as the vortex of mind-bending chaos and the occasion of at least one psychotic break (testimony furnished on request), the Museum of Mental Decay is now back by popular demand. Re-appropriating the concept of the "haunted house" from candy-ass civic groups who can barely be trusted with pancake breakfasts or a car wash, Cacophonist perpetrators have emptied out their closets and turned their minds inside out in search of materials of an extreme and psychologically repellent nature."

—Press release for the Los Angeles
Cacophony Society's haunted house, 1997

Yes, the fireballs, chocolate, and clowns going after the audience with vacuum cleaner hoses were real. No, they did not obey fire codes. Yes, the haunt was a raging success the three years it flew under the radar, and no, it's not still around (never say never).

Atrocity Alley. The Lunatic Petting Zoo. Goat Parlor. The Catholic Closet. Sadists' Kitchen. We're not in the Magic Kingdom anymore. The first Cacophony haunt was staged in 1994 and the second in 1997, where audiences told stories of "slogging through curtains of beef tongue and being pissed on by cartoon dogs." In 2000's show, they promised "implant flashbacks, militaria collectors on ether, and dumpster-dwelling hair merchants." The events were advertised, not as haunted houses, but as walking tours of the diseased soul.

Whose drug-riddled nightmare are we in?

"When I was a kid, I was particularly intrigued by museums, particularly natural history museums as they existed into the 1960s and early 1970s—their stillness, darkness, the dioramas' tiny glowing windows into the past."

This is Al Ridenour, founder of the Los Angeles branch of the Cacophony Society. "It all seemed very dreamlike and otherworldly to me. As a little kid, I even turned my bedroom into a 'museum,' setting up displays with rocks and arrowheads and plastic dinosaurs, and tried to convince my older brothers to take tours of it."

The Museum of Mental Decay was Ridenour's idea, but he had help. Their curtain of beef tongue, for instance, was the work of a performance art group from Oklahoma who, he says, "reveled in their meat-eating non-Californian ways." The chocolate-covered body belonged to a volunteer who went to parties naked. "Just normal parties, even," explains Ridenour. "It wasn't even really a sexual thing, but some part of his psyche that just needed expression. And the clown who spit chocolate syrup on him had done that chocolate-sauce-spitting stunt on numerous occasions, so you see it really was a natural outcome of putting together people who delight in unnatural tendencies. I was just lucky to find myself in the center of those circles."

It's clear that these folks didn't give two seconds' thought to the classic "touch no one and no one touches you" haunted house rule. Or any of the rules normally listed outside haunted houses.

"The element of danger was essential," says Ridenour. "Ideally it would have been some sort of dark-night-of-the-soul shamanic initiation. We dearly wanted to maximize the psychological thrills and spills, and, had it been possible, I would have preferred sending every visitor through naked and on heavy doses of psychedelics, but, sadly, this was not to be."

Titillation has always been part of horror; peeling away layers to find what's forbidden, to see what's normally locked away from us. As Ridenour says, "I suppose if someone bothers burying it, it must be worth digging up.

"I know in the old days they used to give what were supposed to be informative or edifying tours of bedlam to more fortunate thrill-seeking Londoners, so I kind of envisioned the Museum of Mental Decay as something like that, the same questionable combination of education and titillation you'd experience in the old dime museums or freak shows."

Maybe this is what's driving the success of current television reality shows. All that is private, vulnerable, or broken is broadcast, just like the bearded ladies who were carted town to town and put on display. The public surgeries, celebrity fights, weight loss and rehab struggles—are these the freak shows of the twenty-first century?

What were people hungry to see? I ask. What sorts of rooms did they really respond to?

"In a sense, it's kind of predictable," says Ridenour. "The hands-on, rough-and-tumble stuff. Perceptual overload, like the massive military-grade strobe lights, nudity. Shock and awe."

So why do you think that is? Why are people so drawn to the extremes?

"Finding the extremes of nature helps you outline things, gives you some handle on everything that lies in between. Freakish represents the big picture. What makes people most *upset*, if not *afraid*—after all, no one was assaulted, bankrupted, or rejected by those they love in the course of [the MMD] tour, at least not that I know of—is not knowing what's going on. It's the idea that this haunted house isn't following the rules, and therefore, any number of terrible things are possible. People are afraid when they

don't know what their peers think, when there's not a common acceptable reaction to things. Is this scary, is it funny, is it in bad taste? The confusion can cause a sort of panic.

"And speaking of peers, no one that I know of came to take the tour by himself. So maybe that's the big fear—being alone, or the confusion of a common ground—rationality?—slipping away."

The Scream Bone's Connected to the Head Bone

It was at a Halloween Convergence in Sleepy Hollow, New York, that I first truly understood blood splatter. About seventy of us sat on a plastic sheet spread out on the floor of a hotel conference room. The people in the front row wore disposable white Hazmat-like suits, and the excitement built as haunt designer and Jackson Pollack-of-blood John Burton filled bucket after bucket with red paint. Then he started whipping the stuff around. Look, he explained, the shape and color of the blood on the walls of a haunted house scene—to be realistic—should match what's happened in the room. A gunshot wound leaves more of a misting of blood—here Burton flicked tiny drops of red paint on the sample wallboard as we imagined one sharp pistol shot through the temple—and larger drops indicate blunt force. Hammers, tire irons, and frozen sides of beef came to mind.

Then he dipped both hands in the paint and hurled it at the wall; the paint splattered audibly, spread, and dripped down the surface in glossy rivulets. The crowd ooohed. This, Burton told us, would be the splatter pattern for recent violence. But what if the murder happened a while ago? Burton drybrushed a dark color around the edge of the stain. Blood dries there first, he explained, so the stain would be brownish-red at the edges and deep crimson in the center where it was still fresh. The devil's truly in the details. Haunted house audiences demand a level of realism way beyond funhouse buzzers and flashing lights.

So much of the substance of our Halloween haunts has to do with carnage and death, torture and madness. What is it exactly we're afraid of here? Is it that we as a species are capable of a range of perversity, that there really is evil in the world? Is Halloween gore the physical embodiment of a violent America? We use blood, bone, organs, fingers—we use *us*—to scare *us*. In an unrelenting onslaught of wounds, surgery, and insides on the outside, our skins are no longer boundaries.

But this is what we demand, an experience so raw we can feel it through layers of viscera all the way down to our bones, a physical

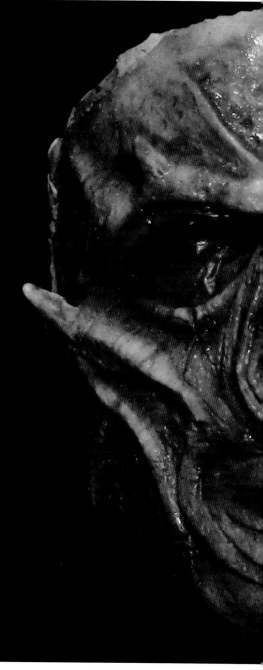

Inner Demon, *constructed of foam latex by Tony Miguez of Vertigo Industries. Bringing fears into a visual 3-D form helps people deal with what scares them, Miguez believes.* (Photograph by Tony Miguez)

jolt. Something extraordinary, in the sense that it's outside ordinary life, but at the same time, real. A fake chainsaw that sparks when it scrapes against metal; monsters that careen over your head on zip lines; a floor that shakes under your feet; or truck headlights that barrel toward you. It's dangerous, but in a good way. The borders between real and pretend, between terror and terror-tainment, between chaos—that can decimate and destroy—and the thrill—that can exhilarate and heal—remain intact on Halloween. You're not really in the presence of a serial killer, and you're not really being shoveled into a shallow grave. At Halloween, fear is fun.

Psychologists even say it's good for you.

"Very few children have to be taught not to play with spiders."
—Rush W. Dozier, Jr., *Fear Itself*

"People fully aroused will tell you that this is when they feel the most alive. There's something to be said for that experience that pushes the arousal beyond typical levels." This is Dr. David Zald talking here. Zald works with the Affective Neuroscience Laboratory at Vanderbilt University, which studies the neural basis of emotional processing. But not only is Zald a professor who has worked with the fear response, he also decorates his house for Halloween. ("My favorite holiday. How could I not say yes," was his response when I asked if I could talk with him.)

Shock and startle are two of the most common fear responses you find in haunts. Shock is a defensive, physical reaction—you can't suppress it—and startle is a reflexive response to something sudden. If any haunted house entertainment lights up just a fraction of the areas of the brain involved in shock or startle, we turn into supermen and women. Our eyes widen (super sight), blood pressure increases and breathing quickens (super strength), and our heart rates rise and we sweat (super speed). But the fear response is a powerful one, maybe the most powerful emotion we have. So how did fear, which is essential to keeping us alive in dangerous situations, become recreational?

"Ah," says Dr. Zald. I sense this may not be the first time he's been asked to explain this. "You can put this question into the bigger picture of movies, TV, things that make us experience emotions that are generally considered negative emotions; for example, watching sad movies. Why would someone choose to watch a sad movie? Why would someone choose to do something that is scary? There is a concept that we gain mastery of our emotions by having these simulated experiences that we know are

only partially real. The haunted house situation takes this to that next extreme because it involves such an autonomic response."

Fear starts in an older, primitive part of the brain, in the amygdala. We inherited this small part from our animal ancestors, and its job is to scan constantly for danger, even while we sleep. Once it registers "threat"—whether it's a real threat or not (e.g., striking rattlesnake vs. fake wolf pack in a corn maze)—it's going to buzz like a high-powered burglar alarm, activating hormones, which flood the brain and trigger physiological reactions (those super powers mentioned above).

But the amygdala is also involved in learning connections, says Zald. Therefore, if you've learned that a Doberman pinscher can hurt you and you see a Doberman pinscher, the amygdala will cue the brain to provide a maximum fear response.

So, the amygdala is where the scary clowns live? (Or, in my case, snakes.)

"Yes, definitely. If there's something that occurs early in one's life where one made an association that clowns are creepy, and now you put them in this context [of a haunted clown house], it's going to push that sense of anxiety."

But we're not the proud owners of opposable thumbs for nothing. Fractions of a second later, the rational parts of the human brain jump right in and begin what Zald terms "reappraisal." It's only a shadow, just an actor, not a real fire. In Zald's opinion, reappraisal is nothing less than a natural selection success story.

"One can argue that is one of the brilliant adaptations humans have, to overcome that anxiety and fear based on the ability to say, 'Oh, in fact, this situation's okay.'"

Haunted attractions and scary Halloween celebrations in general are rehearsals for dealing with real fear. They help us work out the terrors we've been carrying around for a millennium or more.[8] As a species, Dr. Zald explains, humans—all mammals really—are easily startled. But we, unlike turtles or tree shrews, can laugh after we jump. This laughter diffuses our sense of fear and turns it into a sense of mastery. As a bonus, surviving a scare triggers the release of opiate-like neurochemicals to rebalance our bodies. Win-win.

The Halloween we celebrate today is more visually dangerous than the Halloweens of our childhood because it is largely driven by the explicit content of state-of-the-art horror films and video games. Film scholars theorize that this super-graphic horror is popular because it's able to present the real terrors of our world with some honesty, and that horror films can be seen as a way to cope with the way we live now. (As film director Wes Craven once said, "I don't think people like to be scared. I think they are scared or have been scared."[9]) Slasher films and gore cinema are a way to exorcize the rage and terror that fester just below our skins. And in some ways, haunted houses can do this too; they follow the same cultural drifts and ride on the same anxieties that horror films do.

But there is a real difference between a horror film and a haunted house experience. At a haunt, you're fighting for mastery of the situation with other people in the real world. Haunts, in a way, build communities of warriors. Rather than using Halloween's horror-filled imagery to indict the holiday, we could honor this one night when we can be the powerful, bloody creatures we are. When we can let the monsters out.

Part IV. Subversive Halloween:
Monsters and Pranksters

Ryan West from Lichfield, Connecticut, at the Vampire's Ball in Salem.

Chapter Nine
Bats, Tats, Twirlers, and Thrashers

 It's Poe-dark in the ballroom where DJ Addam Bombb looms over a sound system setting up his tracks for the Vampire's Ball. He's the go-to guy for dance music during Salem's high season, a sought-after alternative DJ whose talent has earned him the title "King of Halloween" among his fans in the club scene.

Bombb cements in a pair of fangs, draws a thick line of black under each eye, and cues Vitamin String Quartet's version of "A Vampire's Lament."

"The reason our Goth culture has borne out—not as a horror culture but as an underground culture—is because of the ideology," Bombb tells me. "We feel like we're being told only a portion of the truth, and we don't trust our politicians or the media. Wouldn't it be great to be the great justice-bringer, the vigilante vampire? You want to be the one—not who eats the innocent people—but the one that eats the wicked."

For Bombb, monsters are the supermen of counterculture, heroes who will help bring down the corporate giants who poisoned our earth and kicked all but the very rich to the curb. Monstrosity, like alternative culture, is at the vanguard of change.

"Except our superman is much darker, our superman is something that is vastly more real to us, in that we not only want to see the bad guys lose, but we want to see the power reclaimed and transformed into something else."

Our monsters come from serious places. They emerge not only from our culture, but also from deep within our psyches. After the trauma of World War I, Americans went in droves to see films with new creatures, such as *Dracula* (1931), *Frankenstein* (1931),

175

and *Freaks* (1932). The Wolfman—Hitler's totem animal was the wolf—was the World War II monster; mutants and aliens were our postatomic villains; horrific man-monsters erupted after Vietnam; vampires obsessed us during the AIDS epidemic; and a spate of violent beasts took over after 9/11.[1] Monsters are, psychologists say, our repressed "evil twin" or our collective nightmares.[2] To deal with the monstrosity in our lives, we make the monster real, externalize it, animate it, and kill it to rob it of power.

But here's where our current relationship with monsters takes a left turn. Some of us don't externalize. We emulate. We want to *be* monsters, to get so far out of mainstream culture that no one can mistake us for being part of it. Joining the fraternity of the monstrous becomes an ideological stand, a way of saying, "I'm *not* you, *not* that." Through symbols and aesthetics, we find our own tribe, build alliances, and create our own world. A world that, interestingly, looks a lot like the one we create at Halloween.

Monsters, by nature, live outside the rules. It makes sense that they resonate with the spiked, pierced, corpse-painted, and tattooed. It's no wonder they are legion at Halloween, the rule-bending holiday that opens its arms to fringe and mainstream alike. And who, on this night of nights, can tell the difference? "On Halloween," says a Goth friend, "Everyone looks like us."

"I dress this way just to keep them at bay
'Cuz Halloween is every day."

—"(Every Day Is) Halloween," Ministry

Monster Ink

"I wanted to take my white privilege and throw it down the toilet and be tattooed, and wow, when you get that first tattoo and it doesn't kill you it's almost like being reborn in to this new subculture. I become that guy. That guy with the tattoos."

—Joseph Boo

The Boston Tattoo Convention has a mellow vibe. Customers recline, shirts up around their heads, bending forward over supports that look like massage chairs. Or they stare into the middle distance, arms bravely splayed like they're giving blood. A really big guy cradles the elbow of his client, wiping and drawing, wiping and drawing. One woman talks on a cell phone while she's being inked, right behind a sign that says "Tips Make It Hurt Less." Maybe as the night goes on, the music will kick up and the beer

Tattoo artist Joe Boo.

garden will be packed. But now, early in the evening, the Tattoo Con has all the edginess of a bean supper.

"Oh, cool, what's that?" says a spiky-haired woman as she leafs through a book of designs. The artist lights up: "That guy? He steals children, but if you make him spill the water from that bowl-thing on his head, he loses his power. He's really popular right now."

I'm looking through the tattoo sample books for monsters. I figure if I can find people so obsessed that they tattoo these creatures—zombies, devils, skeletons—on their skin, I might be able to find out why these images are so powerful, what they mean, and how monstrosity and Halloween are tied together in our imaginations. I pause on a photo of the word "Taco" tattooed on the inside of a girl's lower lip, with an arrow pointing up toward her tongue.

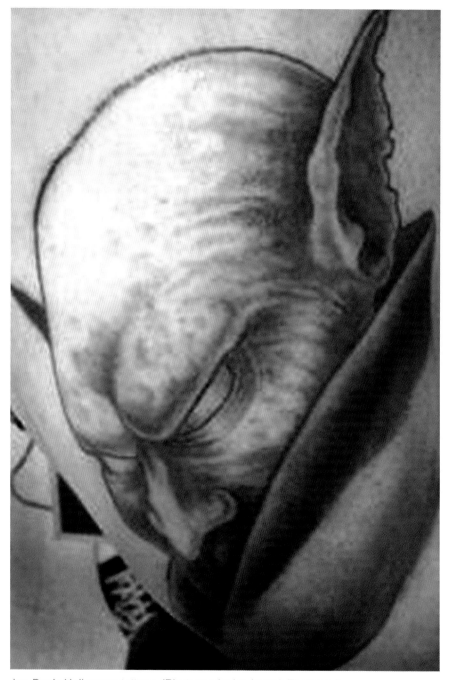
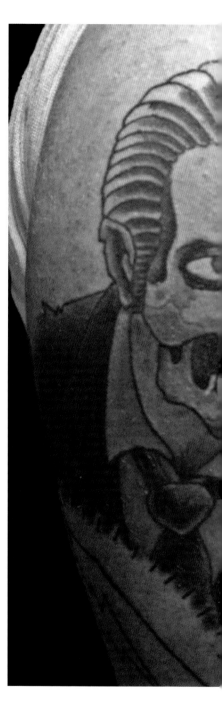

Joe Boo's Halloween tattoos. (Photographs by Joseph Thomson)

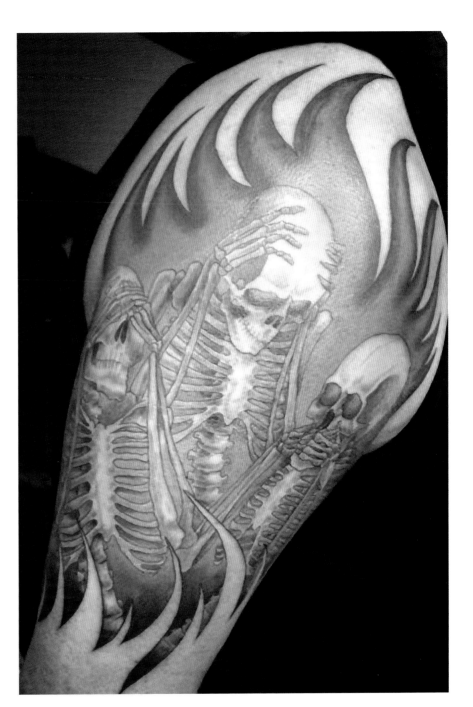

Then I find Joe Boo's book.

"I don't know what it is, but people love Halloween and they love autumn," he tells me. "Even when people want random trees, they want a gnarly, twisted tree with red-orangey leaves or no leaves at all. All I have to say is, 'Kind of Halloweeny?' and their eyes light up and they say, 'Yeeeaaaahhh.'"

When I visit Joe Boo at his workplace, we talk about how he came to be the Halloween tattoo guy.

"I've always liked the darker imagery because I felt it was so much more interesting. Think about all the great classical paintings of any religion or theology; the depictions of damnation and sin are always a lot more interesting than fluffy clouds and angels. Look at the painting of hell by [Albrecht] Dürer—all those classic images of the places you get to go to when you're damned. And all the interesting ideas they have—like you committed a sin so you get this unique form of punishment. I can't remember the fellow that's always pushing a boulder up a hill— oh yeah, Sisyphus. He's tormented. They have these weird, interesting ways to torment people in hell, but heaven is calm and boring. Good stuff always seemed boring to me. The darker stuff always had a lot more pull."

And, of course, he loved monsters as a kid. "We went to church and came home and watched *Creature Features* until our brains were full of all these weird things."

Boo's first tattoo was a "tribally kind of thing" a friend drew on his back. "I so needed not to be a normal civilian. The whole you have to go to school, you have to get a job, you have to have a family, you have to pick out a coffin and die. I was thinking, man, the world is so screwy, I don't want to have anything to do with it."

As I stare in awe at some sharp-looking needles, Boo says, "Yes, it hurts. It's a tattoo, not a handshake. . . . Tattoos should be edgy. Even fifteen years ago you had to deal with some pretty scary people to get a tattoo. Now tattoos are becoming almost p.c. They're too easy."

In a room down the hall, I can hear buzzing.

"Want to see how it works?" Boo asks with a wry smile.

I sure do. I'm tattooless.

We watch as the tattoo machine—about the size of a dremel tool—creates a charge that drives a pin hundreds or thousands of times per minute up and down into your skin, like a fast sewing-machine needle. When the artist dips the point in ink—as you would a quill pen—it gives him about twenty to twenty-five seconds of ink time. For an original tattoo design, he'll usually outline the design first, then use different-sized needles to color and fill.

Visions Tattoo co-owners Canman and Angela Cannistraro both have Halloween tats. Canman's, by Mike Davis, draws inspiration from Big Daddy Roth's monsters and Canman's annual Halloween ritual of stealing a pumpkin and smashing it. For Angela (tattoo by Jamie Cross), it's more about the supernatural aspects of Halloween. "I always watched Scooby Doo. *Trying to find something that not everyone can see. It's scary, it's exciting, and it stirs up emotions that are not every day emotions."*

Boo's got some custom artwork set to go for self-described Halloween nerd Meghan Dahl, who wants a tattoo inspired by vintage holiday images.

"It's a subtle homage to Halloween," the twenty-seven-year-old Dahl tells me, of the piece that includes a mix of traditional symbols like gravestones, a black cat, and a haunted house. "It tells the story of how I think of Halloween, how it's more than just a holiday, more than the candy and costumes. It's about the world of souls passing over."

And that, she thinks, makes the holiday worthy of inking into her skin forever. Halloween stands for something.

"Halloween has its own soul that needs celebrating," Dahl states.

For Boo, though, Halloween evokes darkness and transformation. When people seek him out for tattoos, it's often because they know he's good with monsters.

"I think it stems from their childhood. People want the classics: Michael Myers, the Hammer movie monsters. Portraits of zombies are popular now with the kids—real nasty stuff, stuff I wouldn't even wear on a T-shirt. The consequences are really ugly. I mean, 'Grandpa why do you have a severed head on your chest?' It probably doesn't even look like a severed head by then—probably looks like a piece of steak.

"I think a lot of people get monsters because it has something to do with transformation. We admire monsters because they have things we don't have. To turn myself into a bat and be as smooth as Bela Lugosi? Frankenstein, stronger than seven men, misunderstood, different. I think people relate to monsters not just as a power thing, but on multiple levels. The Creature from the Black Lagoon, he steals chicks in bikinis. He can breathe under water. Wolfman—kind of cursed, a loner, misunderstood. I think everyone thinks they're misunderstood, and everyone thinks they have things to offer like these monsters do. Monsters are cool."

Burn the bridge, lock the door, and don't look back. You can almost guarantee you'll never work on Capitol Hill if you tattoo the word "obey" on your knuckles. To avoid being co-opted by commerce,[3] to outrun the media or any of a million rivulets of mainstream culture—to keep alternative lifestyle *alternative*—you have to transcend the artful exterior and sink down through the skin to the blood. Mark yourself—flay, pierce, rip, decorate (mutilation as creative dissing of normalcy, the ultimate parody of plastic surgery-obsessed America?). Slide right into the frames of those comic books, inked like those beloved creatures, into a reality that feels right.

Monsters, as Boo says, evoke the power of transformation. They're hardwired to hack away at all that's normal, stable, or secure; they're revolutionaries. They're everywhere at Halloween because Halloween is the biggest subversive celebration we've got. Costumes flaunt, vent, agitate, entertain, and give full flight to fantasy. On October 31, you can lampoon massive institutions like government and the church or demand candy from strangers even though you're only three feet tall. Whatever social box you're in—boy/girl, rich/poor—Halloween is your chance to escape it. There is a rampant freedom on this night that is singular, and it comes from being outside your own skin and outside the rules. Monsters and Halloween belong to the same midnight chaos.

Monster Lust

So, then, the worst fears of parents and psychiatrists have come true. EC Comics, *Creature Features* TV movies on Sunday afternoons, and all those weird imaginings *did* damage the psyches of young kids.[4] It was those kids—little Stephen King, George Lucas, Tim Burton, and so many more—who brought their love for creepy tales into the art, film, music, and literature they produced as adults, which influenced the next generation, who grew up to create the latex masks, special effects, music, and gory props that kids today can't get enough of. For anyone born after 1950, Halloween and monsters slid into our imaginations together.[5] We fear them; we love them; we set aside 31 October to celebrate them. And in a sense, they're family. Once we're dead, our flesh melts and falls away, exposing the decay that lies within. We all end up looking like monsters.

Even the most beautiful among us are not immune.

"You can't throw a dead cat without hitting a burlesque dancer in Seattle."
—Evilyn Sin Claire

"I came out looking very quintessential burlesque in red and black with a little top hat and feather bustle skirt. I stripped a little to the first song (Elmer Bernstein's version of "The Man with the Golden Arm"), then at some point I stalked up to a planted audience member. I bit his neck where he had blood packets hidden.

Opposite: *Evilyn Sin Claire performing a "black metal"-themed burlesque act for a theme night at Get Loweded in Seattle.* (Photograph by Vicki Bracken)

The music changed (Mike Patton's "Spider Baby"), and I slowly revealed the blood pouring from my mouth. I continued the striptease . . . and ended up in panties and pasties covered with blood. It was very horrorshow."

Miss Evilyn Sin Claire directs the Sinner Saint Burlesque in Seattle, and her vampire piece is something she's performed as part of the burgeoning neo-burlesque scene, usually around Halloween. Horror burlesque takes traditional striptease and retools it for those who have little patience for glitter and feathers. It has the wink-wink of, say, zombie pinup calendars, as well as the part that goes bump in the night.

"The dark side of female sexuality still really turns me on," says Sin Claire. "But I didn't want to be a Goth burlesque girl. It seemed too easy, and people were already doing it. I definitely had it in the back of my mind that I wanted to do some gore, because I think it's sexy."

Okay. Sidebar here—Sin Claire is onto something. The *New York Times* recently reported that it's women, not men, who make up the majority of the audience at graphic horror films (the *Saw* franchise variety) these days. "Are they ironists?" the article asks. "Masochists?" The story goes on to quote screenwriter Diablo Cody, who explains it this way: "When I watched movies like *The Goonies* and *E.T.*, it was boys having adventures. When I watched [*A*] *Nightmare on Elm Street*, it was Nancy beating up Freddy. It was that simple."[6]

Indie horror film actress Debbie Rochon (*The Good Sisters*, *Satan Hates You*, and *Poultrygeist*, among many others) tells me that she's also seeing more women horror fans now. "We started to see the change towards the end of the '90s. Before that it was a purebred male genre with the occasional sprinkling of female, like in a biker gang—when did you ever see a girl on the front of a bike? Beyond rare. That's why I like to play the crazy or deranged person—and by crazy I'm really saying super strong. Look at *Fatal Attraction*. She's crazy, but she's driving the movie and isn't that great. It's especially good for women to be able to channel that kind of energy. You don't get that opportunity in most material."

Although it's a stretch to make a case for half-naked, blood-soaked girls as the cutting edge of a new feminist movement, that's what some are doing. To take a performance genre—striptease—that represents an era oppressive to women and honor the performers with emulation can be radical. To add horror, revolutionary. We cheer the heroine who picks up the ax and starts

Debbie Rochon and April Burril in the independent horror film The Good Sisters *(2009), written and directed by Jimmy O Burril. (Photograph by Jimmy O Burril)*

whacking; in our hyperviolent world, the vengeance feels much more real than the blood.

"Female sexuality isn't all smiles and glitter; there's also darkness there," Sin Claire says. "The femme fatale, the lioness, harder-edged archetypes and fantasies. I think horror burlesque goes over really well with the punk/metal/alt culture scenes. They want their sexy served with a side of mainstream challenge."

One of Sin Claire's most popular pieces is a zombie act, where at one point she gnaws on an arm filled with hamburger. At the end of the act she runs, roaring, full-bore at the audience.

"Slasher films have gone a long way to turn women into canon fodder and lunch meat. It's not always healthy. But the zombie girl can go from victim to, well, superstar! Why not? And then there's just the absurdness of it, using gross images in a sexy way. It's subversive if you do it right."

"I didn't find the monsters scary. I immediately empathized with them, because as a kid I was the outsider too, the outcast. I identified more with Frankenstein or King Kong than I did with Charlie's Angels," says Carrie D'Amour, aka Devilicia, as I sit in her living room staring at a fake bat's head the size of a trash compactor. Devilicia's part of Black Cat Burlesque in Boston and she, like Sin Claire, performs horror burlesque. But for Devilicia, it's all about the monsters.

"Frankenstein was put in a horrible position. King Kong? Not his fault. Phantom? Tragic. Dracula . . . well, you could argue that he knows what he's doing depending on what movie it is, if he's cursed or if he's just a guy who wants to bite the necks of women in push-up bras."

Put it this way: when other little girls were doodling the names of their best friends on their notebooks in pretty colored markers, Devilicia was drawing a picture of the shark from *Jaws* calling her on the phone; she wanted to *be* a shark so she could date him.

"So they're watching a striptease, watching tassel twirling—there's that sexual connotation—but then they have to accept that the body they're looking at has a Mrs. Creature from the Black Lagoon monster head."

Monsters and Halloween were the perfect pairing for her.

"I grew up in New Hampshire as one of the only punk/Goth chicks, and Halloween was the one time of year I could kick back and relax. Halloween embraces all the outsiders."

The home Devilicia shares with her partner, artist Mister Reusch, is full of Halloween-type props, including the decomposing face she wears for her Inanna, the Sumerian queen act. For that scenario, she created prosthetic-eyeball pasties.

And you twirled them?

"I twirled them."

"They're really gross," affirms Reusch. "Very realistic."

"The more I've been doing this," says Devilicia, "the more I go in for being as gross and disturbing as possible.

The tassel twirling she learned from watching Elvira.

"In *Elvira Mistress of the Dark,* she's wearing this spider web bra and she has two spiders that she twirls and I studied and studied that. Now I twirl bats. Satan's Angel—she's a classic burlesque performer—twirled fire. I changed that to sparklers for my Darth Vader act."

Devilicia says that the link between sex and horror makes a

Opposite: *"Meet Your Favorite Monsters . . . Undead and Undressed"* announces a horror burlesque show flier. (Poster art by Mister Reusch)

kind of sense. "It's kind of like being a little drug addict," she says. "There was a study done that showed people are more apt to be sexually aroused after watching a horror or an action movie because adrenaline or endorphins kick in, and I think that comes into play. There's always some element of sex in horror movies, whether it's Catholic guilt or some statement on sex and death. It's definitely there."

Standing at the Gates of Mordor

"They say the old bluesman Robert Johnson sold his soul to the devil at the crossroads, and when he came back he had some kind of notoriety. Punk rock, black metal, hard rock, everything since then has blues riffs from Johnson. Black Sabbath, if you want to break it down, is a blues band. It's all the same riffs, just heavier."

—Ross Karpelman, House of Shock

So suddenly, out of nowhere, Rob Zombie leaps up onto the bar, shining a hand-held spotlight at the audience while his guitarist rips through a solo on stage. Images of bloody creatures play across giant video screens as Zombie leaps down into the crowd, using the light as you would use a torch to keep monsters away.

A girl next to me grabs my arm, nearly breathless. "Oh, my God. I touched him!" she screams, tears welling up in her eyes. "It was just skin. But it was AMAZING skin!"

Up on stage, the guitarist riffs on "The Star-Spangled Banner," Hendrix style, as the entire back wall lights up in pentacles and the mosh pit is pulsing like an angry beast with fists throwing devil horns at the stage.

Zombie climbs back onto his platform in time for the final chorus, flipping his hair as the drummer tears up the snares. I grab onto the pillar next to me, but it's vibrating like crazy. The video screens are filled with fire, the people in the balconies are slamming against the railings, and the whole place looks like it could come tumbling down in a second.[7]

Draw a circle around a heavy metal concert and all its effects—fire, fog, monsters, makeup, costumes, satanic symbols, death lyrics—then draw a circle around Halloween, and where those two circles overlap you'll find the bad-assed parts of both, the area that's a cocktail of rebellion and tribe. Halloween and metal music have been dark bedfellows since Black Sabbath first cracked open the gates of Mordor and urged the children of disobedience to take back the night.[8]

Headless Metal Horseman. (Illustration by Scott Jackson)

Pyrotechnic Armageddon that ends the occult-themed stage show at the House of Shock in New Orleans, Louisiana. The show usually begins with a performance by a live band. (Courtesy House of Shock)

"Big black shape with eyes of fire
Telling people their desire
Satan sitting there he's smiling
Watches those flames get higher and higher"
—"Black Sabbath," Black Sabbath

"What's so monumental about Black Sabbath is that they were the first of their kind."

This is Mike Einziger, cofounder and guitarist for the platinum-selling band Incubus, whose eclectic music you'll find everywhere from pop radio stations to metal shows like the seventy concerts they played with Ozzy.

What is it, I ask Einziger, about the iconoclastic, creatures-of-the-night, doom-and-death gestalt that is so seductive and dangerous in both metal music and Halloween?

"That concept you're talking about, the impending unknown, I think that extends into everything. Fear of death is actually a survival mechanism, that's why it's so powerful. It evokes really strong images, and we're conditioned in an evolutionary sense to run from it to survive. It goes back billions of years. We're obsessed with it because it's key to our survival."

The over-the-top stage shows and music work together, says Einziger, like a sound score and a film. The visuals enhance the music. "It's sensory overload . . . and the fantasy element of it is very thick."

Like a good haunted house, the music serves as a massive, skull-tattooed steam valve, releasing a Dionysian mania. It's theatrical and sensory-loaded to hammer both mind and body with a defiant, raw energy that projects you into another reality, a monster among monsters.

To be honest, says Einziger, people's adverse reactions to bands like Black Sabbath or Marilyn Manson or movies such as *The Rocky Horror Picture Show* are what make them so great. "If people didn't react the way they did, other people wouldn't get off on it."

I can't let Einziger walk away yet. I have to ask: But what about Ozzy? A nice guy?

"Yeah. He's really lovely. Like a little puppy dog."

It makes sense that the first inklings of modern Goth culture appeared in clubs a few years after Steve Jobs and Steve Wozniak were camped out in Jobs' parents' garage building a microprocessing system that would become Apple Computer, Inc. The inspiration for the original Gothic—a genre of eighteenth-century literature—was a quiet rebellion against the rise of science and reason. Halloween, too, both then and now, is a throwback. It cavorts with magic and imaginary beings, superstition, and the past. Halloween, like the monster, is bloody, iconoclastic, dramatic, and full of the unexplainable.

It feels good to align yourself with the creatures who gather at nights' edge; there's a freedom and passion there. There's joy in living by a code, no matter how offbeat or temporary, and in celebrating who you are with your tribe. And all monsters, be they myth, symbol, or metaphor, obliterate an old order. Their very presence means a change is coming.[9]

Those on the outskirts of our culture have developed their own language of creativity and rebellion. For the rest of us, there is Halloween, and on this night, the connections between us become visible, like a giant web that stretches from tattoo parlor to Goth/industrial club to your kids' cafeteria, where on Halloween, and only Halloween, the lunch ladies wear horns.

DJ Addam Bombb. (Photograph by gregm cooper.com)

Insider Info: Dance Party Music for Zombies, Witches, and Vampires
Addam Bombb, DJ

Music for Zombies

I started the Zombie Ball with Nina Simone "I Put a Spell on You" and followed up later that night with Marilyn Manson's take on it. Zombies, they lurch. I played $\frac{6}{8}$ timing and a lot of triplets, a lot of stuff that's lurch-oriented. Zombie movies always have guitars and saws in them. So I'm thinking brains and green earth and rotting flesh. Iggy Pop's "Nightclubbing." "Living Dead Girl," by Rob Zombie; "Put a Lid on It," by Squirrel Nut Zippers; the Love Spit Love cover of "How Soon Is Now," which was the theme song for [the movie] *The Craft."*

For Witches

In the early part of the night, I try to reach for stuff that really holds true over the decades. Ella Fitzgerald singing "Ding Dong the Witch Is Dead," or 'Spooky' by Classics Four. I realize it's a popular Halloween track, but I'm looking for things that pin you to the right place. Frank Sinatra's "Witchcraft," Dead Can Dance, "The Ubiquitous Mr. Lovegrove."

For Vampires

I like to go for the more seductive, romantic side. I look for bigger operatic sounds—smooth, deep and dark. The track everybody always asks me about is "Mitternacht," by E Nomine. Then there's "Kiss," by London After Midnight; "Bela Lugosi's Dead," by Bauhaus; Siouxsie and the Banshees' "Peekaboo"; The Cure's "Lullaby." They're my favorite songs, my Halloween-is-every-day music.

Hackers broke into this Austin, Texas, electronic road sign and reworked the message one night in late January 2009. Within the week, pranksters in at least two other states followed suit. In Collinsville, Illinois, hackers changed a sign along I-255 to read, "Daily lane closures due to zombies." In Hamilton County, Indiana, a sign appeared flashing "Raptors ahead—Caution." (Photograph by Chris Nakashima-Brown)

Chapter Ten
Trick and/or Treat?

"In the town that I live in we don't even erect an altar anymore where we can torture animals as a warning to the spectral realm."

"Why, oh, but why?"

"Someone complained about the howling."

"Yes, but the howling is the whole point. How else are you going to scare the demons away?"

—The Onion News Network, 2008 Halloween Internet broadcast

At the 2000 Democratic National Convention in Los Angeles, there was an area set up for protesters and media. Among the crowd was a group of ragged zombies playing ball with a rubber brain and carrying a crudely painted placard reading "Zombies for Gore." An MTV reporter thrust her microphone into the group and asked them what their message was. They drooled and growled. No really, she insisted, this is your chance to get your message out, what is it? The zombies surrounded her, growled some more, and chewed on her shoulders.

A few years earlier, a press release went out to national media announcing that religious groups would be protesting the opening of the movie *Fantasia* at the Castro Theatre in San Francisco. According to the release, one group, Sensitive Parents Against Scary Movies (SPASM), was angry at the glorification of Satanism inherent in the "Night on Bald Mountain" section, claiming their children had nightmares for weeks afterwards. *Time Magazine* picked up the story.[1]

Riiiiggghht.

Zombies for Gore and SPASM were both pranks perpetrated by members of the Los Angeles Cacophony Society, an anarchic group with its roots in California and its own special take on Halloween (see Psycho Haunting in chapter 8).

The point is this: the trickster's tools have changed from chalk, soap, toilet paper, and eggs to fictional press releases, staged events, YouTube videos, hacked electronics, and, for reasons I'll never understand, clowns. (Cacophonists once dressed forty members as clowns and scattered them at San Francisco bus stops so that each time the bus stopped, more would get on until the bus was full of clowns.[2]) Because we don't always know our neighbors anymore, we trick "culture" or "media" or "them" in order to shock, wake up, or amuse. Since Halloween is no longer about hiding your identity so much as revealing an alternate self, the anonymous trick is fading.

But tricks were what first defined American Halloween—removing porch steps, setting mailboxes on fire, covering church pews with molasses, switching street signs, stealing fences, and dumping a one-ton pile of tomatoes in the middle of Main Street. Traditional Halloween pranks are a) subversive, b) done under cover of darkness, and c) involve someone getting the fright of their life, injured, annoyed, or stuck with cleaning up a mess. Some of the youngest pranksters in this chapter fit the definition most accurately. The Massachusetts Institute of Technology hackers work exclusively at night, aim to subvert everything, and, as a thoughtful twist, leave instructions for how to clean up and patch back together what they've done.

Pumpkin Pi

"It's not that we can run faster than you can. It's that we can manipulate the physical world to do things you hadn't imagined were possible."
—MIT hacker, quoted in *Nightwork*

Dawn on Halloween, 1994. The sun's first glitter hits the Charles River and rakes along the Cambridge bank. One of the first things it lights up is the Great Dome at the Massachusetts Institute of Technology, somehow transformed into a giant jack-o'-lantern. Triangular eyes and nose, big grin, all plastered to the crown of the university's signature building.

Hackers.

It's MIT's word for pranksters, a pastime so storied there are creeds, secret languages, archives, and even books. Halloween is one of their high holy days.

Not that there aren't pranks throughout the year. Pedestrian

Student hackers turned the MIT dome into a jack-o'-lantern. (Courtesy MIT Museum)

traffic signs near campus can blink from "DON'T WALK" to "CHEW" at random. Who's to say when a lecturer's amplified voice will increase in pitch until he's talking in an inhaled-helium-like squeak? Or when all 199 seats in a classroom will be reversed and rebolted to face the back of the room? For that matter, you'll never know when you'll find a dinghy in the moat surrounding the campus chapel, a band of hackers attacking a tour bus with *Star Trek* phasers, or a nipple set atop a university dome to form "The Great Breast of Knowledge."[3]

"There were times of the year when we always knew something would go up. You could pretty well count on stuff happening around Halloween."

I'm talking with the very savvy Anne Glavin, who was on the MIT police force for twenty-seven years, fourteen of them as chief. She's chief of police at California State University, Northridge now, but the MIT hackers still hold a fond place in her heart. "The jack-o'-lantern face on the dome—that was a no-brainer, you just peeled the junk off. But the cool thing about hackers was that they always left these elaborate instructions on how to disassemble whatever the hack was, and get it off the roof safely."

Odd but affable bedfellows, cops and hackers. As a new chief, Glavin unlocked her office door one morning and found a bottle of wine and a card on her desk. "I'm looking at the bottle, thinking who the hell was in my office? It's from the MIT hacking association: 'Dear Chief . . .'" She laughed and then installed an alarm system.

Halloween inspired some classic seasonal icons. A twenty-foot-tall witch's hat atop a smaller-domed building. A giant jack-o'-lantern face created with lit windows on the twenty-three-story Green Building (using what the hackers call "Greenspeak"—turning lights on and off and raising and lowering window shades to create words or images). Four large gargoyles secretly installed on a ledge high up in a university lobby. A lit jack-o'-lantern hanging from the apex of a ninety-foot-tall vaulted ceiling.

Campus police stared up at it and marveled. How did they do it?

"You could access it from the roof," explains Glavin. "You could go to the fourth- or fifth-floor level and come in through a catwalk. MIT buildings were filled with elaborate tunnels and all kinds of weird entryways that went through walls and closets, so kids were able to get up inside the structures of buildings and get into places you and I wouldn't think of going. It's the reason we could rarely catch these guys."

Students passing through the grand foyer in MIT's main building were used to hacks: bubble wrap welcome mats, a rope swing, a downpour of sixteen hundred pink and green ping-pong balls. However, on Halloween eve in 1992, the hack was especially clever.

The Cathedral of Our Lady of the All-Night Tool was erected, like most pranks, under cover of darkness. Panels of pseudo stained glass were hung over existing windows. Pews were dragged in. A makeshift organ was installed and there was a confessional where you could confide your secrets to a computer that had to reboot when it was overwhelmed with sins. There were prominently displayed commandments:

Though shalt keep holy the hour of *Star Trek.*

Thou shalt not decrease entropy.

Thou shalt not divide by zero.

Thou shalt not sex toads.

One couple, according to MIT lore, was legally married there that night.

Chief Glavin can't help but admire the ingenuity, not to mention the engineering, it took to pull off a particularly fine prank, such as getting a realistic-looking police car through a three-by-four-foot hatch and set it atop the Great Dome (they used pieces of a junker Chevy Cavalier passed through the hatch and reconstructed with wooden framing) or building a genuine snowman in August.

"We didn't want people going out and arresting these kids like they were criminals. The hackers made very sure they didn't deface property. In fact, that's how you could tell it was an official MIT hack—these kids wouldn't break locks. They'd pick 'em. And they wouldn't hurt them when they picked them because they knew how."

Zombie Claus originator Mark Maynard was successful with his event, he thinks, partially because there's an anonymity that goes along with becoming a zombie that's liberating. (Photograph by Mark Maynard)

"That grinning, globular invader of your living room is an inhabitant of the pumpkin patch, and if your doorbell rings and nobody's there, that was no Martian. It's Halloween."

—Orson Welles, final speech, 1938 broadcast of "The War of the Worlds" (Six million people heard it; 1.7 million people believed it was really happening.[4])

Zombie Claus
FOR IMMEDIATE RELEASE

Ann Arbor, Michigan: It has come to our attention that the North Pole and the International Mall-Santa Training Grounds (IMSTG) have been attacked by the undead. The arrival of the undead into these areas of normal holiday cheer has caused a mass revolt of Santas around the world. "They are now protesting the over-commercialization of the Christmas holiday

and its encroachment into the traditional Zombie holiday of Halloween," stated the IMSTG president in exile, Claude H. Smoot.

—Media release posted on markmaynard.com

Zombie Claus is the love child of Santarchy—a mob of people dressed like Santa Claus invading shopping districts around Christmas time—and a Halloween-style zombie crawl.

I tracked down the creator of the original Zombie Claus event, blogger and artist Mark Maynard from Ypsilanti, Michigan, to ask him this: in the battle between Christmas and Halloween fought by Zombie Clauses, who deserves to win?

"Who would win? I'd like to think that good wins out in the end," answered Maynard. "That's what keeps me going. I actually have two tattoos, and one of them says 'Good Will Win.' The other says 'Evil is Bad.' The woman who did the second one was in a hurry because she wanted to get home and watch the Chris Farley movie *Tommy Boy* with her boyfriend. It wasn't too good of a design to begin with, as it took about twenty seconds to draw, but her rushing made it look like 'Evil is Bao.' I think people probably assume I'm making some kind of statement about the actor Scott Bao."

Maynard put together his first and only Zombie Claus prank event in 2005. ("Don't make eye contact. If you encounter a person, stare at their ear," instructs the Zombie Claus training instructions.) "I thought that maybe there would just be the few folks who had written in to say that they'd be coming. But there were a lot more. At the end, a lot of zombies kind of swarmed around a police car menacingly. That's when I took off. I didn't want to see any zombies tasered after trying to flip the cruiser or something."

Since Maynard's event, there have been others, as well as a demand in southern Michigan for a repeat performance.

"I think we're all so used to fast-moving danger that there's a novelty in Zombie Claus, a surreal kind of quality that's fun. I think, given the choice, most people would prefer a different kind of adversary, one that we at least had a fighting chance against. And I think that people have always enjoyed dressing up in ghoulish ways and tempting fate. It kind of takes a little power away from the dark unknown that's all around us and puts us back in control, at least to some little degree. You kind of feel more alive when you're dressed up like you're dead, you know?"

"Many troublemakers and dangerous people come out on Halloween night. To be safe, trick-or-treat in early March."

—*The Onion*, Halloween safety tips

Guerrilla Masquerade Party

"After high school, a couple friends and I who shared the costume bug used to dress up for any occasion we could, from rock concerts to just a night out for drinks," says Dan Garlington from Seattle, Washington, who works as a business analyst for Amazon by day. "My good friend Zac did amazing drag, and our friend Serenity had a black Christmas tree with orange lights that she kept up year-round. We all inspired each other to make our costumes more and more elaborate. But there weren't enough opportunities to dress up without being the only one in the crowd."

Garlington threw his very first Guerrilla Masquerade Party (GMP) in 2003. That's "Guerrilla," as in take over an unsuspecting bar for a night; "Masquerade," as in put together your most fabulously weird costume; and "Party," as in show up with hundreds of strangers at one bar on the same night and have a ball. GMP's motto: "Dress up, go out and take over. Because Halloween isn't often enough."

Since then, Garlington has thrown thirty-three parties and invaded forty-five bars, five private parties, four restaurants, two parades, one park, one theater, and a bowling alley. "People in costume are really difficult to pigeonhole," says Garlington. "You can't make assumptions about someone dressed as a parrot, other than that they are someone who is willing to dress as a parrot. Race, age, socioeconomic status, even gender became secondary to what great costumes people wore—and this led to a lot more mixing at the parties than would usually happen.

"There were some really funny costumes, like the group of four people who showed up dressed as a rapper, two prostitutes, and a big brown bottle with three Xs on it. They were Yo, Ho, Ho, and a bottle of rum. There was a karaoke night where everyone dressed for the theme Monsters of Rock, and Björk in her swan dress did duets with Axl Rose, Madonna, and a dead Elvis. There was the Circus of Insanity party where two clown troupes and some of the cast of Teatro ZinZanni showed up, including a very loud, very rowdy, armless mime.

"I think the fact that we're all dressed up on a night when people aren't expecting it gives the group more camaraderie, and a feeling that we're doing something a little crazy. On Halloween night, people expect to see costumes as they sip their beer or drive down the street, but on a Saturday night in July, seeing a crowd of people in togas and Viking helmets smoking outside a bar throws people off and usually delights passersby."

Garlington is now out of the GMP but is happy to report that his

Guerrilla Masquerade Party goers, Seattle, Washington. (Photograph by Dave Matthews)

year-round Halloween party is being kept alive in Las Vegas and in coastal Oregon.

Mass Sabbath

"Halloween is the night where too much is never enough."
—Nicholas Liivak

There's this house out in middle of nowhere, in the shadow of the Blue Ridge Mountains near Charlottesville, Virginia, where a couple of bands practice upstairs. One year, when Halloween was rolling around, they came up with an idea for a great party. Not a bunch of cover bands, like they'd already done, but one cover band made up of all the musicians in all the bands, playing the music of only one band.

"Anyone who's ever picked up a guitar or drum set knows half a Black Sabbath song, whether they admit it or not," says Horsefang guitarist Nicholas Liivak, one of the originators of the annual Halloween Mass Sabbath concert.

"We built a stage outside the house in a field that first year, and three hundred to four hundred people came by over the course of the evening. We were playing outside to a throng of costumed people, thrashing away in this tranquil setting. There were train tracks nearby, and when an Amtrak train came past we could see the passengers' heads all lit up inside the cars, looking at us. I wonder what they were thinking. The police said they could hear us three miles away."

The band grew. "You find people (or they find you) really interested in the material and who are dedicated to a hellish six to eight weeks [of rehearsal]," explains Liivak. "You're willing to jam yourself into a basement and blow your ears out."

Two Halloweens later, Mass Sabbath had moved to an indoor concert venue called the Satellite Ballroom. The stage was packed: two drummers, two bass players, four guitarists, a front man, two electric violinists, a cellist, keyboardist, fog machines, a Buddy Holly look-alike on harmonica, go-go dancers, and a wizard.

A wizard?

"Kurt was this wizened guy with a gray beard who always answered direct questions with non sequiturs, and it looked like he should be walking with a staff all the time. We had Kurt walk across the stage with a staff for one song.

"We had Jesus on guitar, with a crown of thorns. There was a dead Elvis, a terrifying black widow on violin, Bettie Page on guitar, and a Rastafarian warrior on bass. Butch Klotz, the front man, looked fantastic with his body painted white with a crude, black skeletal ribcage and a *Blade Runner* stripe across his eyes."

They started the night with the first song on Black Sabbath's first album.

"There is thunder in the background, and a church bell tolling, and then it starts with the Devil's Tritone—a root note plus the octave plus a diminished fifth—it's an ominous squall. It's a Halloween-appropriate song, demons collect their dues and all. We only did Black Sabbath songs off the first five albums, because most aficionados—and the band members—consider those the best."

"We had jugs of fake blood at the sides of the stage so if you felt your costume was lacking you could pour it on your head or take a mouthful and spray it."

Those of you who've ever tried Liivak's recipe for fake blood—Karo Corn Syrup and food coloring—can just imagine what it's like to take a shower in this stuff. "Your body hair will come off before the blood does," confirms Liivak.

"It's very much about taking it over the top. You can't be too ridiculous on Halloween. Everyone's going to the same circus that night. We make it as decadent as we can. We were all afraid to look at our guitar cases and drum sets the next morning. There was hair stuck to things hair shouldn't be stuck to," Liivak laughs.

Could Mass Sabbath happen at any time *other* than Halloween? Or is Sabbath/Halloween the mix that makes it all work?

"Halloween and heavy metal are tied together," says Liivak. "Heavy metal has the same vivid imagery—Vikings with swords, ghosts, Satan. I think heavy metal bands take Halloween more seriously. Skulls, broomsticks, and witches are pretty ripe material. And Halloween is a real freak fest. It's time to go overboard, when everyone really lets it hang out. If I said let's do Mass Sabbath on Arbor Day, I'd probably be playing by myself. Nothing against trees."

Mass Sabbath concert. (Photograph by Anthony L. Childs)

"Be sure child closes eyes before you drill eye-holes in mask."
                    —*The Onion,* Halloween safety tips

Tipping outhouses and ringing doorbells are relics. Most little kids don't even know that Halloween is a red-letter trick day and couldn't imagine exploding pipe bombs, building pyramids of stones on streetcar tracks, tying the doorknobs of opposing apartments together, mowing down shrubs, or greasing trolley rails (all things our grandfathers and great-grandfathers were up to). On the other hand, we grownups can't imagine stealing corpses from a medical school to display in a butcher shop window or frying pennies and throwing them out onto the street for little ones to grab (ask your sweet-natured grandmas and grandpas about that, too).

The decades-long campaign to divert kids from pulling Halloween tricks has, for the most part, succeeded. It's a good thing grownups have taken up the mantle.

The Invisible Rope

Peekskill, New York, Halloween, 1901. Joseph Hudson strides out of his house to see who is making such a racket in the front yard. He slams open the front door, only to trip on a rope stretched across the top step. He falls, and at two hundred pounds, he falls hard. Damn kids. Damn Halloween.

A few years ago, Dan Podosek and Yuki Palermo, two Chicago-area college students, found a video of the rope trick on YouTube. But the perpetrators used an invisible rope, which the guys thought was hysterical. They tried it. On a flat, orderly, suburban street, Podosek crouched down on one side and Palermo on the other. A car sped toward them. The guys pulled as hard as they could on their invisible rope and the car slowed, cautiously, then stopped. It waited. If a car could look irritated, this one did. There was an angry honk. Shouted Palermo, "There's nothing there!"

Female drivers generally thought the rope trick was funny.

Guys didn't.

Podosek and Palermo took their invisible rope out a few more times and then made a video. Here's where life changes: the video was featured on comedy sites like collegehumor.com and ebaumsworld.com, where it began its trek around cyberspace. The guys had created a Web site, theinvisiblerope.com, and when the video went viral, they got twenty thousand hits from sixty different countries in a month, along with a request from MTV for the rights to show it. At no other time in our evolution could two guys with a pretend rope entertain so many people around the globe with so little effort.

Back to Halloween night: "We'd get on opposite sides of the sidewalk and pull the rope when trick-or-treaters went by," says Podosek.

"Kind of like you're reeling something in," adds Palermo.

"They'd stop and talk to each other like we couldn't hear them," Podosek continues. "'What are they holding, should we go past?' Some people would go around us and some people would step over the rope that wasn't there. It was hilarious."

Did you ever ring doorbells or soap windows?

"Yes, maybe when we were a little younger," laughs Podosek.

"Guilty," says Palermo.

New dogs. Old tricks. All for it.

Halloween tricks are still subversive. They're risky (think scaling the dome at MIT), and many still incorporate some element of truth (like *The Onion* parodies or Zombie Claus). What's changing is that they're not so personal or vindictive. The tricks that had to hide in the dark, that had to be delivered hit-and-run style, are being replaced by quirky performances that are, for the most part, entertaining. Humor, rather than revenge, seems to be what we crave in a twenty-first-century prank.

Haunted Subway Car

So there you are, heading into the city on the number 6 train from Brooklyn on Halloween night. The subway stops at Brooklyn Bridge, the doors open, and twenty people barge on board, looking five shades of horrible and bloody. They stretch cobwebs across the car and hang green and pink saran wrap from the poles. That girl from *The Ring*—in the white dress with long dark hair over her eyes— she's crawling on her hands and knees down the aisle, and there's a Jason wannabe glaring at you from behind a hockey mask in the very last seat. Some wacko clown on roller skates grabs clumsily at the overhead straps as the subway bumps along its route. People get on, shocked to see the second-to-last car of the 6 completely and totally haunted. Some dude in a grim reaper cape with a megaphone welcomes everyone "to the scariest car on the Lexington Avenue line."

That would be Charlie Todd, creator of Improv Everywhere, the urban pranking organization responsible for inspiring and organizing the nine hundred people who rode these same New York subways pants-less (No Pants 2K8). The organization was born from Todd's day job as a theater instructor at the Upright Citizens Brigade Theatre in New York City. Its missions are now legend, like the fake U2 concert it staged on the roof of Todd's Manhattan apartment building or Frozen Grand Central, where more than two hundred people froze in place at the exact same moment for five minutes in the train station's main concourse.

Opposite: *Haunted subway car by Improv Everywhere.* (Courtesy Charlie Todd, improv everywhere.com)

But the Halloween subway haunt? Todd's pal Neil Casey came up with the idea. Todd remembers, "As soon as I heard it, I knew we had to make it happen."

The haunt was a hit. It wasn't exactly scary, despite all the theatrics and the boombox playing the theme from the movie *Halloween,* but it made people laugh. "Giving out free candy made people happier," says Todd.

The twenty Improv Everywhere agents—including a dead Lincoln and that creepy *Ring* girl—disembarked after nineteen stops, taking every trace of the haunt with them. The subway riders waved and smiled as they left.

As for the MTA? Says Todd, "I don't think they noticed."

D'oh!

"Homer, tell me again why we're spending our vacation on the Island of Lost Souls?"

—Marge Simpson, from *The Simpsons'* episode "The Island of Dr. Hibbert"

And again we have to come to parody—Halloween's precious gift to the ritual year. On the longest-running sitcom in television history, *The Simpsons,* the most highly rated episode of the year is the Halloween special, "Treehouse of Horror." What does that say about us? Does it have something to do with the fact that "Treehouse" is outside the regular Simpsons canon, teetering off the edge of normal, just like you know what?

In various "Treehouse of Horror" episodes, Homer dies, neighbor Ned Flanders is decapitated, and their hometown is destroyed by a French nuclear missile. By the following week, all is back to normal. What happens in "Treehouse" stays in "Treehouse."

The show takes on real world trends. The episode "Heck House" is a parody of conservative Christian churches' hell house attractions, in themselves a kind of parody of haunted houses. (To cure the neighborhood kids of tricking, Homer's Christian neighbor Ned Flanders, incarnate as Satan, imprisons them and conjures up the horrors of the seven deadly sins. Let's just say pride involves a "My child was an honor student" bumper sticker.) And the allusions to literature and pop culture come fast and furious, from sources as wide ranging as Stephen King's *The Shining* to W. W. Jacobs's classic story "The Monkey's Paw." ("Homer, there's something I just don't like about that severed hand.")

The show has been on for so long that if you bring up any

(Courtesy Charlie Todd, improveverywhere.com)

subject with fans, there's a joke about it. *The Simpsons* writer Mike Reiss told me there's a lawyer at Google who can speak entirely in lines from the show.

Reiss has worked as writer and producer on *The Simpsons* since the early days. Every Wednesday, he heads for the office at 20th Century Fox Studios in Los Angeles, where "Treehouse of Horror" was born. Before work, he hits the treadmill. That's where I caught him on the phone.

Here's what I'm curious about: On Halloween, *Simpsons* characters decapitate, stab, hang, and shoot each other with assault weapons. They are eaten by alligators and aliens, and the entire world gets sucked into a black hole. So where, I wonder, does this wacky, ultraviolent take on Halloween come from?

"For whatever reason," Reiss tells me, "there's always been a big overlap on our staff between comedy writers and horror film fans. In our first and second seasons, we'd go all together to see *Terminator 2.* We just like this stuff. But there's an influence on top of that. We delight in destroying the characters. We get a kick out of hurting and killing them. I guess we had the most fun during 'A Most Dangerous Game,' when Burns goes hunting. [Homer's boss, Mr. Burns, invites all the regular characters to his hunting lodge and murders them one at a time.] We were delirious watching the characters get killed one by one."

Okay, how about this: The kids on "Treehouse" get nicotine gum, raisins, travel-sized toothpaste, and library cards in their trick-or-treat bags. Does this come from experience? Maybe a bad childhood Halloween?

"I grew up in Bristol, Connecticut. I didn't like Halloween. It was just a personal thing. I was very shy. I didn't like dressing up, and going out for candy didn't appeal to me—nothing thrilled me about it. In fact, in high school I made a complete ass of myself at the rerelease of *The Exorcist.* Every high-school kid in town was there, and I bolted halfway through the movie.

"I started enjoying horror movies sometime in my twenties, I think. My brother loved them. I wanted to spend time with my brother, so we would rent horror movies like *I Drink Your Blood* and *I Eat Your Skin.* Actually once we rented *I Drink Your Blood, I Eat Your Skin,* and *I Spit on Your Grave.* Now I'm steeped in the stuff. On my first date with my wife, I dragged her to *Texas Chainsaw Massacre II.*"

Marge's curtain speech on the first "Treehouse of Horror" episode: "Kids worshipping ghosts, pretending to be devils." She tells the viewers not to let their children watch the show and not to write letters to complain about the violence. Do you get letters about the Halloween show being too outrageous?

"We don't get complaints. There was one executive producer who worried we'd get complaints when we first started, so we wrote Marge's opening speech, which is a parody of the original Frankenstein movie. If you know it, you can see we matched the curtain speech shot for shot."[5]

I tell Reiss I'm trying to picture the writer's room at Fox, but all I've got in my head is the old *The Dick Van Dyke Show,* where Maury Amsterdam and Rose Marie shot one-liners at each other from desks on opposite sides of the room.

Yeah, Reiss says, it *is* a little like that.

"We're not class clowns jumping around. There are funny people around a big table in a roomful of garbage and old food and old scripts, but it's not unorganized. It's a system that shouldn't work but it works very well. We go through the script—we need something here, need to be funnier here. There is constant pitching of jokes until someone says something that makes us all laugh. By the end of the process, there probably are fifty jokes pitched for every line that goes in the final show.

"There are two rooms now [in 2008], with eight to ten writers in each. And we've always had a woman on staff—it's not a quota, it just works out that way. Right now, we have 2.5 women writers. One is pregnant with a daughter."

Speaking of women and men writers, it seems to me that guys rhapsodize about *Simpsons* episodes, and girls . . . not so much.

"It's true, but less and less," says Reiss. "I've been giving lectures for about eight years, and it used to be 90 percent men in the audience. When a woman said 'I've watched my whole life,' I'd say, 'Really?' Now it's fifty/fifty—and if you're twenty years old, you've grown up with *The Simpsons.*"

Have you got a favorite "Treehouse" episode?

"'Halloween 3D Homer.' You know how there are three segments to each show? One is usually great, one is mediocre, and one sucks. On that show, all three segments clicked. At the time that show was done, the animation cost a half-million dollars for three minutes of Homer walking around in 3D. Now I think that's a free program you can download."

Reiss is off to work, and I'm left with the urge to create some historical Halloween context for *The Simpsons.* The scene of kids trapped in chairs in "Heck House" resembles a scene in an Irish myth. The plotline in "Reaper Madness," about a world without death, might have come from a folktale I know. But, I ask myself, should I really be analyzing *The Simpsons?* I mean, seriously? I think my answer can be found in the words of Edgar Allan Poe on the very first "Treehouse of Horror" episode: "Quoth the raven: eat my shorts."

Naked Pumpkin Run

What makes a tradition? Who decides? The town of Nederland, Colorado's, Frozen Dead Guy Days was inspired by the cryogenic freezing of a local resident, Bredo Morstoel, and consists of three days of parades, parties, coffin races, and a polar plunge (as some call it, cryonics' first Mardi Gras). Is Frozen Dead Guy Days any less worthy a tradition because the guy it commemorates is only recently dead?[6] How about New York City's Annual April Fools' Day Parade? Is it any less a tradition because in all the years it's been held—since 1986—it's never actually happened? How about if a holiday tradition—say, a naked pumpkin run—is fleeting because it has to be? (There should be an ironic font. If there was an ironic font I would be using it right now.)

> *"Get down there, put your clothes in a trash bag and we'll run."*
> —Instructions to the 2006 Naked Pumpkin Runners

. . . 4-3-2-1-RUN! The Boulder, Colorado, Naked Pumpkin Run is exactly that—running naked, except for your shoes, through the crowded Pearl Street pedestrian mall on Halloween night. You run as best you can with one hand balancing a carved-out pumpkin completely covering your head, and the other clutching the white trash bag that holds your clothes.

Yes, technically it's a misdemeanor. And yes, people get ticketed by the police. Those who run take their chances because where else are you going to find a gang this intrepid?

> *"2002: Three feet of snow coated the intersection of 13th and College as the first guardians of pumpkin-derived nudity ran through. Struggling to stay upright, these stallions charged through the crowds, shouting and stumbling from pure exhaustion . . . and pure exhilaration. And the crowds exploded in delight as the radiant Naked Pumpkin Runners kept coming, strung out and separated over more than a block. Forty-five naked bodies flailed in every direction, falling and sliding over the snow, and running! Running! Running!"*
> —nakedpumpkinrun.org

Ty Tuff, a biologist in his late twenties, helps organize the run.

Since the Boulder police outed him by releasing his name as one of the twelve ticketed for indecent exposure at the 2008 run, he no longer needs to remain anonymous.

"The pumpkin on your head gives you a whole level of anonymity you don't normally have," says Tuff. And you can tell who's really shy by how they carve their pumpkin. "They'll have these tiny little eye holes and this tiny mouth hole, and you can't really see much of their face.

"In Boulder, Halloween is pretty much the biggest holiday of the year. It's a college town and everyone plans on going out and doing something." (I should mention here that Halloween is in Tuff's blood. His family runs haunted houses around Denver and supplies the haunt industry with special effects. Tuff spent his high-school summers packaging and shipping "black holes.")

But, I ask Tuff, how do you get from "doing something" to running naked with a pumpkin on your head?

"There's that Halloween tradition of running up to doors and ringing doorbells and smashing pumpkins? So, when he was bored one Halloween, a friend of mine carved a pumpkin, put it on his head, ran up to this door, rang the doorbell, and ran away. That was the first year."

The second year, six friends decided to strip naked, put pumpkins on their heads, and run a one-hundred-yard dash. By the fourth year, forty runners sprinted through the streets of downtown Boulder. People poured out of restaurants and bars and cheered.

Details of the run—what time and where—are spread discreetly via the Internet, a kind of twenty-first-century whispering in the back of class. The runners convene at a house party where everyone carves their own pumpkin and drinks beer. (In fact, Tuff says, people drink in direct proportion to how comfortable they are running naked.)

"Then we have this parade to the staging area, a location we keep as secret as possible. Only the planning committee knows where it will be. People scream and yell and sing and holler—it's got kind of a sports arena feel—you're just screaming as loud as you can.

"When we get there, we count down, people get undressed, put their clothes in a trash bag and a pumpkin on their head. Everybody gets quiet. The pumpkins are heavy, and it's really cold outside. But every single person I've ever talked to (including myself) never feels cold during the run. We've had ten inches of snow on the ground or it's been snowing and you just don't even feel it. You try to scream and yell, but really all you can hear inside the pumpkin is your own breathing."

Despite the weather, year after year, the crowd of naked

runners grew. By 2008's tenth annual run, there were well over two hundred runners and hundreds more costumed spectators—space aliens, a Jolly Green Giant, Red Riding Hood, and a great big Lifesaver candy—who waited hours to catch the pack on their cameras. The crowd cleared a narrow, serpentine pathway and the runners padded through, arms uplifted with the exultation of marathon winners crossing the finish line. The onlookers cheered and the runners reveled, then slipped back into the night.

Tuff says they've tried running naked at other times of the year and with other fruits on their heads—watermelons for instance—but it just isn't the same. There's something about Halloween (the darkness, the chill, the pumpkin?) that gives the run its good-natured audacity.

But, says Tuff, "It's so crowded now that you can't really run anymore. It's like a single-file march through the crowd."

The pure exhilaration of *running* is now out of the mix, and Tuff misses it.

"Yeah I do. Absolutely. There are conflicting views even among the people who plan the run. Some like it as a community art project, the shock value of it, and the rest like the fame value of it, and want as broad an audience as possible."

Regardless of how it's managed, the Naked Pumpkin Run will abide, Tuff thinks. "It would be hard to stop. It would just become less organized."

The twenty-first-century Halloween trick—be it spectacle, joke, entertainment, or clever subversion—is really a treat in disguise, an offering that's as much fun for the tricked as it is for the trickster. For those not fond of sodden toilet paper or burning poo, this is good news. But we should thank the pranksters who came before us for setting up an expectation at Halloween, for staking it out as a day to cause a little mayhem, mock anything, and make the haves give to the have-nots, the old to the young, or at least shine a light on the fact that they should. This, we still need.

The real genesis of Halloween tricks is not the belief that mischievous spirits roam around on this night. It's festivals like carnival and the feast of fools, when the the ordinary people remind those in power that no one's property—no matter how beloved the family or how locked the gates—is unbreachable. That no one ruler is completely safe if enough people are massed together in the dark. Halloween tricks remind those in authority that it's the rest of us who let them remain there.

Notes

Chapter One: What Does Halloween Celebrate?

1. Halloween is seen as a secular children's holiday in Sweden and Catalonia and has been criticized as American imperialism in Slovenia and Russia. Most often, it seems to creep into another country's calendar through American army bases or theme parks, Irish pubs and nightclubs, movies and television, and via elementary-school teachers looking for holidays that appeal to young children. Essays on Halloween in different countries are collected in Malcolm Foley and Hugh O'Donnell, eds., *Trick or Treat? Halloween in a Globalising World* (Newcastle upon Tyne, U.K.: Cambridge Scholars Publishing, 2009).

2. Halloween—although it feels medieval and that's one of the things we love about it—only recently took the shape we recognize. Trick-or-treating, for example, wasn't a coast-to-coast phenomenon until the mid-twentieth century, and the proliferation of haunted houses came even later. The North American Free Trade Agreement and open trade agreements with China in the 1990s, says Ricky Dick of Castle Blood Haunt Couture, created the first flood of affordable, higher-quality costumes for adults.

To complicate the holiday's American history, the customs we associate with Halloween were not exclusive to October 31. There were costumed kids out begging for money on Thanksgiving in New York City as late as the 1930s, and there still are a few towns with costumed "Horribles" parades on the Fourth of July. Masquerades were popular year-round in the early twentieth century, and it wasn't unusual for social clubs to host Valentine's Day or New Year's Eve costume parties. And it was Christmas, more than

Halloween, where you'd find ghost stories. Ghosts migrated toward Halloween in the nineteenth century, when Christmas was retooled from a drunken brawl to a family-centered, gift-giving celebration.

Chapter Two: Ghosts

1. In her book *Spook: Science Tackles the Afterlife* (New York: W. W. Norton, 2005), Mary Roach gives a full account of MacDougall's experiments as well as several extraordinary efforts made on the part of science to prove the existence of the soul. The one she holds out the most hope for involves a laptop computer installed high up in an operating room at the University of Virginia Hospital. It displays images, but you wouldn't be able to see them unless you were floating on the ceiling, which is the point. C. Bruce Greyson (editor of the *Journal of Near-Death Studies*) keeps the laptop running in the event that, someday, a patient who claims to have had a near-death experience will be able to describe the images on the screen. Bingo!

2. Religious studies scholar Douglas E. Cowan points this out in *Sacred Terror: Religion and Horror on the Silver Screen* (Waco, TX: Baylor University Press, 2008), 55-56.

3. The new rite of exorcism includes prayers, blessings, and a Q & A. It replaced the ritual of 1614, and, according to Cardinal Jorge Arturo Medina Estevez, the main difference between the two is that the new one has fewer adjectives. See "Vatican Releases New Rite for Exorcism," *Catholic World News*, January 1999.

4. Kolek is referring to this passage in 1 Corinthians, 12:8, 10-11: "For to one is given through the Spirit the word of wisdom . . . and to another the word of knowledge . . . and to another prophecy; and to another discernings of spirits . . . but all these worketh the one and the same Spirit."

5. Ghosts were important to the medieval church, since building a relationship between the living and the dead helped establish moral and social norms (like fear of retribution from a ghost you offended in life or helping enforce laws of inheritance). Souls in purgatory were considered members of the church, and through alms given in their names, they brought considerable profit. In medieval thinking, individual ghosts appeared for any number of reasons (unfinished business, unexpiated sins, to warn or admonish, or to acknowledge prayers said for them) and at any time of year. Microbursts of supernatural activity—that is, the dead en masse—were associated with darkness and winter. Jacques Le Goff's *The Birth of Purgatory* (trans. Arthur Goldhammer. Chicago: University of Chicago Press, 1984) contains a detailed description

of the relationship between the living and the dead in medieval times, as does Jean-Claude Schmitt's *Ghosts in the Middle Ages: The Living and the Dead in Medieval Society* (trans. Teresa Lavender Fagan. Chicago: University of Chicago Press, 1998), especially "The Development of the Liturgy of the Dead," 33-34, and "The Invasion of Ghosts," 59-78. On the calendar of ghostly appearances, Schmitt is also good, 173-76.

6. November 11, St. Martin's Day, celebrated in countries such as Germany, is known to scholars as the beginning of popular winter. "The day when the bear and the wild man came out of the caves, which symbolized the land of the dead" (Schmitt, *Ghosts in the Middle Ages,* 175). What's interesting about this in relation to Halloween is that a) St. Martin's Day is celebrated with costumes, masks, lantern-lit processions, and witch imagery—in other words, with customs resembling Halloween (or vice versa); and b) countries accepted the Gregorian calendar at different times, meaning there was a period when October 31 in Britain and November 11 in Germany would have been the same day. (Britain and the American colonies were among the last to accept the new calendar, which they did around 1752. In fact, folklorist Jack Santino found people living in Northern Ireland who still remember celebrating "Old Halleve" on November 11; see Santino, *The Hallowed Eve: Dimensions of Culture in a Calendar Festival in Northern Ireland* [Lexington, KY: University Press of Kentucky, 1998], 88-89.) It's intriguing, too, that November 11, Armistice Day in England and Veterans Day in the United States, commemorates the dead in a way that resembles All Souls/All Saints. In a general way, these mid-autumn holidays are of a piece. They are essentially inspired by seasonal change and agricultural/pastoral cycles. And although it may seem superfluous to talk about the weather, changing seasons did move early peoples to ritual. Historian Ronald Hutton writes that it would have made sense to propitiate the spirit world at Samhain, or summer's end (*The Stations of the Sun, A History of the Ritual Year in Britain* [Oxford: Oxford University Press, 1996], 369-70). The medieval church, too, eventually set All Souls' in the fall for a seasonal reason—the abundance of food at harvest—so that monks could feed the poor, who were stand-ins for the dead.

7. When the Reformation (beginning in the sixteenth century) ripped All Souls' Day from many calendars (Protestant reformer John Calvin called ghosts "sleights of Satan"), people still kept their ghosts and remembrances. They rang church bells to honor the dead even though it was illegal and lit bonfires to comfort them

(Hutton, *Stations*, 371-73; also David Cressy, *Bonfires and Bells: National Memory and the Protestant Calendar in Elizabethan and Stuart England* [London: Weidenfeld and Nicolson, 1989], 29-30). Even when the eighteenth century brought science and reason, ghosts did not vanish; they just slid farther out into the realm of superstition. Lady Gregory, who wrote in the early twentieth century, found people in Ireland who believed the shadows of the dead gathered round at Samhain to see if there were anyone among their friends saying masses for them (*Visions and Beliefs in the West of Ireland* [Gerrards Cross, U.K.: Coln Smythe, 1970], 196). Santino found the same thing in Northern Ireland as recently as 1960 (*The Hallowed Eve*, 90).

8. Drew Faust, *This Republic of Suffering: Death and the American Civil War* (New York: Vintage Books, 2008), xi, 102.

9. Lesley Pratt Bannatyne, *A Halloween Reader: Poems, Stories, and Plays from Halloweens Past* (Gretna, LA: Pelican Publishing Company, 2004). There are several examples of Halloween ghost stories from the mid- to late-nineteenth century included, and many more listed in the bibliography.

10. The code words are "Rosabelle, believe." But Rosen says there's another theory: a second, secret code that was known only to Bess and Theo, Houdini's brother, and that Theo passed it on to Houdini collector Sid Radner. Radner is still alive, and may be the only person who would recognize a true message from Houdini.

11. A recording of the 1936 Knickerbocker Halloween séance, along with commentary, can be heard at http://cdn3.libsyn.com/pointofinquiry/10-31-06.mp3?nvb=20090120212247&nva=20090121213247&t=019661d9be1beb06c2a7b (accessed 8 October 2010).

12. Roach's *Spook* chapter, "Hard to Swallow," 123-48, delves into ectoplasm. The scuffle between Margery and Houdini is also detailed, 134-38.

13. There are reports of séances that employed magical tricks as early as the 1700s, such as those of Leipzig coffee shop proprietor Johann Schropfer, who used projections on smoke, sound effects, electric shocks, sensory deprivation, disorientation techniques, and drugs to conjure supposed spirits. Schropfer developed a cult following in Europe until his suicide in 1774.

Chapter Three: Witches

1. Information and photos of WITCH can be found at the Web site of Jo Freeman, feminist scholar and author, www.jofreeman.com/photos/witch.html (accessed 8 October 2010); also see "The Revolution is Happening in our Minds" via the same site, www.

uic.edu/orgs/cwluherstory/jofreeman/feminism/happening. htm (accessed 20 October 2010).

2. Ronald Hutton, *The Triumph of the Moon: A History of Modern Pagan Witchcraft* (Oxford: Oxford University Press, 2001), 341. WITCH's manifesto declared that before Christ, witchcraft was the religion of all Europe, a theology that was suppressed by the ruling elite; that nine million sexually liberated women died in a church-engineered genocide meant to wipe out female power; and that to be free, modern women need to get back to the business of witchcraft. The idea works politically but the historical facts are incorrect. Research done since 1968 has put some myths to rest: 1) the number of deaths from the witch trials is estimated to be closer to sixty thousand; 2) secular courts were as culpable as church courts; 3) men as well as women were prosecuted (although women do represent the majority of victims); 4) the trials were not the result of the Catholic Church squashing a resistance; 5) witches weren't persecuted healers; and 6) the people tried for witchcraft during the fifteenth through eighteenth centuries were not practicing a paganism that had survived from pre-Christian times. (Jenny Gibbons is very good on summarizing the recent scholarship in "Recent Developments in the Study of the Great European Witch Hunt," http://draeconin.com/database/ witchhunt.htm/ [accessed 16 October 2010], as is Brian Pavlac, "Ten Common Errors and Myths about the Witch Hunts" http:// departments.kings.edu/womens_history/witch/werror.html [accessed 29 December 2009].)

3. Hutton writes, "By uniting paganism with the figure of the witch . . . it automatically pre-empted any easy reconciliation of the result with Christianity or with conventional social mores; it was full-blown countercultural religion." Also, he notes, giving the divine feminine an edge over the masculine was a radical innovation (*Triumph,* 235-36).

4. In Polanski's film, Rosemary and her actor-husband, Guy Woodhouse, move into an apartment in Manhattan that shares a wall with the leaders of a coven who are plotting to use Rosemary to bring the son of Satan into the world. The "witches" are mostly older. They're dentists, grandparents, people you trust, except they murder anyone in their path to domination. In the film's creepiest scene, the coven chants, nude, in the smoky halflight of a nightmare, and Satan's brackish fingernails are glimpsed digging deep into Rosemary's perfect skin as the son of hell is conceived. (And lest we underestimate the role of popular culture, consider that most people had never heard of occultist Aleister

Crowley until Ozzy Osbourne mentioned him in the song "Mr. Crowley" on *Blizzard of Ozz*, 1980.)

5. Judy Klemesrud, "Witchcraft: Some People Find it a Serious Matter," *New York Times*, 31 October 1969, 50.

6. Special to the *Times*, "At a Witchcraft Museum, Halloween. Is More Than Trick or Treat," *New York Times*, 30 October 1972, 27. Buckland's estimate, in retrospect, is likely high. Trying to get a head count on pagans has never been an exact science.

7. It was Egyptologist Margaret Murray who named Halloween as one of the quarterly witches' Sabbaths, basing them on the four Scottish "quarter days" mentioned in the seventeeth-century trial testimony of Isobel Smyth of Forfar—November eve (All Hallow E'en), February 2, May eve, and August 1. Murray was criticized for evolving her theories about Sabbaths on the testimony of only one source (Murray, *The God of the Witches* [London: Sampson Low, Marston & Co., Ltd., 1933], 78). Scottish trial testimony does include mentions of gatherings on All Hallow's Eve, but there are several other days mentioned as well. "The Survey of Scottish Witchcraft, 1563-1736" (Julian Goodare et. al, www.shc.ed.ac.uk/Research/witches/, [accessed 8 October 2010]) contains the names of nearly four thousand people who were accused during the years the Witchcraft Act was in effect. Detailed records exist for around a tenth of them. Of those, thirty-two confessions mention Halloween as a time when witches gathered or when magic was effective. The next most popular days were Candlemas (February 2, named twelve times) and Whitsunday (in May, named ten times). What sorts of Halloween activities were imagined and described? The most famous was a plot to sink King James I's ship (North Berwick trials, Scotland, 1590-91), but most were more mundane, along the lines of giving advice (sprinkle drops of blood over a sheep to save it; Jonet Forsyth, 1629) or healing (use linen cloth and a hair to protect cattle; Issobell Sinclair, 1633).

Gerald Gardner, twentieth-century witchcraft practitioner, adopted Murray's calendar. He wrote his Halloween ritual sometime between 1948 and 1952, using original material as well as the works of Aleister Crowley and fiction such as a sorcerer's incantation he found in a thirteenth-century play (Hutton, *Triumph*, 232-34). Gardner's ritual dealt with the fate of the soul; it addressed death and the possibility of reincarnation. American author Aidan Kelly (his 1991 *Crafting the Art of Magic* was a study of the origins of modern witchcraft) gave the seasonal festivals new names, and Halloween became better known among modern practitioners as Samhain (Ronald Hutton, "Modern Pagan Festivals," keynote lecture at the conference Forging Folklore: Witches, Pagans and Neo-Tribal Cultures, Harvard University, May 3-5, 2007).

8. Julie Steenhuysen, "U.S. Scientists Learn How to Levitate Tiny Objects," Reuters, www.reuters.com/article/idUS TRE50672320090107 (accessed 7 January 2009).

9. Len Fisher, *Weighing the Soul: The Evolution of Scientific Beliefs* (London: Weidenfeld & Nicolson, 2004), 5, 150.

10. The seven principles from *The Kybalion* (published anonymously by "The Three Initiates," 1912) is what Schuster was referring to here. Briefly, these are the principles of Mentalism (all is mind), Correspondence ("As above, so below; as below, so above"), Vibration (everything moves, and to change one's mental state is an effort of Will), Polarity (everything has its opposite; everything is and isn't at the same time), Rhythm (there is a rhythm between opposites), Cause and Effect (there is no such thing as chance), and Gender (everything and everyone contains both).

11. It was no small moment when, on October 29, 1982, Rev. Pat Robertson looked right into the television cameras on the set of *The 700 Club* and said, "I think we ought to close Halloween down. Do you want your children to dress up as witches? The Druids used to dress up like this when they were doing human sacrifice. . . . [The children] are acting out Satanic rituals and participating in it, and don't even realize it." Although he cited (erroneous) Druid rituals as the reason—there is no evidence that Druids dressed in costume and made sacrifices on Halloween; Druids weren't Satanists; and Satanists don't have any investment in trick-or-treating—Robertson tapped into the exact right cultural moment for proposing an end to Halloween. Just four weeks before, newspapers broke a story about five people in the Chicago area who'd been poisoned by cyanide tamped into Extra-Strength Tylenol capsules. By October 3, seven people were dead and one hundred state and federal agents dispatched to find a "random killer." Within a week, the investigation moved from California to Philadelphia to Wyoming, and on October 25, cyanide turned up in an eighth bottle. The Chicago Tylenol tamperings were unsolved by October 31, and the media headlined the potential danger of trick-or-treating on Halloween. Robertson's plea to "close Halloween down" made sense to many already alarmed by the Tylenol crimes. Vineland, New Jersey, and five towns in Massachusetts, for example, banned trick-or-treating, and Greenwich and Vernon, Connecticut, moved it to the daytime.

12. The most famous invective against witchcraft is this biblical quote: "Thou shalt not suffer a witch to live." Pagan scholar

Isaac Bonewits pointed out that in the original Hebrew, the word does not translate to "witch" but rather "poisoner" or "herbalist," and that, not surprisingly, it was translated as "witch" in the more modern King James Bible, since King James I of Scotland had a well-documented witch phobia. Interview with Isaac Bonewits by Christian Day, "Hex Education," blogtalk radio, 7 June 2009.

13. By 1986, a federal appeals court recognized Wicca as a religion in America, justifying its protection under the Civil Rights Act of 1964 (Religious Tolerance, www.religioustolerance.org). By 1999, it had a legitimate presence in the military, which famously prompted Georgia congressman Bob Barr to snipe, "Will divisions be forced to travel with sacrificial animals for Satanic rituals?" (S. C. Gwynne/Killeen, "I Saluted a Witch," *Time,* 5 July 1999.) As of 2007, the federal Department of Veterans Affairs allows gravestones of Wiccan soldiers to be marked with a pentacle. (Samuel G. Freedman, "Paganism, Slowly, Triumphs Over Stereotypes," *New York Times*, 31 October 2009).

Chapter Four: Pumpkin Obsessions

1. This fastest-carved time is a 2006 Guinness World Record; the most pumpkins carved, a 2008 GWR; and the heaviest, a GWR in 2009.

2. Dr. Alan Hirsch, the Smell and Taste Treatment and Research Foundation, www.smellandtaste.org (accessed 4 January 2010).

3. Michael C. LaBarbera, "The Biology of B-Movie Monsters," (Fathom Archive, University of Chicago, 2003), http://fathom.lib.uchicago.edu/2/21701757 (accessed 4 January 2010).

Chapter Five: Dead Man Rising

1. Psychologist Shulamith Kreitler at Tel Aviv University studied the death-fear responses of eighty-seven people and found that there were interesting variations ("Fear of Death," *New Research on the Psychology of Fear* [2005]: 59-62). The most common fears were of the pain of death (59.80 percent), of dying before being ready (52.90 percent), and of the unknown (57.50 percent). The least common fears were being bored (9.20 percent), stuck in a bad dream (1.15 percent), looking for a lost body (3.45 percent), dying without finding out why we were born (3.45 percent), finding out we were wrong about it all (5.75 percent), and being closed up in a narrow, dark hole for eternity (1.15 percent).

2. Images of the Danse Macabre throughout history are collected at the Cornell Institute for Digital Collections, Division of Rare and Manuscript Collections, Cornell University Library,

http://fantastic.library.cornell.edu/ (accessed 2 January 2010).

3. Joanna Bourke, "Death," in *Fear: A Cultural History* (London: Virago Press, 2005), 25-50.

4 Ibid., 316-21.

5. Zombies are hungry pretty much because George Romero made them so, according to Kim Paffenroth, associate professor of religious studies at Iona College. Haitian/voodoun zombies don't eat flesh, Paffenroth points out; Romero used the dining habits of ghouls instead, which is what he called the monsters in *Night of the Living Dead*. Personal e-mail to author.

6. Lily Huang, "Rise of the Bugs," *Newsweek*, 20 June 2009.

7. According to Ed Jones, editor of the ezine *Zombie Times*, when British media ran warnings about avian flu and mad cow disease, some newspapers estimated that a third of the population might get struck down and that there would be field hospitals in public parks and makeshift morgues set up in schools for the number of the dead and dying. Jones notes that many zombie films use this same pandemic scenario to drive tension and plot and it very much mirrors fears that are real and recent. Personal e-mail to author.

8. David Gilmore, *Monsters: Evil Beings, Mythical Beasts, and All Manner of Imaginary Terrors* (Philadelphia: University of Pennsylvania Press, 2003), 186-90.

9. E-mail correspondence with author.

10. The Zombie Fest and Walk of the Dead at Monroeville Mall is a charity event created by *The It's Alive Show*, an independent horror and sci-fi television show produced in Pittsburgh. The event spawned World Zombie Day, when organizers collect canned goods from zombie walkers to donate to local food banks. Monroeville Mall's Walk of the Dead is a three-time Guinness World Record holder for Largest Gathering of Zombies (nearly nine hundred in 2006, over one thousand in 2007, and 1,341 in 2008). However, according to the Guinness World Record site, the one to beat is now The Big Chill Festival in Ledbury, England, that event clocked in with 4,026 zombies in August 2009.

Chapter Six: Caution: For Halloween Wonks Only

1. John Brand, *Observations on Popular Antiquities: A New Edition with the Additions of Sir Henry Ellis* (London: Chatto and Windus, 1900), 803. Other will o' the wisp documents online at http://ina midst.com/lights/wisp/archives (accessed 16 October 2010).

2. Not only wandering lights, but lanterns and candle flames were associated in Europe and the British Isles with All Souls' Day and purgatory; so too, the idea of using a light to remember the

familial dead or to keep away the evil dead is a common one. Obi-wan's UFO-Free Paranormal Page is an excellent source of both historical documents explaining lights and contemporary reports of encounters with them, www.ghosts.org/ghostlights/ghost lights.html (accessed 13 December 2009).

3. Peter the Venerable wrote *De Miraculis (Book of Miracles)* while he was abbot of Cluny (1122-56). The volume is a collection of six-ty tales, ten of which involve apparitions of the dead. Irish beliefs about the lights being souls of the dead were recorded in *The Comical Pilgrim* (attributed to Daniel Defoe, 1723), found in Brand's *Observations on Popular Antiquities*, 800.

4. Poppy Z. Brite, "Lantern Marsh," in *October Dreams: A Celebration of Halloween* (Baltimore: Cemetery Dance Publications, 2000).

5. Carleton first published "The Three Wishes" in *Dublin University Magazine* in 1839 and later included it in his book *Tales and Sketches, Illustrating the Character, Usages, Traditions, Sports, and Pastimes of the Irish Peasantry* (Dublin: James Duffy, 1845). *Tales and Sketches* went through fifty editions with different tales added and removed, but "The Three Wishes" was rarely printed and not published in an American edition until the twentieth century. Its audience of readers grew exponentially, though, when W. B. Yeats, who thought Carleton the greatest Irish novelist of the century, included "The Three Wishes" in his *Fairy and Folk Tales of Ireland* (W. Scott of London, 1888). The story then reached a readership on both sides of the Atlantic, coming as it did at the time when people were clamoring for folktales and the public was newly fascinated with Ireland.

6. In folklore studies, this story is referred to as the Aarne-Thompson Tale Type 330, "the smith outwits the devil." The Aarne-Thompson system catalogues several thousand folk tales from around the world and organizes them into motifs and types. Richard Dorson, in *Buying the Wind: Regional Folklore in the United States* (Chicago: University of Chicago Press, 1964), reports that the Irish Folklore Commission has 359 texts of this story, the Finnish Folklore Archive has 146, and there are 200 German versions (429). The story exists in collections of folklore in Shropshire, Corsica, France, Wilshire, North Dorset, and in the famous *Kinder und Hausmärchen (Folk Tales for Children and the Home)*, by the Brothers Grimm, in two versions, although neither explains the wandering light.

7. Newell's article, "The Ignis Fatuus, Its Character and Legendary Origins," (*Journal of American Folklore* 17 [1904]: 39-60) traces the story of the jack-o'-lantern from medieval sources through several modern American versions. It also explains a huge amount of folklore, worldwide, about the lights, their spiritual meanings,

and how they relate to death and the soul. Interestingly, Newell points out that those most likely to get lost in bogs following lights were inebriated, which led to tales that describe the ghost—Jack of the jack-o'-lantern—as a drunk (49).

8. In the medieval Irish tale, the heroic Fians were supernaturally stuck to chairs and only a drop of royal blood could free them. (Patrick Kennedy, "How Fann Mac Cuil and His Men Were Bewitched," in *Legendary Fictions of the Irish Celts* [London: Macmillan and Company, 1866], 208. Stith Thompson talks about similarities in older Hebrew tales in *The Folktale*, [Berkeley: University of California Press,1977], 45-46). The Fisherman of Arabian tales tricks a Genii into a bottle by suggesting that the Genii was incapable of making himself so small, much like the smith traps the devil in a purse (W. A. Clouston, *Popular Tales and Fictions: Their Migrations and Transformation* [Santa Barbara: ABC-CLIO, 2002], 191). Storyteller and folklorist Joseph Daniel Sobol points out the smith is a direct descendant of Lugh ("'Whistlin' Towards the Devil's House': Poetic Transformations and Natural Metaphysics in an Appalachian Folktale Performance," *Oral Tradition* 21, no. 1 [March 2006], 5. *eOT* = http://journal.oraltradition.org/articles/show/7/, accessed 1 January 2010). St. Dunstan was a goldsmith, and when the devil takes the form of a woman to seduce him, he grabs the devil's nose with hot tongs just as Jack did (William Hone, "St. Dunstan," in *The Every-Day Book,* ed. Kyle Grimes, University of Alabama e-text, www.uab.edu/english/hone/etexts/edb/day-pages/139-may19. html, accessed 1 January 2010). As for Sisyphus, he cheats death twice: first, he tricks Hades into handcuffs and second, Sisyphus instructs his kin not to bury him or place a coin beneath his tongue. Without a proper burial, Sisyphus argues, he cannot be dead. When Hades does catch up with him, Sisyphus's penance is the basest of hard labor. He must push a boulder up a steep hill and watch as it tumbles back down, for all eternity.

9. Harris published two versions of the blacksmith story. He writes that the first, "Jacky-My-Lantern" (*Uncle Remus: His Songs and His Sayings* [1880; reprint, University of Virginia American Studies Program 2003-2004, http://xroads.virginia.edu/~HYPER/ Harris2/ch32.html, accessed 11 October 2010]) was popular in the South and that there were several versions in circulation. In the second, "Impty-Umpty and the Blacksmith" (*Uncle Remus Returns* [Boston: Houghton Mifflin Company, 1918]), Uncle Remus tells his young friend that he got the story wrong when he told it to the boy's daddy. The smith in this story bests Impty-Umpty (that's Satan, who in this version is club-footed, double-jointed, and laughs

so hard smoke comes out of his nose) by daring him to turn himself into a black cat, which he then bags. The last line of "Impty-Umpty" remains in most American versions: "Go git 'im a chunk er fier an' let 'im start a sinner fact'ry er his own." In 1935, Zora Neale Hurston published "How Jack-o'-lanterns Came to Be" in *Mules and Men* (reprint, Bloomington, IN: Indiana University Press, 1978), her collection of Negro folklore gathered from stories told by the people of Eatonville, Florida. She records a story different from Harris's, but with a similar last line: "You ain't comin' in here," says the devil's widow. "Here, take dis hot coal and g'wan off and start you a hell uh yo' own." The story become "Wicked John and the Devil" in Richard Chase's *American Folk Tales and Songs* (New York: New American Library, 1956) to distinguish the smith from a heroic trickster named Jack who appears in other American folktales. Chase's version, which he says he got from a Mrs. Yowell in Virginia, is more akin to the Irish/British story (with the substitution of a prickly fire bush for the purse—again, ouch). However, he took his last line from Hurston: "Here, take dis hot coal and g'wan off and start you a hell uh yo' own."

10. Richard Chase, *The Jack Tales* (Boston: Houghton Mifflin Company, 1943), x.

11. "Wicked John and the Devil" was a signature tale of Ray Hicks, known since 1973 as the unofficial heart of the National Storytelling Festival in Jonesborough, Tennessee. Hicks used the story to explain a phenomenon called the Brown Mountain Lights, an occurrence near his Beech Mountain, North Carolina, home. Sobol's "Whistlin' Towards the Devil's House" includes many details of twentieth-century versions of the tale and the transcript of a telling by Hicks.

12. The October 31, 1866, edition of the *New York Times* reports on a Halloween parade in Scotland where "the boys form themselves into long processions, each bearing hollowed turnips with devices marked on the shell and illuminated by candles, while the girls form in the same manner, bearing tall 'kail' stalks [curly cabbages] having candles burning in the centres of the heads." In an 1890 *Harper's Magazine* story by William Black, "A Halloween Wraith," children with turnip lanterns carved with faces frighten a traveler on Halloween night. Children in Somerset, England, carved turnips on both Halloween and on "Punkie Night" as recorded in the early twentieth century (Kingsley Palmer, *The Folklore of Somerset* [New Jersey: Rowman and Littlefield, 1976], 105). American folklorist Jack Santino found carved turnips used on St. Briget's Day as well as Halloween in Northern Ireland from the

late 1800s through today (*The Hallowed Eve*, 39, 49, 80, 126). *Harper's Weekly* reports that turnip heads on sticks were still carried on Guy Fawkes Day in nineteenth-century Britain ("The Pumpkin Effigy," November 23, 1867, 1), and British historian Ronald Hutton reports carved turnip lanterns to be common in Ireland and some areas of England in the late nineteenth century at Halloween (*The Stations of the Sun,* 382-83). Carved beet lanterns are still part of Christmas Eve processions in northern France. Some—Hutton is one—have noted that reports of carved lanterns on Halloween are few and far between in the major published folklore collections until the early twentieth century. I'd agree; although many sources describe them as a medieval custom, I've been unable to find any primary record of Halloween (or All Hallow's) carved lanterns before the early nineteenth century.

13. Whittier's poem, although first published in 1850, was set in his youth, real or imagined, some thirty-odd years before. The lines that apply are as follows: "When wild, ugly faces we carved in its skin / Glaring out through the dark with a candle within!" (*The Poetical Works* [Boston: Houghton Mifflin, 1894]).

14. This trick done with the turnip was well enough known in England of 1820 to be part of a political cartoon showing a parson terrified by three boys holding a turnip lantern draped in ghostly white cloth. An illustration of the cartoon, captioned "The Village Retort—or Ghost of Small Tythes," can be found in Caricatures vii. 21. #14087, *Catalogue of Political and Personal Satires Preserved in the Department of Prints and Drawings in the British Museum,* vol. x, 1820-1827.

15. According to *Forrester's Boys' and Girls' Magazine and Fireside Companion,* all you need do is "put a small amount of phosphorus in a retort, filled with a moderately strong solution of caustie potash"—heat to boiling and bam! ("Will-o'-the-Wisp" or "Jack-o'-lantern," April 1, 1856, 133). For adults, there were pieces like "Observations on Ignis Fatuus," by Rev. John Mitchell, which explained the lights' motion as an optical illusion (*American Journal of Science and Arts,* January 3, 1929, 246).

16. A toast given at the Federal Republican Young Gentleman's meeting recorded in 1810 in Walpole, New Hampshire: "The President of the United States; instead of following the Jack-o'-lantern of Jefferson, may be guided by the polar star of Washington" (*The Farmer's Museum,* July 9, 1810, 2-3).

17. Children's magazines helped teach what jack-o'-lanterns were and how to make them by embedding information into stories. Take, for example, "Cooking a Ghost," by Sophie May in *Merry's Museum and Wordsworth's Cabinet* (January 1, 1867), where little

Jennie is terrified by a lit jack-o'-lantern and her cousins confess, "'Twas only us, just we two! And this thing is nothing but a jack-o'-lantern,' they continued, holding up a hollow pumpkin with a candle inside." In "The Jack O' Lantern" (the *Youth's Companion*, February 19, 1840) there is an entire how-to: "He prepared to make his Jack-o'-Lantern. He got a knife, cut off the top, and scraped out all the inside, and made another hole in the bottom, put a candle in, and another in the top, to let the smoke out. He then cut, on the several sides of the pumpkin, the outline of three faces, with their eyes, noses and teeth." The magazine must have liked the idea, because it's repeated in another story two years later, with even more tips. "Then with the knife you must cut in deep, all around where I have marked, and then the cap will come off if you pull by the handle. Then you must dig it all out inside, until the shell is only as thick as your hand." ("The Cow and the Jack o' Lantern," *Youth's Companion,* March 18, 1842.) The jack-o'-lantern returns again in its July, 1873, issue ("A Lark"), and appears in several other magazines for both children and adults, notably *Harper's Weekly* (in December 1, 1865, "Farmer Bell's Thanksgiving," and again in the November 23, 1867, issue, "The Pumpkin Effigy").

18. Halloween how-to articles and books starting in the 1890s and continuing through to October 2010's *Martha Stewart Holiday* nudged the jack-o'-lantern from trick toward party decoration. Manufacturing companies created decorations with a pumpkin face for Halloween parties (and, initially, for Thanksgiving parties as well, where jack-o'-lanterns were occasionally part of decor as late as 1900). Called happy john, pumpkin head, pumpkin face, john pumpkin head, pumpkin jack, and finally jack-o'-lantern, lanterns, candy containers, decorations, masks, and greeting cards featuring pumpkins with faces were created for a market eager to celebrate Halloween in America. According to Halloween collectibles author Mark Ledenbach, the jack-o'-lantern was the most popular image on Halloween ephemera. Then came cats, witches, skeletons, and owls. The rarest were ghosts, veggie people, bats, and, the rarest of all, devils. For details and images of these objects see Mark B. Ledenbach, *Vintage Halloween Collectibles* (Iola, WI: Krause Publications, 2003), or Ben Truwe, *The Halloween Catalog Collection: 55 Catalogs from the Golden Age of Halloween* (Medford, OR: Talky Tina Press, 2003).

19. The first reference I could find to a Halloween-specific carved pumpkin in the United States is this: "A flood of light began to pour in on the subject, illuminating their craniums as a tallow candle lights up the interior of a hallow-e'en pumpkin"

(Laramie Boomerang, "That's All Right: An Interesting Story from the Wild West," *Macon (GA) Telegraph,* 20 January 1884, 1). The date may move earlier as more and more archives and materials become digitalized and searchable.

20. Silver Ravenwolf, *Halloween* (St. Paul, MN: Llewellyn Publications, 1999), 38-41.

21. Quoted in Truwe, *The Halloween Catalog Collection,* fn. 55, xx.

22. Setting the movie on Halloween was key to its success, according to film historian Adam Rockoff. "In retrospect, the element most integral to *Halloween*'s success may have been its title. The singularity of the name 'Halloween' seemed to strike a collective chord within the consciousness of American moviegoers, conjuring up haunting images of ghouls, mystery, death, and most importantly, evil. It's hard to imagine *The Babysitter Murders [Halloween*'s original title] or some derivation of, eliciting the same response" (*Going to Pieces: The Rise and Fall of the Slasher Film, 1978-1986* [Jefferson, NC: MacFarland & Company, 2002], 53).

23. The angry pumpkin may be part of a greater fear of nature, as our consciousness awakens to what we're doing to the planet. Mikita Brottman theorizes that movies like *The Ruins* (2008) and *The Happening* (2008) are a backlash against the green movement or, more likely, a projection of "green guilt." She writes, "We cultivate plants solely in order to eat them, or to cut them off in their prime and enjoy the way they smell as they slowly die. With no Parliament of Trees to defend their rights, perhaps we can't help but unconsciously imagine plants to be, at some level, voiceless, resentful, and oppressed." ("When Good Plants Go Bad," *The Chronicle Review,* December 12, 2008, B12-13). And in another twist on the postmodern pumpkin, in October 2008, pro-Kremlin youth in Moscow used jack-o'-lanterns carved with the names of war victims to protest what they saw as America's responsibility for the war in Georgia.

Chapter Seven: Kindred Spirits

1. Rochelle Santopoalo, "Hallowe'en: Playtime for Adults" (Ph.D. thesis, Fielding Institute, 1996).

2. Ehrenreich's book, *Dancing in the Streets: A History of Collective Joy* (New York: Metropolitan Books, Henry Holt & Company, 2006), examines ecstatic ritual and its place in various cultures. She writes that up until around the twelfth and thirteen centuries people (and priests) in the Western world used to dance in church. Catholic leaders eventually purged the behavior and sent people outside to celebrate, inadvertently inventing carnival (and by carnival she's

talking festivity, not just pre-Lent). The thirteenth to fifteenth centuries, says Ehrenreich, were one big outdoor party ("From the Churches to the Streets: The Creation of Carnival," 77-95). But then came both the Reformation, which suppressed carnival on moral grounds, and industrial capitalism, which required fewer holidays and more work days. The elite came to see revelry as vulgar and dangerous, rife with fights, drunkenness, and crime. At the same time—starting in England in the seventeenth century—there was an epidemic of emotional depression that Ehrenreich thinks could have been cured by festivity and ecstasy. "The immense tragedy for Europeans . . . and most acutely for the northern Protestants among them, was that the same social forces that disposed them to depression also swept away a traditional cure. . . . They had completed the demonization of Dionysus begun by Christians centuries ago and thereby rejected one of the most ancient sources of help—the mind-preserving, lifesaving, techniques of ecstasy" ("An Epidemic of Melancholy," 129-153).

3. Three artists—Susan Bartolucci, Christy Silacci, and Ginny Betourne—developed Halloween and Vine into a national show. Together with Scott Smith, they built the event to the point where it has a waiting list of interested artists. Other Halloween folk art shows have since appeared, such as the now-defunct Halloween Opera in Jim Thorpe, Pennsylvania, and the new Goultide Gathering, outside of Detroit.

4. German artisans were encouraged by early American merchandisers such as Woolworth and Kresge to create Halloween party goods for American markets. German productions reached a zenith between 1919 to 1935, and many folk artists use them as inspiration. Mark Ledenbach's German ephemera history is at www.halloweencollector.com/history/.

5. "Halloween's 24/7/365 presence on the web has grown exponentially [since the late '90s]," says artist Chad Savage of the visual design company Sinister Visions. "Websites, message boards, discussion lists, community sites, podcasts, video channels, you name it. The savvy companies have been there from the start, but (literally) every day we see haunted houses, prop companies, special effects services, Halloween vendors and enthusiasts, musicians, artists, designers, and more surfacing on Twitter, Facebook, MySpace, YouTube, Flickr and other services. It has literally never been easier to find other Halloween enthusiasts than it is right now." Personal e-mail to author.

6. Don Bertino passed away on December 17, 2008, in Elk Grove, California. When the news hit the lists, there was an outpouring of

appreciation for "Papa Don." Listers believe that every Halloween list and regional gathering that exists today can trace its roots to Bertino and the L.

7. Teary Thunder lived in a tiny town in Georgia, and Koumajutsu (their screen names) in arid southern California when they met on hauntforum.com. She posted a video as a joke; he liked her sense of humor. Koumajutsu eventually took a bus to Georgia, and a week later, Teary loaded what she could onto a moving van and the two headed west. They got matching skull tattoos and, after a few years, married in Las Vegas, where they could stream the ceremony live to all their Internet friends.

8. It's possible to learn the "Thriller" dance steps by downloading the choreography walkthrough from thrilltheworld.com, an organization responsible for a late October, worldwide "Thriller" zombie dance event.

Chapter Eight: Terrortainment

1. John Carpenter's 1978 movie *Halloween* was the first to use the holiday as a theme; it also forged a relationship between Halloween and violence that didn't exist in earlier movies. Up until then, Halloween was used for atmosphere or was the focus for a scene or two, like in *Meet Me in St. Louis* (1944), *A Tree Grows in Brooklyn* (1945), or a caper involving Donald Duck's nephews called *Trick or Treat* (1952). For a complete synopsis of Halloween in film, see "Halloween on Screen," in David J. Skal's *Death Makes a Holiday: A Cultural History of Halloween* (New York: Bloomsbury, 2002), 155-81.

2. *HauntWorld Magazine* estimates there are around 1,200 professional haunts, 300 amusement parks with Halloween or haunt events, and 3,000 charity attractions (www.americahaunts.com). Leonard Pickel of *Haunted Attraction Magazine* estimates somewhere between 3,000 and 5,000 Halloween-season haunted attraction events, of which maybe 30 percent are professional. The number of haunts is hard to pin down because it varies drastically year to year, says Pickel.

3. David J. Skal, *The Monster Show* (New York: W.W. Norton, 1993), 221.

4. I don't say retching idly. Professor Trevor Cox of Salford University in Britain tested thirty-four "horrible sounds" on more than one million people, worldwide. He discovered that the sound of someone vomiting was voted the most horrible of all, followed by microphone feedback, babies crying, and the sound of a metal garden tool scraping across slate. Other oddities emerged, like the fact

that Australians couldn't abide the sound of arguments and North Americans found the sound of retching more horrible than did the rest of Europe. Squeaky seesaws and bad violin playing also made the top ten (Roger Highfield, "Sound of Vomiting Tops Poll," *London Telegraph,* 25 January 2007). The actual experiment is detailed at Salford University's Acoustic Research Centre's Bad Vibes Web site, www.sound101.org/badvibes/ (accessed 4 January 2010).

5. Scientists theorize that most "prepared" fears developed 100,000 years ago and that they once served to protect us. Even fear of public speaking may have come from this time, when any individual who stood out was a potential target for violence (Rush W. Dozier, Jr., *Fear Itself* [New York: St. Martin's Press, 1998], 234-35).

6. Internet researcher Bill Tancer looked into the most common searches that began with the words "fear of." From more than one thousand unique fears, he came up with a top ten of searched terms: flying, heights, clowns, intimacy, death, rejection, people, snakes, success, and driving. The whole study is detailed in "What Are You Afraid Of? and Other Telling Questions," in Tancer's 2008 book *Click: What Millions of People Are Doing Online and Why It Matters* (New York: Hyperion), 101-17.

7. The Los Angeles Cacophony Society proclaims to be a disorganized group of klowns, guerrilla artists, kitsch hounds, slackers, and noisemakers in search of experiences beyond the mainstream. The Los Angeles Cacophony Society Web site, about page, http://losangeles.cacophony.org/aboutlacaco.htm.

8. There's a lot of primitive mishigas going on when it comes to fear. Science has recently learned, for instance, that there's a good chance humans can smell fear in each other. For years, it's been clear that fish can; clever fathead minnows use odor to warn others of a nearby fathead-minnow-eating pike. Bees use fear-scent, too, and rats can pick out the smell of a stressed rat. So the question is, if animals can send out warning scents, can humans? Yes, according to a team of scientists at the Institute of Anthropology at the University of Vienna, who created the scent of fear by having female subjects wear "under-arm axillary pads" as they watched scary films. The scientists then asked others to identify the fear-scented pads, which they easily did. That fear is contagious is surely not news to the folks who design haunted attractions. Kerstin Ackerl, Michaela Atzmueller, and Karl Grammer, "The Scent of Fear," *Neuroendocrinology Letters* 23, no. 2 (April 2002).

9. Wes Craven, television interview on *Anatomy of Horror,* August 22, 1995, as cited in Isabel Cristina Pinedo, *Recreational Terror: Women and the Pleasures of Horror Film Viewing* (Albany: SUNY Press, 1997), 66.

Chapter Nine: Bats, Tats, Twirlers, and Thrashers

1. Issues forced by war and its aftermath—such as economic depressions, nuclear fear, and epidemics—are mainly what drives horror in America, says David Skal in *The Monster Show* (386). "In the early '60's," he writes, "children turned instinctively to Dracula and Frankenstein as protective amulets during the death-loving days of the Cold War. In the age of AIDS, the vampire myth offers a similar strategy to adults (gay or straight) for processing the widespread, inescapable reality of death at an early age" (347). The comment about Vietnam, 9/11, and movies is by director Eli Roth, who thinks that horror films are more popular when the country is experiencing severe stress. *Texas Chainsaw Massacre* and *Last House on the Left*, he believes, emerged from the tensions of the Vietnam era, and after 9/11, there was a spate of violent horror films like his own *Hostel*, which he claims is a favorite with soldiers in Iraq (Stephen T. Asma, *On Monsters: An Unnatural History of Our Worst Fears* [New York: Oxford University Press, 2009], 197.)

2. And here's another, not unrelated, take. Anthropologist David Gilmore studied monsters around the world (including one called, yes, the were-octopus) and came up with a theory about what exactly makes a monster monstrous. There are two main things: size (monsters are usually large and looming, and therefore powerful) and the use of their mouths as weapons (they eat, swallow, or bite you). A monster, he says, is in essence a cannibalism fantasy (*Monsters*, 175-85).

3. It's just a matter of time before you find wolfmen in your kid's animal crackers. There's been an uptick of horror/Halloween-themed products offered year-round, such as an armchair with embroidered blood-splatter pattern (Amy Lau for *Dexter*), a coffee set covered in bloody prints (Antonio Morado), Skelanimals (undead plush toys), bloodstained shower curtains (The Geekiest Link), and SPLAT! Road Kill carpet (Studio OOOMS). Not only graphic elements, but whole concepts have been borrowed. During a 2008 Fashion Institute of Technology show in New York, vamp/Goth-inspired clothes were set in exhibits similar to rooms in a haunted house, including a laboratory scene and a ruined castle (Karen Rosenburg, "Where Too Much is Never Enough [and Black is Still the New Black]," *New York Times*, 19 December 2008).

4. Just a few for-instances: TV writer Mike Reiss admits that a *Tales from the Crypt* comic book was inspiration for at least one "Treehouse of Horror" episode (Personal e-mail to author). Movie producer Irwin Yablans, who convinced John Carpenter to name his 1978 movie *Halloween* rather than *The Babysitter Murders*, was

an "Inner Sanctum" and "Lights Out" horror-radio addict as a kid (Rockoff, *Going to Pieces,* 53). Steven Spielberg read EC Comics and allegedly terrorized his sister Nancy by cutting off her doll's head and serving it to her on a bed of lettuce (Skal, *The Monster Show,* 272). In addition, Stephen King credits *Famous Monsters of Filmland* with sparking his career (Film Radar, www.filmradar.com).

5. Historian Nicholas Rogers dates the wedding of Halloween, horror, and monsters as early as Orson Welles's radio broadcast of "The War of the Worlds" on Halloween eve in 1938 and points to occasional scary Halloween episodes in early *Shock* comics starting in 1950 (*Halloween: From Pagan Ritual to Party Night* [New York: Oxford University Press, 2002], 106). Forrest Ackerman's *Famous Monsters of Filmland* magazine (inaugurated in 1958) published an annual Halloween issue, further cementing the bond between Halloween and monsters. Universal Studios began marketing Halloween tie-ins for franchised characters of Dracula, Frankenstein, the Mummy, and the Wolfman in the early 1960s (Skal, *Death Makes a Holiday,* 157).

6. Michelle Orange, "Taking Back the Knife: Girls Gone Gory," *New York Times,* 6 September 2009, 7.

7. This account is from Rob Zombie's HellBilly Deluxe 2 touring show at House of Blues in Boston, December 2, 2009.

8. The legions of the beast—monsters—fight against righteousness at Armageddon and lose. They're confined to a lake of fire for one thousand years, after which the evil one is able to have his way with the "children of disobedience," who have fallen to earthly temptation. For more on monsters and Armageddon, see Asma, *On Monsters,* 67-69.

9. Monsters were portents to the ancients; the appearance of a monster meant something, good or bad, was coming. Even the word "monstrous" comes from the Latin *"monere"* to warn (Asma, *On Monsters,* 13).

Chapter Ten: Trick and/or Treat?

1. These pranks and many more are detailed in interviews with the Cacophony Society in V. Vale's *Pranks 2* (San Francisco: Re/ Search Publications, 2006) on pages 75 and 66-67, respectively. The *Time Magazine* piece was "Exculpations Crybabies: Eternal Victims," August 12, 1991. The full quote must have delighted the Cacophonists, as it describes the event deliciously: "How many ways can crybabies parse shame and blame? In San Francisco last month, a motley flock turned out to picket the classic Disney movie *Fantasia.* One man complained that the spooky 'Night on

Bald Mountain' scene had terrified his child. Members of an organization called Dieters United objected to the tutu-clad hippos frolicking to the music of 'Dance of the Hours'; the protesters felt the sequence ridiculed fat people. Conservationists were appalled at the waste of water in the 'Sorcerer's Apprentice' scene. Fundamentalist Christians bewailed the depiction of evolution in 'Rite of Spring.' Anti-drug forces suspected something subliminally pro-drug in the 'Nutcracker Suite' episode featuring dancing mushrooms."

2. The clowns on the bus prank is described in an interview with John Law in *Pranks 2* (49). Prank as art, as a communal or media event, came out of the counterculture of the 1960s and seems to be gathering steam. Huge pillow fights appear suddenly in public parks (www.pillowfightday.com); hundreds dress as Santas and swarm through downtowns (santarchy.com); or a crowd freezes absolutely still at the same time in the same place for a short period of time (improveverywhere.com). You can find or suggest pranks at http://urbanprankster.com. To see innovative pranksters in action, watch Tim Jackson's documentary *Radical Jesters* (www.radicaljesters.com).

3. All the hacks mentioned here are described in detail in T. F. Peterson, *Nightwork: A History of Hacks and Pranks at MIT* (Cambridge, MA: MIT Press, 2003). More MIT hacks can be found at Interesting Hacks to Fascinate People: The MIT Gallery of Hacks, http://hacks.mit.edu.

4. Richard J. Hand, "Stay Tuned for Tricks, Threats, and Terror: Halloween and Horror Radio in the Golden Age of American Live Broadcasting," in *Trick or Treat? Halloween in a Globalising World,* eds. Malcolm Foley and Hugh O'Donnell, 223 (Newcastle upon Tyne, U.K.: Cambridge Scholars Publishing, 2009).

5. Universal Studios insisted that the 1931 film *Frankenstein* include a prologue to appease censors. The prologue ends, as does Marge Simpson's speech, with the words, "Now's your chance to . . . well, we've warned you!"

6. Maintaining the frozen body of Nederland, Colorado, resident Bredo Morstoel, who died in 1989, is something of a community event; each month, sixteen hundred pounds of dry ice are delivered to the wooden shed housing Morstoel's body and it takes the efforts of several people to pack the ice around the sarcophagus.

Resources

This section will tell you where to find more information about the people and events in this book.

Part I. Celebrate!
   Chapter One: What Does Halloween Celebrate?
Brown, Eric S.: www.myspace.com/esbrown4
Camp Sunshine Pumpkin Festival:
   www.campsunshine.org/pumpkinfestival
Devilicia: http://blackcatburlesque.com
Dick, Ricky, Castle Blood: www.castleblood.com
Einziger, Michael, official Incubus site: www.enjoyincubus.com
Giant Pumpkin Carve: www.giantpumpkincarve.com
Guiley, Rosemary, Visionary Living: www.visionaryliving.com
Keillor, Garrison, A Prairie Home Companion with Garrison
   Keillor: http://prairiehome.publicradio.org
Landry, Ryan: http://www.facebook.com/golddustorphans
Lawrence, Kristin, Halloween Carols: www.halloweencarols.com
Ledenbach, Mark B., the Mark B. Ledenbach Halloween Collec-
   tion: www.halloweencollector.com
Maberry, Jonathan, official site: http://jonathanmaberry.com
Ridenour, Al, Los Angeles Cacophony Society:
   http://la.cacophony.org
Rochon, Debbie, official site: www.debbierochon.com
Savage, Chad, Sinister Visions, Inc.: www.sinistervisions.com
Skal, David, official site: www.monstershow.net
Von Hallenborg, Griffin, Great American Gothic:
   www.greatamericangothic.com

Part II. Icons of Halloween
Chapter Two: Ghosts
Cacek, P. D., official site: www.pdcacek.com
Dreshman, Janice, official site: www.spiritmessagework.com
Lily Dale Assembly, Inc.: www.lilydaleassembly.com
New England Ghost Project: www.neghostproject.com
Rosen, Paul, Houdini Club of Wisconsin:
    www.houdiniclubofwis consin.com;
    http://www.myhistorymuseum.org/houdini/

Chapter Three: Witches
Barrett's Haunted Mansion: www.bhmansion.com
Day, Christian, Festival of the Dead: www.festivalofthedead.com
EarthSpirit: www.earthspirit.com
Schuster, Ellie: write to at lyttlewyng@aol.com
Witches in Bikinis: www.witchesinbikinis.com

Chapter Four: Pumpkin Obsessions
Big Pumpkins, a resource for growers: www.bigpumpkins.com
Cambridge Brewing Company:
    www.cambridgebrewingcom pany.com
Cummins, Scott, Pumpkin Gutter: www.pumpkingutter.com
Great Pumpkin Commonwealth:
    www.greatpumpkincommon wealth.com
Luck, Hugh, Pine Street Studios, Inc.: www.pinestreetstudiosnj.com
MIT Glass Lab: http://web.mit.edu/glasslab
New England Giant Pumpkin Growers Association: write to at
    negpga@yahoo.com
Topsfield Fair: www.topsfieldfair.org/
Wickstrand, Ryan, Zombie Pumpkins: www.zombiepumpkins.com

Chapter Five: Dead Man Rising
Ann Arbor World Zombie Day: www.myspace.com/zombiewalka2
Bough, Geoff, *Revenant: The Premiere Zombie Magazine:*
    www.revenantmagazine.com
Brown, Eric S. Brown: www.myspace.com/esbrown4
Burrello, Dan: Ashtoberfest ZombieWalk:
    www.myspace.com/ashe villezombiewalk;
    www.myspace.com/ashtoberfestzombieday
Deadite Empire, Florida's premiere zombie social club:
    www.thedeaditeempire.com
Di Stefano, Jaime, Corpses for Sale, Di Stefano Productions:
    www.corpsesforsale.com

Finlay, Jo, WZD London: www.wzdlondon.co.uk
Jacksonville Zombie Walk: www.jaxzombiewalk.com
Monroeville Mall Zombie Festival: www.theitsaliveshow.com
Paffenroth, Kim, Gospel of the Living Dead: gotld.blogspot.com
Schlozman, Steven, Grand Rounds: Why We Do the Things We
     Do, a *Psychology Today* blog:
     www.psychologytoday.com/blog/grand-rounds
Terror4Fun, worldwide zombie resources such as the *Zombie Times*
     and UK zombie events: www.terror4fun.com
Zombie Harmony:
     http://mingle2.com/zombieharmony/free-dating-sites

Part III. Creating Halloween: Frights of Fantasy
   Chapter Seven: Kindred Spirits
Bartolucci, Susan, Tinsell and Whimsy: www.tinsellandwhimsy.com
Batte, Charles: www.chasbattestudio.com
Betourne, Ginny, Trout Creek Folk Art: www.troutcreekfolkart.com
Bezek, Will: www.williambezek.blogspot.com
Cunningham, Allen, Dolls by Allen W. Cunningham:
     www.dollsbyallenwcunningham.com
East Coast Haunt Club: www.hauntclub.net
Edgar and Edgar: www.edgarandedgar.typepad.com
Garage of Evil: http://garageofevil.com
Ghost Ride Productions: www.ghostride.com
Halloween and Vine: www.halloweenandvine.com
Halloween Forum: halloweenforum.com
Halloween-L list: www.wildrice.com/Halloween-l
Harden, Laurie: www.lauriehardinsaccents.blogspot.com
Haunt Forum: hauntforum.com
Haunt Space: hauntspace.com
Haunt World: hauntworld.com
HAuNTcon: www.hauntcon.com
Haunted Enterprises, The Last Ride, Haunted Village:
     www.hauntedvillage.com
Iron Kingdom: www.theironkingdom.com
Lightfoot, Vergie: write to at anapaw@msn.com
Madonna Estate Winery: www.madonnaestate.com
MoonHowler Productions: www.moonhowler.com
New York's Village Halloween Parade: www.halloween-nyc.com
NightScream Studios: www.nightscreamstudios.com
Parker, Johanna, Johanna Parker Design:
     www.johannaparkerde sign.com
Rice, Chuck, WildRice: www.wildrice.com

Rocky Mountain Haunters: http://rockymountainhaunters.com
Rucus Studio: www.rucusstudio.com
Superior Concept Monsters: www.superiorconcept.org
Venturella, Paul: http://halloweenpropmaster.com
Webber, Katherine: www.katherinewebber.com
Wisconsin Feargrounds: www.wisconsinfeargrounds.com
Zombie Army Productions: www.zombiearmyproductions.com

Chapter Eight: Terrortainment
Chamberlin, Brian, Nightmare New England:
   www.nightmare newengland.com
Gore Galore: www.goregalore.com
Haunted Overload: www.hauntedoverload.com
Los Angeles Cacophony Society: http://la.cacophony.org
Midnight Syndicate: www.midnightsyndicate.com
Midsummer Nightmare: http://midsummernightmare.com
Millet, Bruce: www.myspace.com/spookylobo
Nightmare New York: www.hauntedhousenyc.com
Spooky World: www.spookyworld.com
Vertigo Industries: http://vertigoindustriesllc.com
Zald, David, Psychological Sciences Department, Vanderbilt
   University: www.vanderbilt.edu/psychological_sciences/zald

Part IV. Subversive Halloween: Monsters and Pranksters
Chapter Nine: Bats, Tats, Twirlers, and Thrashers
Bombb, Addam, official site: www.addamidiom.com
Boo, Joe: www.myspace.com/joseph_boo
Canman and Angela, Visions: Tattoo, Piercing, and Art Gallery:
   www.visionstattoogallery.com
Cannibal, J.: www.jcannibal.com
Delivicia: http://blackcatburlesque.com
Einziger, Michael, official Incubus site: www.enjoyincubus.com
Karpleman, Ross, House of Shock Horror Show:
   www.houseof shock.com
Reusch, Mister: http://spooksbyreusch.com
Sin Claire, Evilyn: http://thelaurarose.com;
   www.sinnersaint burlesque.com

Chapter Ten: Trick and/or Treat?
Boulder Naked Pumpkin Run: http://nakedpumpkinrun.org
Guerrilla Masquerade Party: www.myspace.com/gmppdx
Improv Everywhere: www.improveverywhere.com
Invisible Rope: www.theinvisiblerope.com

Mass Sabbath: http://www.myspace.com/masssabbath
Maynard, Mark: http://markmaynard.com
MIT Gallery of Hacks: http://hacks.mit.edu
Reiss, Mike, Greater Talent Network page:
    www.greatertalent.com/MikeReiss

Selected Bibliography

General Halloween/Holiday

Bonewits, Isaac. "The Real Origins of Halloween." Isaac and Phaedra Bonewits' Neopagan.net. www.neopagan.net/Halloween-Origins.html. Accessed 12 October 2010.

Chizmar, Richard, and Robert Morris, eds. *October Dreams: A Celebration of Halloween.* Baltimore: Cemetery Dance Publications, 2000.

Cross, Gary. *The Cute and the Cool: Wondrous Innocence and Modern American Children's Culture.* Oxford: Oxford University Press, 2004.

Finlay, Richard J. "The Burns Cult and Scottish Identity in the Nineteenth and Twentieth Centuries." In *Love and Liberty. Robert Burns: A Bicentenary Celebration,* edited by Kenneth Simpson. East Linton, Scotland: Tuckwell Press, 1997.

Foley, Malcolm, and Hugh O'Donnell, eds. *Trick or Treat? Halloween in a Globalising World.* Newcastle upon Tyne, U.K.: Cambridge Scholars Publishing, 2009.

Hutton, Ronald. *The Stations of the Sun: A History of the Ritual Year in Britain.* Oxford: Oxford University Press, 1996.

Nissenbaum, Stephen. *The Battle for Christmas.* New York: Vintage Books, 1996.

Rogers, Nicholas. *Halloween: From Pagan Ritual to Party Night.* New York: Oxford University Press, 2002.

Santino, Jack. *The Hallowed Eve: Dimensions of Culture in a Calendar Festival in Northern Ireland.* Lexington, KY: University Press of Kentucky, 1998.

Santopoalo, Rochelle. "Halloween: Play Time for Adults." Ph.D. thesis, Fielding Institute, 1996.

Skal, David J. *Death Makes a Holiday: A Cultural History of Halloween.* New York: Bloomsbury, 2002.

Chapter Two: Ghosts

Blackson, Robert, ed. *Soul.* Sunderland, U.K.: Reg Vardy Gallery in partnership with Satellite Arts, Inc., 2007.

Faust, Drew. *This Republic of Suffering: Death and the American Civil War.* New York: Vintage Books, 2008.

Fisher, Len. *Weighing the Soul: The Evolution of Scientific Beliefs.* London: Weidenfeld & Nicolson, 2004.

Kaye, Marvin, ed. *Ghosts: A Treasury of Chilling Tales Old and New.* New York: Doubleday and Company, Inc., 1981.

Roach, Mary. *Spook: Science Tackles the Afterlife.* New York: W. W. Norton, 2005.

Schmitt, Jean-Claude. *Ghosts in the Middle Ages: The Living and the Dead in Medieval Society.* Translated by Teresa Lavender Fagan. Chicago: University of Chicago Press, 1998.

Willis, Danielle. *Dogs in Lingerie.* Oakland, CA: Zeitgeist Press, 1990.

Chapter Three: Witches

Gardner, Gerald B. *Witchcraft Today.* New York: Magickal Childe, 1982.

Goodare, Julian, Lauren Martin, Joyce Miller, and Louise Yeoman. "The Survey of Scottish Witchcraft, 1563-1736." The University of Edinburgh, School of History and Classics. www.shc.ed.ac.uk/Research/witches. Archived January 2003. Accessed 8 October 2010.

Hutton, Ronald Hutton. *Witches, Druids and King Arthur.* London: Hambledon & London, 2003.

———. *The Triumph of the Moon: A History of Modern Pagan Witchcraft.* Oxford: Oxford University Press, 2001.

Kinahan, Frank. *Yeats, Folklore and Occultism: Contexts of the Early Work and Thought.* Boston: UNWIN Hyman, 1988.

Murray, Margaret. *The God of the Witches.* London: Sampson Low, Marston & Company, Ltd., 1933.

Simpson, Jacqueline. "'The Weird Sisters Wandering': Burlesque Witchery in Montgomerie's 'Flyting.'" *Folklore* 106 (1995): 9-20.

———. "Margaret Murray: Who Believed Her, and Why?" *Folklore* 105 (1994): 89-96.

Thuente, Mary Helen. *W.B. Yeats and Irish Folklore.* New Jersey: Barnes and Noble, 1981.

Chapter Five: Dead Man Rising

Bourke, Joanna. *Fear: A Cultural History.* London: Virago Press, 2005.

Cowan, Douglas E. *Sacred Terror: Religion and Horror on the Silver Screen.* Waco, TX: Baylor University Press, 2008.

Maberry, Jonathan. *Zombie CSU. The Forensics of the Living Dead.* New York: Citadel Press, 2008.

Roach, Mary. *Stiff: The Curious Life of Human Cadavers.* New York: W.W. Norton & Company, 2003.

Rockoff, Adam. *Going to Pieces: The Rise and Fall of the Slasher Film, 1978-1986.* Jefferson, NC: MacFarland & Company, 2002.

Chapter Six: Caution: For Halloween Wonks Only

Blain, Mary E. *Games for Hallow-e'en.* New York: Barse & Hopkins, 1912.

Brand, John. *Observations on Popular Antiquities: A New Edition with the Additions of Sir Henry Ellis.* London: Chatto and Windus, 1900.

Briggs. Katharine M. *A Dictionary of British Folk-Tales in the English Language.* Part A, vol. 1 and part B, vol. 1. London: Routledge and Kegan Paul, 1970-71.

Brottman, Mikita. "When Good Plants Go Bad." *The Chronicle of Higher Education,* December 12, 2008, B12-13.

Brusca, Maria Cristina, and Tona Wilson. *The Blacksmith and the Devils.* New York: Henry Holt Company, 1992.

Calvino, Italo, ed. "Jump into My Sack." In *Italian Folktales.* translated by George Martin. New York: Harcourt Bruce Jovanovich, 1980.

Campbell, J. F. *Popular Tales of the West Highlands: Orally Collected with a Translation by the Late J. F. Campbell.* Vol. 4. 1893. Reprint, Detroit: Singing Tree Press, 1969.

Campbell, John Gregorson, comp. "The Fians, or Stories, Poems, and Traditions of Fionn and His Warrior Band." In *Waifs and Strays of Celtic Tradition.* Argyllshire Series, No. 4. London: David Nutt, 1891.

Carleton, William. "The Three Wishes. An Irish Legend," *Tales and Sketches, Illustrating the Character, Visages, Traditions, Sports and Pastimes of the Irish Peasantry.* Dublin: James Duffy, 1845.

Chandler, Harris. "Jacky-My-Lantern." In *Uncle Remus: His Songs and His Sayings.* 1880. Reprint, University of Virginia American Studies Program 2003-2004. http://xroads.virginia.edu/~HYPER/Harris2/ch32.html. Accessed 11 October 2010.

Chase, Richard, comp. "Wicked John and the Devil." In *American Folk Tales and Songs.* New York: New American Library, 1956.

———. *The Jack Tales.* Boston: Houghton Mifflin Company, 1943.

Clouston, W. A. *Popular Tales and Fictions: Their Migrations and Transformations.* Santa Barbara: ABC-CLIO, 2002.

Cressy, David. *Bonfires and Bells: National Memory and the Protestant Calendar in Elizabethan and Stuart England.* London: Weidenfeld and Nicolson, 1989.

Croker, Thomas Crofton. *Fairy Legends and Traditions of the South of Ireland.* London: John Murray, 1828.

Dalyell, John Graham. *The Darker Superstitions of Scotland.* Edinburgh: Waugh & Innes, 1834.

Danaher, Kevin. *The Year in Ireland: Irish Calendar Customs.* Dublin: Mercier Press, 1972.

Dasent, George Webbe, ed. "The Master Smith." In *East o' the Sun and West o' the Moon: Fifty-nine Norwegian Folktales.* New York: Dover Publications, Inc., 1970.

Dorson, Richard, ed. "Pedro de Ordimalas." In *Buying the Wind: Regional Folklore in the United States.* Chicago: University of Chicago Press, 1964.

Fanning, Charles, ed. *The Exiles of Erin (The Irish in America): Nineteeth-Century Irish-American Fiction.* Indiana: University of Notre Dame Press, 1987.

Gregory, Lady Augusta, ed. *Visions and Beliefs in the West of Ireland.* Gerrards Cross, U.K.: Colin Smythe, 1970.

Henderson, Lizanne, and Edward J. Cowan. *Scottish Fairy Belief: A History.* East Linton, Scotland: Tuckwell Press, 2001.

Helfenstein, Ernest. "Hallowe'en, Or the Fountain." *Graham's American Monthly Magazine of Literature, Art and Fashion 27,* no. 1 (January 1845): 34.

Hooks, William H. *Mean Jake and the Devils.* New York: Dial Press, 1981.

Hurston, Zora Neale. *Mules and Men.* 1935. Reprint, Bloomington, IN: Indiana University Press, 1978.

Ledenbach, Mark B. *Vintage Halloween Collectibles.* Iola, WI: Krause Publications, 2003.

Le Goff, Jacques. *The Birth of Purgatory.* Translated by Arthur Goldhammer. Chicago: University of Chicago Press, 1984.

McNeill, F. Marian. *The Silver Bough.* Vol. 3. Glasgow: William MacLellan, 1959.

Morton, Lisa. *A Halloween Anthology: Literary and Historical Writings Over the Centuries.* Jefferson, NC: McFarland & Company, Inc., 2008.

Murphy, Michael J. "Willy the Wisp." In *Irish Folktales,* edited by Henry Glassie. New York: Pantheon Books, 1985.

Newell, William Wells. "The Ignis Fatuus, Its Character and Legendary Origin." *Journal of American Folklore 17,* no. 64 (1904): 39-60.

Opie, Iona, and Peter Opie. *The Lore and Language of School Children.* Oxford: Clarendon Press, 1959.

Orne, Martha Russell. *Halloween: Its Origin and How to Celebrate with Appropriate Games and Ceremonies.* New York: Fitzgerald Publishing, 1898.

Palmer, Kingsley, ed., "Saints and Settlers," "The Daily Round," "But Once a Year," In *The Folklore of Somerset*. New Jersey: Rowman and Littlefield, 1976.

Pourrat, Henri. "Dearth and Poverty." In *French Folktales from the Collection of Henri Pourrat,* edited by C. G. Bjurstrom. New York: Pantheon Books, 1989.

Ravenwolf, Silver. *Halloween*. St. Paul, MN: Llewellyn Publications, 1999.

Simpson, Jacqueline, ed. "My Jon's Soul." In *Icelandic Folktales and Legends*. London: Batsford, Ltd., 1972.

Sinex, Margaret. "'Tricksy Lights': Literary and Folkloric Elements in Tolkien's Passages of the Dead Marshes." *Tolkien Studies* 2 (2005): 93-112.

Sobol, Joseph Daniel. "'Whistlin' Towards the Devil's House': Poetic Transformations and Natural Metaphysics in an Appalachian Folktale Performance." *Oral Tradition* 21, no. 1 (2006): 3-43. *eOT* = http://journal.oraltradition.org/articles/show/7/. Accessed 1 January 2010.

Thompson, Stith. *The Folktale*. Berkeley: University of California Press, 1977.

———, comp. "The Master Smith." In *One Hundred Favorite Folktales*. Bloomington: Indiana University Press, 1968.

Thuente, Mary Helen. "From Fairy to Folk: *Representative Irish Tales* and *The Celtic Twilight*." In *W.B. Yeats and Irish Folklore*. New Jersey: Barnes and Noble, 1981.

Truwe, Ben. *The Halloween Catalog Collection: 55 Catalogs from the Golden Age of Halloween*. Medford, OR: Talky Tina Press, 2003.

Yolen, Jane, ed. "Wicked John and the Devil." In *Favorite Folktales From Around the World*. New York: Pantheon Books, 1986.

Chapter Seven: Kindred Spirits

Ehrenreich, Barbara. *Dancing in the Streets: A History of Collective Joy*. New York: Metropolitan Books, Henry Holt & Company, 2006.

Chapter Eight: Terrortainment

Dozier, Rush W., Jr., *Fear Itself*. New York: St. Martin's Press, 1998.

Gower, Paul L., ed. *New Research on the Psychology of Fear*. New York: Nova Science Publishers, Inc., 2005.

Phillips, Kendall R. *Projected Fears: Horror Films and American Culture*. Westport, CT: Praeger, 2005.

Tancer, Bill. *Click: What Millions of People Are Doing Online and Why It Matters*. New York: Hyperion, 2008.

Chapter Nine: Bats, Tats, Twirlers, and Thrashers

Asma, Stephen T. *On Monsters: An Unnatural History of Our Worst Fears.* New York: Oxford University Press, 2009.

Gilmore, David D. *Monsters: Evil Beings, Mythical Beasts, and All Manner of Imaginary Terrors.* Philadelphia: University of Pennsylvania Press, 2003.

Hitchcock, Susan Tyler. *Frankenstein: A Cultural History.* New York: W.W. Norton & Company, 2007.

Marriot, James. *Horror Films.* London: Virgin Books Ltd., 2004.

Pinedo, Isabel Cristina. *Recreational Terror: Women and the Pleasures of Horror Film Viewing.* Albany: SUNY Press, 1997.

Skal, David J. *The Monster Show.* New York: W.W. Norton, 1993.

Steele, Valerie, and Jennifer Park. *Gothic: Dark Glamour.* New Haven: Yale University Press, 2008.

Chapter Ten: Trick and/or Treat?

Boese, Alex. *The Museum of Hoaxes.* New York: Dutton, 2002.

Peterson, T. F. *Nightwork: A History of Hacks and Pranks at MIT.* Cambridge, MA: MIT Press, 2003.

Vale, V. *Pranks 2.* San Francisco: Re/Search Publications, 2006.

Index